THE
PERSIAN GULF
CRISIS

THE
PERSIAN GULF
CRISIS

Power in the
Post–Cold War World

Edited by
ROBERT F. HELMS II
and
ROBERT H. DORFF

PRAEGER

Westport, Connecticut
London

Library of Congress Cataloging-in-Publication Data

The Persian Gulf crisis : power in the post–cold war world / edited by
   Robert F. Helms II and Robert H. Dorff.
      p.   cm.
   Includes bibliographical references and index.
   ISBN 0–275–94120–5 (alk. paper)
   1. Persian Gulf Region—Politics and government.   2. Persian Gulf
War, 1991.   3. World politics—1989–   I. Helms, Robert F. (Robert
Francis).   II. Dorff, Robert H.
   DS326.P4734   1993
   956.704'3—dc20   92–9120

British Library Cataloguing in Publication Data is available.

Library of Congress Catalog Card Number: 92–9120
ISBN: 0–275–94120–5

First published in 1993

Praeger Publishers, 88 Post Road West, Westport, CT 06881
An imprint of Greenwood Publishing Group, Inc.

Printed in the United States of America

The paper used in this book complies with the Permanent
Paper Standard issued by the National Information Standards
Organization (Z39.48–1984).

10 9 8 7 6 5 4 3 2 1

Contents

**PART III: RESPONSES TO THE IRAQI
INVASION OF KUWAIT**

**PART IV: IMPLICATIONS FOR THE
RESOLUTION OF CRISES IN THE
POST–COLD WAR WORLD**

Preface

The purposes of this volume are twofold. First, it examines the events, actions, and policies that led up to the Iraqi invasion of Kuwait and the subsequent response by the United States, the United Nations, and other national and international actors. Second, and most important, it seeks to move beyond a simple case study of the Middle East and the crisis itself to a more general analysis of the search for security in the post–Cold War world. The chapters in this volume examine the crisis from different perspectives to provide a set of potential lessons about issues such as the uses of national and international power (economic, political/diplomatic, and military) by individual nations, multilateral coalitions, and supranational organizations (the United Nations) that may be applied on a more general level.

As the Cold War moves further into the past, it is important that we seek answers to questions of crisis management and resolution that are at the very core of what many believe will be a fundamentally altered international system. Whether and to what extent that system will reflect both long-standing, historical characteristics of international relations and new, as yet only partially understood characteristics, are questions that the chapters in this volume seek to address.

THE
PERSIAN GULF
CRISIS

1

Introduction

Robert F. Helms II

The brutal invasion and military occupation of Kuwait by Iraq on August 2, 1990 represented yet another chapter in the turmoil of the Persian Gulf and the Middle East. The conquest of Kuwait with its oil resources and the threat that Iraq then represented to the oil fields of Saudi Arabia presented the industrialized nations with serious challenges. Clearly, the concern over continued access to reasonably priced oil was a major factor in the international response to the invasion. However, continued access to oil was only one of the factors that was included in the decisions that shaped the international responses to the invasion. There were other, perhaps more important issues that were being challenged.

The invasion took place in a world that was exalting and basking in the passing of the Cold War. Global attention was riveted on the historical events that were occurring at breathtaking speeds on the Eurasian land mass. These events included the breaking up of the Soviet empire in Eastern Europe—symbolized by the fall of the Berlin Wall, the reuniting of Germany, and the first signs of the crumbling from within the Soviet Union. The events of time even included historic arms control agreements that would have been unthinkable only a few years earlier. The order of the day was for declaring victory and self-congratulations. It was a time for a collective sigh of relief in a belief that mankind may have survived the threat of nuclear destruction: It now might even be possible to move the hands on the doomsday clock back from the dreaded count of midnight. It was a time for declaring that peace was breaking out all over and for forecasting greater cooperation among nations. It was time for great confidence and hope.

   The invasion of Kuwait by Iraq was out of step with the events of the time. This invasion was a throwback to earlier eras of using brutal military force in naked aggression against weaker nations. It was yet another example of *might making right*. It represented a direct challenge to those espousing the emergence of a *new world order*. Saddam Hussein was, in effect, flaunting the new world order. The actions of Iraq, if successful, would have made a mockery of any new order and threatened to turn back the clock to earlier times. Therefore, the international reactions were not just about reliable access to reasonably priced oil, they also were in defense of a new order that was perceived to be emerging with the passing of the Cold War. The responses also were shaped by the frustrations of nations that someone would try to deny entry into this new environment that so many had worked and sacrificed so long to achieve. Finally, the responses represented the intention of nations to be a good midwife to the new order even if this birth meant resorting to the use of military force. In this sense, the responses can be viewed as a broad international attempt to confront aggression in defense of what was hoped to be a new world order.

   The chapters in this volume seek to move beyond a simple case study of the Middle East and the crisis itself to examine the extent to which it represents a model for security in the post–Cold War world. These examinations address the challenge of Iraq's invasion to the new world order and alternatives that might be pursued to confront these challenges. Although there are many factors that influenced decision making during the events leading up to the war, the military conflict itself, and the post-war actions, there are a number of potential conclusions that may be drawn and applied on a more general level. These include the use of national and international power in the post–Cold War world by individual nations, multilateral coalitions, and supranational organizations such as the United Nations.

   If a fundamentally altered international system is emerging to replace the one that existed during the Cold War, then it is critical that we understand crisis management and resolution to ensure that actions taken are appropriate for this new international system. Otherwise, the responses to crises that can be expected to occur from time to time will be grounded in the lessons learned during earlier periods such as the Cold War. These responses from earlier times may be inappropriate and very easily could be counterproductive, leading to the very conditions that nations are attempting to avoid.

   Our examination begins with a historical overview of the search for security in the international system. The nations of today and tomorrow are the products of their history. The inclusion of a historical overview establishes a basis for understanding the present and forecasting the future. It enables us to understand better the similarities and discontinuities of events. It provides a basis for concluding whether the Persian Gulf war was an aberration or the product of a larger set of trends that is shaping our destinies.

The overview poses a series of questions and observations from the earlier periods of upheavals associated with 1815, 1918, and 1945 to provide a historical perspective for possible future international security experiences. It also includes an analysis of the search for collective security arrangements in the twentieth century. These analyses seek to address the issue of whether the remarkable coalition that was created and waged the war against Iraq represents a collective security model for the post–Cold War world or whether it was aberration. The extent to which the successful formation of the coalition to oppose Iraq was the product of a unique situation or represents a post–Cold War model is one of the key questions that has to be addressed in this context.

The great powers of the nineteenth and twentieth centuries have been involved in shaping the present-day Middle East situation. It is not possible to conduct any meaningful examination of the war with Iraq without including the interplay between internal and external forces in the region. For example, the historic rivalry between the United Kingdom and Russia in the Middle East and the decline of the British Empire provided the setting for the emergence of the United States as a major actor in the region. The rivalry of the Great Powers and the British Imperium is examined to establish a basis for understanding the evolution of outside interests and influences in the Middle East. This examination is followed by a review of the U.S. experience in the Persian Gulf and the emergence of the United States as a major power in the region.

The Iraqi invasion of Kuwait and the perspectives of the Arab nations are a major part of the scenario that unfolded and is continuing to emerge. In the second part of the book, the internal Arab perspectives are examined to develop a greater understanding of the crisis from these points of view. These examinations describe the political currents in the Arab world before the Iraqi invasion of Kuwait and the Arab perspectives of it. Since Iraq was the pivotal nation in the crisis, this latter examination proceeds from the basis of the motivations of this nation as the center of analysis.

In the third section of the book, the examination turns to international responses to the invasion. The search of the U.S. administration for a policy and appropriate responses is described to develop how the United States might be expected to manage similar scenarios in the post–Cold War world. The responses of nations and the United Nations were much broader than the traditional use of military forces. Their responses also included an earnest attempt to impose an international economic embargo. If this means of behavior control is ever to be effective, the embargo imposed on Iraq might be considered a model—particularly in view of broad support for it, scope of this action, and the vulnerability of the targeted nation to such an embargo. The success, failure, and future use of economic embargoes as a means for controlling the behavior of nations in the post–Cold War world is explored to develop implications for using this form of power in the upcoming eras.

When it did not appear that Iraq had any intention of withdrawing from Kuwait, the United Nations sanctioned the use of military force and the coalition of nations used military means to free Kuwait from Iraqi control. The final examination of this section describes the use of military forces to wage war against an Iraq that, apparently, did not believe that the international community had the will to undertake these steps to free Kuwait.

The final and fourth section of this book develops the implications of the lessons that were learned during this conflict for the resolution of crises in the post–Cold War world. The examination includes the role of military forces in the emerging national security environment and how military forces are expected to be used in the post–Cold War world. These examinations compare and contrast the roles and uses of military forces in the post–Cold War environment with that of earlier periods. The impacts of major trends are described to suggest how they are influencing the use of military forces. The use of advanced technologies to alter the battlefields and the ways that wars will be fought is developed to determine the implications of using this instrument of national power for crisis resolution. Finally, this section includes a discussion of the implications for the use of other means of national and international power in the post–Cold War world.

The final section summarizes the key findings of the chapters and suggests implications for the resolution of crises in the post–Cold War world.

NOTE

The authors gratefully acknowledge the Triangle University Security Seminar and the Research Triangle Institute for hosting the conference at which the following papers were initially presented. Funding for the conference was made possible by the Chief of Staff, U.S. Army's Strategic Outreach Initiative. Finally, Colonel Karl Robinson and the members of his staff at the Strategic Studies Institute, U.S. Army War College at Carlisle Barracks, Pennsylvania, are to be commended for their extremely helpful assistance in making preparations for and conducting the conference.

PART I
HISTORICAL PERSPECTIVES

2

The Search for Security in the International System: Historical Perspectives from 1815, 1918, and 1945

Samuel R. Williamson, Jr.

Much has changed in the world since the summer of 1990, or so it appears. Certainly our armed forces performed with skill and courage during the Persian Gulf crisis. Yet we must be careful what lessons we now draw, for the disparity of the odds may have been more akin to the Germans and the Poles in 1939 than against a truly formidable foe. As we now face the process of creating a new world order (at best an unfortunate turn of phrase that sounds like something once heard from Hitler at Nuremberg rallies), the Middle East seems likely to dominate concerns and policy agendas. On the other hand, the search for security remains understandably far more encompassing and more Eurocentered than the months of the Gulf crisis suggest. The revolutions in Eastern Europe in 1989–1990 and their consequences will probably loom far larger in determining whether we really achieve a new measure of international security in the last decade of the twentieth century.

The use of historical perspectives has shaped much recent work. I, thus, will not apologize for bringing a set of historical categories to the discussion, as I analyze the reconstruction of international security systems after periods of acute upheaval. These categories, however labeled, will frame many of the issues confronting policymakers as they seek to reshape an international environment profoundly altered by the events of the late 1980s and early 1990s. In this discussion some debts must be acknowledged early, especially to David Kaiser, Joseph Nye, Michael Porter, Paul Kennedy, Robert Art, and Robert Jervis for their willingness to think provocatively about change in international systems.[1]

I want to pose a series of questions and observations, drawn from earlier periods of upheaval, to ponder possible future international security experiences. Necessarily, the discussion will be incomplete and sometimes contradictory. But I hope the power of the exercise will come from the identification of issues that must be considered in any new security system.

I begin with the first of the categories dubbed *preventing the last war*, or *lessons apparently learned*. Foremost among these, whether in 1815 or 1918 or 1945, has been a desire to create some continuing form of collective security, an attempt to regularize the cooperation that had brought the recent victory and that would ensure a future peace. In 1815 the task appeared simple: Contain France and prevent a new Napoleonic aggression. But the desire for a collective approach also aimed to contain Russia while giving Austria and Britain dependable roles to play. Even before the war ended had come the Quadruple Alliance of Britain, Austria, Russia, and Prussia. France itself would be reintegrated into the system later to form what came to be called the Concert of Europe. Initially, this collective arrangement sought to prevent a resurgent France. By the early 1820s it had become the mechanism for checking Russia and for legitimizing Austrian and French efforts to squash revolutionary threats in Italy and Spain. Although the Holy Alliance had the same participants, its obtuse intentions left no lasting imprint. By contrast, the Concert of Europe approach lasted—despite ups and down, to be sure—until the Crimean War and even later.

The end of the Great War in 1918 saw a new attempt to institutionalize collective security, this time with a new structural approach in the shape of the League of Nations. With more popular verve behind it (after all, the loss of so many lives had to bring some lasting change in the very system that had brought the war), the League represented President Woodrow Wilson's lasting contribution to a new vision of American idealism and self-interest. Even without the United States as a participant, the League initially served as a collective security arrangement against Germany and, more distantly, against Russia. Yet almost from the start, given the absence of the United States, the League had problems. Soon local balance of power arrangements against Germany, including Locarno and the Little Entente, undermined the League; but the ideal remained.

During the Second World War, President Franklin Roosevelt, anxious to do what his earlier patron had not completed, committed Washington to collective security in a new United Nations. President Roosevelt and then President Harry Truman managed the domestic process to secure American participation. Yet almost immediately the Soviet Union became less willing to participate, and the United

Nations (UN) played only a peripheral role in the Cold War containment of Moscow. To be sure, there was a hint of collective security during the Korean War. However, UN involvement in international problems after 1953 came chiefly on issues in which the two superpowers had little direct interest or wish to become involved. Nor did the United Nations play any part in the recent upheavals in Eastern Europe. On the other hand, the United Nations remains more popular in Europe than in the United States; and it probably is still so, despite all of President Bush's recent talk about UN resolutions and their implementation. That the United Nations would emerge to play a role, even if possibly that of a fig leaf for recent actions in the Middle East, suggests how continuing is the urge for collective security.

However phrased, *preventing the last war* has led to persistent efforts to achieve a set of understandings that facilitates defense against a possible new hegemony. A collective arrangement becomes a means to an end. The continuing vitality of this desire in the 1990s, thus, should not surprise us. Nor should we be surprised to see the concept turned against the United States if it claims in this decade to be the sole arbiter of international security.

The containment of revolution and thwarting of sudden political change at home constitute the second lesson from preventing the last war. After 1815, conservative governments lost no time in trying to set the clock back on two decades of revolution; they were only partially successful. The desire to freeze the status quo, or indeed return to the status quo ante, permeated Metternich's efforts to keep the Austrian position intact. He sought to divert Russia from supporting national movements while acting in Germany and Italy to snuff out any possible change.[2]

It is not surprising, given the magnitude of the First World War and Soviet efforts to exploit the situation for widespread revolution, that the peacemaking in 1918–1919 also possessed strong antirevolutionary dimensions. Not only did the victors seek to keep the Soviets out of the new successor states, especially after Béla Kun in Budapest, but they actively intervened in the Russian civil war. Nor did the victors stop there. London especially worked to curb any aspect of change in its colonies, particularly in India.

After 1945, the Western powers once again feared the prospect of revolutionary change, once more identified with the Soviet state. In this case, the Allies were more successful in their reconstruction efforts in Western Europe and in Italy. On the other hand, they could do nothing to prevent the gradual expansion of Soviet power in Eastern Europe and were equally ineffectual in changing the tide of events in China. Still later would come the hesitant and destabilizing effects of the end of colonialism.

With the utter collapse of the Soviet Union and the disintegration of Yugoslavia, the United States and Western Europe confront an unexpected, unparalleled opportunity to reshape the international system. Already the first German steps in this environment have provoked concern, even apprehension. Washington, full of the hubris of the Gulf war and the disappearance of the Soviet state, now talks in Roman imperial terms of keeping all other powers (including Germany and Japan) in a state of dependency on American military power. Such an effort will almost certainly prove self-defeating; on the other hand, historical understanding and balance of power politics have not always been well appreciated by the Pentagon in the last decade or more.

If one set of perspectives deals with *preventing the last struggle*, a second set focuses—often fuzzily—on the *consequences* of the recent upheaval. One consequence soon appreciated, though not readily or with grace, is the sheer exhaustion of one or more of the victors. Closely aligned with this set of outcomes are those of new configurations of economic power. Britain emerged from the Napoleonic wars the undisputed winner. Rid of Napoleon and the French naval menace, London also saw the two decades of war give impetus to industrialization. The results were staggering. When the wars were over, Britain had a preeminent position, which would only gradually erode late in the century. Pig iron production, for instance, stood at 68,000 tons in 1788; in 1811 it had risen to 325,000 tons. Customs receipts went from $13.5 million to $44.8 million in twenty years.[3] On the Continent, meanwhile, the Russians now became the strongest power. Through most of the century—in the context of the Eastern Question—Britain and Russia confronted each other. The third victor had been victorious but in reality was an exhausted loser. Austria under Metternich's guidance had won but became exhausted. Henceforth, Vienna's foreign and security policy were those of the defensive, containing liberalism and nationalism while seeking to hold an increasingly restive multinational state together.

In the First World War, the French won but actually lost. Indeed, the losses were devastating; the French economy, French manpower, French production, and the French psyche all suffered. And the British were in an only marginally better position. This sense of defeated victory would bedevil both of the Western powers as they sought to confront the defeated victor in the form of Adolph Hitler. Of course, the real winner in 1918 was the United States, now the triumphant world economic power. Again, the numbers tell the tale very simply. If the manufacturing indices for 1913 show Europe, the old USSR, and the United States at 100, then by 1920 the indices showed 77.3 for Europe, 12.8 for Russia, and 122.2 for the United States.[4]

The pattern repeated itself after 1945. This time, as Churchill realized more acutely than most of his countrymen, Britain was now a dependent, second class power. The exhausted victor was London; the United States reigned supreme in all areas. Indeed, even in 1950 the gross national product (GNP) of the United States exceeded that of the rest of the industrialized powers. Kennedy and Kaiser and the retorts to them make clear that the American position was unnatural and exaggerated. Still, the power shifts were fundamental.

Paradoxically, Soviet Russia also emerged as a great military power. It would now pose the same challenge to Washington that Russia had posed a century before to London. Once again, the Eastern Question or its legacies became one of the major points of contention. Currently, even after the Gulf War, Paul Kennedy's analysis about the possibility of the United States being the new exhausted victor continues to stir debate. Here the evidence is far less clear-cut, despite Joseph Nye's claims, given the domestic economic problems of this country. The Cold War has ended, but President George Bush would scarcely go for a walk near the White House after dark—so much for triumph. Perhaps more paradoxical still is the question of whether non-participation might be more rewarding—in the case of Japan—than actual participation in the struggle itself. In any event, the question of exhaustion and the consequent shifts of power constitute a set of analytical considerations.

A second major consequence of upheaval, appreciated early by Metternich and his German counterparts, are the explosive dangers of nationalism. In this instance nationalism is more than revolution; it is unthinking, patriotic zeal and nationality mixed with pride and self-fulfillment. With the appeal to liberty, equality, and fraternity, the French had stirred themselves and others during the course of the struggle. Not least were the German peoples stirred by their resistance to the French, a result that terrified the Habsburgs and the rest of the crowned heads as well. During the ensuing decades the rise of nationalisms—Italian, German, Irish, and particularly those of Eastern Europe—displayed the power of state, *Volk*, a misty past, in galvanizing popular attitudes.

The First World War, caused in large part by nationalism, enshrined national emotions still further. From the Baltic states, which reappeared after centuries of absence, to a nostalgic recreation of Poland (too much like the current popularity for comfort), nationalism reigned supreme. Everywhere nationalism became the order of the day, everywhere manipulated by rulers for their own ends. Later, its divisive character would make cooperation against Hitler less effective. Ironically, the League of Nations magnified the principle, not reduced it, by treating all states—great and small—as if they were equals. In 1945 nationalism would be more muted, though de Gaulle's presence suggested its potent power, as did the national Communist movements in Eastern Europe. If the four decades plus since 1945 have seen nationalism become less virulent in Western Europe, some credit must grudgingly be allocated to the Soviets and some to the generous spirit of Jean Monnet and others who worked for European cooperation as a way to curb a future European war.

Since 1989 nationalism has returned in its most contagious variety. In Eastern Europe, nationalism—with Soviet acquiescence—toppled the tottering Soviet empire; in the Balkans nationalism has ripped apart the fragile Yugoslav state. The recent Gulf crisis has strengthened, not dampened, the fires of nationalism, including those of patriotic zeal in the United States. And there are more than enough indications that Japanese and German nationalism, hedged so carefully for decades after 1945, has now returned as a political force in both countries. Closer to home, the United States, while often bewailing the nationalism of others, has buttressed its own. The question now becomes how to contain, once again, the more anarchical forms of nationalism and thereby build a more secure international system. John Mearsheimer correctly argues, in my opinion, that the future may be far more dangerous than when the two superpowers could check or contain irrational nationalism. Nor should we assume that the United States will be spared. We may well find ourselves with a black foreign policy, a Hispanic one, a Jewish one, a Greek one, and so forth. The sense of nationalism and ethnicity has been loosened; each can have corrosive effects.[5]

A third consequence of periods of upheaval may be less clearly appreciated; it is the militarization of approaches to international politics, along with the transformation of the military role itself. No one doubted Napoleon's contributions to warfare. He had mobilized, fed, and led hundreds of thousands of troops; his counterparts had gradually done the same. New staff techniques, a more professional study of war (not least by Clausewitz and Jomini), and a willingness to put the entire nation into the equation, as did the Prussians after 1806, were some of the results. If the mechanics of warfare were not much changed during the two decades, the elements of leadership, command, and ruthlessness were. These attitudes left strong impressions on both the French and German peoples and were not lost on the other states as well. The wars of German unification reinforced an easy acceptance of militarism. Later in the century, imperialistic drives, along with Social Darwinism (like fascism and Naziism later), saw publics worship the principle of force and aggression.

After two world wars, average soldiers hated the war yet still found themselves forever changed by the experience—and not necessarily made more peaceful. Force did appear to solve problems, even if in an awful fashion. More important, the militarization of the society at war saw many of those attitudes carry over into civilian life. Even in the defeated countries, the old generals (less so the admirals) were objects of veneration; even if, like the Austrian Conrad von Hötzendorf, they had condemned thousands to death by their own ineptitude. Equally important, after both wars the inter-Service rivalries, more or less muted before 1914, came to full throttle; each Service fought for its share of the budget and for its conception of strategic superiority. The two world wars had seen new weapons transform the conduct of the fighting, with the atomic weapon of the summer of 1945 altering the equation in an unparalleled fashion.

The upheavals of 1989–1990 are among the most remarkable in history because of the absence of the military. Instead, we saw the exhaustion of an economic system in the Eastern bloc trying to support a military machine that finally ran out of gas. The military had to be checked if there was to be any domestic economic reform. In that sense, Paul Kennedy's thesis seems unassailable; the question remains whether the United States will be able to do the same in an orderly fashion. Given recent events and with a successful American war president, militarism and the militarization of attitudes remain questions for the new world order. How strong will the temptation be, as Robert Art has recently warned, for the United States to become the new Rome, enforcing its views worldwide?[6]

I have suggested two types of historical perspective to this point: *preventing the last war* and *incorporating the consequences*. Now let me pose a third set of categories, those of *altered contexts*. First among these is enhanced public involvement in wars and their aftermath; closely linked with this is the role of public opinion as such. The French revolution and its wars stirred emotions and peoples; these were harnessed by Napoleon for his benefit. In the process, the people returned to the fray. During the subsequent century, as conscription became the norm in Europe, the average family and person were more deeply involved in the process. Moreover, the cost of weapons systems by the start of the early twentieth century meant that taxes and tax issues would involve the public. The wars of this century have reinforced each of these points.

But other features have reinforced them as well. The telegraph, the camera, the telephone, and then the radio brought the home front and the war front closer. Then came the movies and television and now Cable Network News (CNN) real-time war. In this, the issue of communications, with the public's right to know, the issue of public support, and the manipulation of information have come to the fore. Some recent attitudes toward the press (both civilian and military) suggest an American version of the stab-in-the-back legacy. That is, like the German military after 1918 blaming the civilians for defeat, so runs the belief that the Vietnam War was lost by the press and not because of General Westmoreland and his superiors. The problems first came to the fore in the early nineteenth century. The issues of public involvement now have real-time and instant impacts, just as they have had—without a full realization—in our nuclear deterrent theories. To put it another way, the horrors of war may now be so realizable and understandable that a new variable has been put into the equation of whether or not to go to war. Certainly, recent concerns about reporting casualties suggest that the mere notion of body counts makes the prospect for the loss of life an even greater, not lesser, constraint on the conduct of military operations.

Another altered context, after each period of chaos, has been the increased power of the state itself. The growth of state power during the Napoleonic era amazed many at the time. That same phenomenon occurred during both world wars in this century; moreover, the Cold War was even more instrumental in its growth. The emergence of the modern bureaucratic state has been a subject of much study and more criticism. While the apparatus permits the achievement of complicated tasks, it also limits options and stifles creativity. Furthermore, in moments of great crisis, the circle of decision makers remains narrow and their options even narrower because of the limited repertoire permitted by the bureaucratic structure. The growth of state power, while castigated by many, has become almost inexorable.

A third altered context (it might also be seen as a consequence) focuses upon ideology. After Waterloo, Metternich and others saw liberalism as a dangerous, radical ideology that could overturn the monarchical system. Indeed, it did eventually, though some governments, like the British, found ways to adapt and survive. And as the nineteenth century continued, socialism became an even more dangerous foe of the established order. After 1918, liberalism and democratic values were constantly challenged by Marxism; the two rival ideologies jousted through the interwar period, indeed until 1989–1990. In the interval, both confronted fascism and Naziism and won. But just as this ideological confrontation has eased and with democratic (though not necessarily capitalist or free market) values victorious, a new element came forward—a potentially far more difficult rival: religion. Generally absent from international politics since the peace of Westphalia in 1648, religion has returned to bedevil relations. Its importance, not least in the Middle East, may be an interesting portent of the future. In fact, it could be argued that Pope John Paul II's elevation to the papacy was at least as responsible for undermining Soviet power as the defense expenditures of the Reagan administration. Religion makes the policymaker understandably nervous; it brooks little compromise and requires patience. In the reconstruction of the Persian Gulf, as we are discovering, religion may be as important as oil and weapons.

The lessons learned from epochal struggles, the corollary consequences, and changed contexts influence the policymaker's search for security. Each state, each statesman, becomes in part a prisoner of individual experiences, able to see only within a narrow set of blinders. The points enumerated thus far represent some of the essential considerations in the reconstruction of the international system. But there are at least three other categories that must be considered. The first might be called the *persistence of history*, for often the military struggle has decided the issue of power only for the moment; it has not really resolved the reasons behind the struggle itself. Thus, while Metternich and the Quadruple Alliance could overcome Napoleon, the essential motive forces behind his power were just momentarily checked: nationalism, popular government, state power, liberalism. The Holy Alliance of Russia, Austria, Britain, and Prussia elevated the victors to a metaphysical relationship; it sought to resist evils the wars could not exorcise. After 1918, the situation was more practical and dangerous. The allies had won the war, but German power remained implicitly intact. The provisions of the Treaty of Versailles only gave a breathing spell should the Germans resume a march to domination. More dangerous still, the war's conduct had led to the installation of a government in Russia far more ambitious than the limited tsarist mentality would have ever dreamed in its desire for power.

In 1945, with the lessons of the interwar period in mind, both East and West without much difficulty found the division of Germany an easy solution. In the Far East, the United States sought to do what the victors had not done with Germany after 1918: Remake a society into a democratic model and limit the military in a nearly permanent fashion. The success of these policies for nearly four decades has been demonstrated anew in the German and Japanese reluctance to become involved in the events of the Persian Gulf and in the domestic debates occasioned by the crisis. On the other hand, as I shall examine in a moment, the Japanese may have achieved a competitive advantage that has given security a new definition.

The *persistence of history* category also addresses the very fabric of the societies involved in the epochs of struggle. Can a state overcome its own history and its own geography? In the case of Japan, the answer may well be yes; and in the case of Germany, the answer must be yes. But what of the other governments in Eastern Europe? The Middle East? Can it be reasonably assumed that the Eastern

European governments can become democratic? Can Warsaw or Bu-
charest or Sofia ignore either their most immediate past or their
longer term familiarity with authoritarian governments? Can Poland
really function as a democracy? And what should we really expect
in the states of the former Soviet Union? Certainly, the belief that
democracy and a free market economy can be achieved represents a
wholly unrealistic set of expectations. The strength of continuity,
even in an era of great change, has far more staying power than we
usually like to concede. Furthermore, when juxtaposed with ethnic
issues, the potential for armed conflict is great. What would any of
the greater powers do if Croatia and Serbia come to full-scale war?
Would the United Nations be effective? Would Bonn or Washington
or Moscow stand aside? To put it another way, the persistence issue
should lead to modest expectations of social and political change. Wilsonian or Leninist or even the new world order: prudence demands
that we not expect too much.

This examination takes us to still a further category, a *new definition of strategic security*. We have already seen the consequences of
upheavals: the exhaustion of victors; power shifts tied to economic,
strategic, and military realities. Yet we live in a time of enormous
economic change with an increasingly interconnected world economy.
Economic strength and national security are in the process, it could
be argued, of being redefined. After Waterloo, Britain's industrialization gave a new definition of power, one that Europe and the United
States spent the rest of the century trying to imitate. Even then, at
the end London discovered it had been leapfrogged by the United
States in a fashion less dependent on the old industrialization than a
new one built on higher technology and the combustion engine. The
two world wars actually changed less in economic competition than
the sheer fact that the United States dominated everything.

In the last forty years, during the Cold War, this country managed
to keep its electronic, communications, and information system advantages; or so it appeared. Now the advantages are less certain as
the microchip becomes the post-modernist equivalent of the steel
plant. Furthermore, the rise of the truly global corporations with their
interlocking directorates and the shifts in capital allocations and control mean that power has become more diffuse, the economy more
important, and competitive advantages (to use Michael Porter's term)
ever more transient and less meaningful. The sudden shocks of October 1987 have been muted in the subsequent performance of financial markets. But the debacle of the savings and loan industry, with
its destruction of capital far in excess of that expended in the recent
Persian Gulf war, suggests anew the fragility of power and the ability
to be secure.

Joseph Nye easily dismissed Paul Kennedy's arguments, while the recent events in the Persian Gulf seem to suggest that military power is the final calculus, as before. But the newest work of Robert Reich offers a difficult and more disturbing perspective in which the symbolic elites of the world are tied together across national lines, while the underclass and Third World countries remain aside. Does this situation mean new imperialism? New friction? Substantial domestic upheaval, even in the United States? Can America's unfinished domestic agenda be ignored indefinitely without challenging the survival of the system? Can we win the Cold War and lose the American dream?[7]

A fifth aspect of the category *new definitions of strategic security* requires some attention to the military systems themselves. Remarkably, the years 1815, 1918, and 1945 displayed, in my opinion, a less dramatic impact on the conduct of warfare than the American Civil War or the wars of German unification. A soldier fighting in 1815 would not have perceived much difference on the battlefield if he had fought with Napoleon in the 1790s. A soldier in the trenches in France would not have seen much difference in 1918 from 1914, though tanks, the airplane, and poison gas were introduced during the war. Their introduction had not fundamentally altered things. Only at sea with the submarine had there been surprises, but these were hard to gauge. Nor would the average American soldier have seen much difference from 1942 to May 1945. A civilian in London, with the V-1 and V-2, might have reacted differently, yet still he probably saw the Battle of Britain as more horrific. It was, of course, the atomic bomb that suggested that warfare and strategy had shifted dramatically by the end of the Second World War.

The atomic era and new delivery systems did alter conceptions of security. But this change came only slowly and ploddingly in the next five years, as the Services began to think atomic as opposed to conventional systems. The Persian Gulf has shown the success of some new weapons systems, even after discounting the nearly total ineptitude of the opponent. Laser-guided weapons, anti-missile weapons, and the Stealth bomber made a difference. For the Army, though there were differences to be sure, a General Patton or Field Marshal Rommel would not have been much surprised had either been riding with the 24th Infantry Mechanized Division. Nor would naval surface officers have seen much difference from Vietnam, though the aviators would have. This line of reasoning may mean that apart from the nuclear deterrent structure, strategic security systems do not change very quickly. The innovations in the systems come less from the wartime experience than from the peacetime developments. Yet even they are less revolutionary than may appear at first glance.

Nowhere does the searing experience of war have more impact than

on the current and next generation of leaders. To this point, while I
have mentioned individuals, I have eschewed the talk of *personalities
and leaders* that must surely constitute a category of historical perspective. The defeat of Napoleon represented the demise of the great
leader; the victors were determined to prevent a repeat performance.
That determination persisted until Bismarck's success; then he became the paradigm to be avoided. But what of Napoleon's opponents:
Castlereagh, Metternich, Alexander, Wellington? They were formidable personalities in their own right. Even if one disregards some of
Henry Kissinger's adulation of Prince Metternich, the Habsburg
statesman remains a seminal figure in European diplomacy; he was
able to judge the odds well and was willing to pursue a long-term
strategy. Without his manipulation, the Fourth Coalition might well
have gone the way of the first three.

In the First World War the generals won reputations, many unde-
served either in terms of praise or condemnation. But only a few leaders emerged, and with fateful consequences. David Lloyd George,
George Clemenceau, and Woodrow Wilson were personalities whose
insights, drive, skill, and ruthlessness made a difference. And no one
equaled Lenin for his exploitation of the exposed jugular of the Russian state for his own ends. In these encounters, the personalities
made a difference. So would be the case with the Big Three of the
Second World War: Churchill, Franklin Delano Roosevelt, and Stalin.
Each stands, even allowing for some diminution by the passage of time
and the savagery of historians, as remarkable if not likeable personalities. In the aftermath of the war, the emergence of Dwight D. Eisenhower, the essential humility yet decisiveness of Harry S. Truman,
and the prestige of George C. Marshall helped to push a new international security system forward.

What of the Cold War era? Mikhail Gorbachev stands as a pivotal
figure; his disappearance has not seen his successors inspire much
confidence in Eastern Europe. In the West the personalities are still
less striking; George Bush can be given high marks for his leadership
of the Gulf coalition but his domestic political skills appear flawed and
inconsistent. Still, in the search for international security, the absence
of strong personalities, familiar with the world and with world economic politics, represents an Achilles' heel for the durability of a
peaceful international system. The paucity of such choices in the
American system is, regrettably, matched by that of most of the industrialized world. Is John Major a Macmillan or a Churchill, even an
Atlee? This is doubtful.

In this connection, one must also ask what intellectual and historical paradigms future leaders will carry in their heads: No more Viet-

nams; the Falkland Islands redeemed; resistance with the help of the United Nations; no more concessions to the Germans; make the Japanese pay their fair share; treat the Middle East as a great imperial game; keep the politicians in their place; use external crises to divert attention from domestic discord? Whatever these images may be, they will be more real than Munich, or Manchuria, or the 1914 analogy.

Finally, I come to the international system itself. Earlier, I noted the urge to form a collective security system in the aftermath of great upheavals, either a Concert, a League, or a United Nations approach. In no case did the attempt last more than a dozen years; usually less. In part, the failure stems from the sheer turnover of leaders; the newer ones have different agendas and new views. In part, the failure comes because the very issues themselves change. In the 1820s, the Greek revolt against Turkish power was hard to defeat, given the historical importance of the Greeks to Western civilization. In the interwar period, the Soviet threat seemed at least as dangerous as the Nazi one, and the League had no chance. After 1945, the United Nations had scant success in dealing with the superpowers while giving them a place to play some of the time. On the other hand, in fairness, the United Nations helped with some of the decolonization issues. How long the current American approach to, and success with, the United Nations will continue will depend in large part on President Bush's continued willingness to stomach Chinese behavior that others would condemn. With Iraq, we may be creating a future war. To put it another way, the persistence of collective security action should not be too easily assumed.

What does this mean for the future of the international system? Samuel Huntington, in a recent article in *Survival*, worries aloud about the need to counter Japanese economic power and to thwart the emergence of a hegemonic power on the Continent aimed at the United States. While this may seem extreme, the logic of the balance of power would dictate that the emergence of one truly global power will eventually see lesser rivals seek some advantage or at least seek to be more equal. What might this mean for the United States? Some conclusions can be ventured. The dissolution of the Soviet Union is a destabilizing event of the first order. The continuance of the North Atlantic Treaty Organization remains unassured. The national struggles in Eastern Europe will also prove fertile ground for the development of a new military strongman, including one in Russia.[8]

The complex interconnection of economic interests will, moreover, constrain the room for maneuver in the international system. Only if all the controlling powers agree will something happen. Thus, quite possibly the Japanese, who in the Persian Gulf crisis went along, might differ on South Africa. At the same time, in a confusion of new regimes, as in Russia, there is also a chance of a nuclear theft, of some unintended consequence of action by one of the smaller powers.

What this emerging situation means is that having won the Cold War and now the Persian Gulf war, the most dangerous war of all— the genuine securing of international peace and security—may be at hand. In this process the United States of the 1990s, unlike the British of 1815 or the United States in 1918 or 1945, has far fewer resources and will face more constraints. To achieve success will require patience, a willingness to measure things with longer term results, and some assurance that the domestic situation (economic, political, and social) is in relative harmony and prosperity. Unfortunately, on none of these points can one be more than tentative. As Robert Jervis is fond of telling us, perceptions are important because they become reality. Perception in this instance requires an understanding that, John Locke notwithstanding, no statesman, no country writes on a blank slate. Rather, the slate is bounded by history, by the immediate past, and by the irascibility of the human spirit. In that latter point lies the danger and the hope.[9]

NOTES

1. The literature on the subject of international systems in change is voluminous; this chapter makes no attempt to survey all of the relevant work. But the following have proved especially helpful. Robert Art, "A Defensible Defense: America's Grand Strategy after the Cold War," *International Security* 15 (1991): 5–53; Robert Jervis, "The Future of World Politics: Will It Resemble the Past?" (1991), unpublished manuscript; David Kaiser, *Politics and War: European Conflict from Philip II to Hitler* (Cambridge, MA: Harvard University Press, 1990); Paul Kennedy, *The Rise and Fall of the Great Powers: Economic Change and Military Conflict from 1500 to 2000* (New York: Alfred A. Knopf, 1987); Joseph Nye, *Bound to Lead: The Changing Nature of American Power* (New York: Basic Books, 1990); Michael Porter, *The Competitive Advantage of Nations* (New York: Free Press, 1990).

2. Henry Kissinger's study of Count Metternich remains invaluable. It also provides extremely useful insights into Kissinger's later political views. Henry A. Kissinger, *A World Restored: Metternich, Castlereagh, and the Problems of Peace, 1812–1822* (Boston: Houghton Mifflin, 1957); see also Enno Kraehe, *The Congress of Vienna, 1814–1815*, Vol. 2 of *Metternich's German Policy* (Princeton: Princeton University Press, 1983).

3. Kennedy, 130.

4. Ibid., 280.

5. John J. Mearsheimer, "Back to the Future: Instability in Europe after the Cold War," *International Security* 15 (1990): 5–56.

6. Art, 44–50.

7. Robert Reich, *The Work of Nations: Preparing Ourselves for 21st Century Capitalism* (New York: Alfred A. Knopf, 1991).

8. Samuel P. Huntington, "America's Changing Strategic Interests," *Survival* 33 (1991): 3–17.

9. Robert Jervis, *Perception and Misperception in International Politics* (Princeton: Princeton University Press, 1976).

3

The Gulf War and Prospects for World Order by Collective Security

Inis L. Claude, Jr.

The idea of collective security was elaborated and gained prominence during and immediately after World War I, when it was associated particularly with President Woodrow Wilson and his plans for world order. For President Wilson and his colleagues, a collective security system was conceived as a new and improved method of maintaining international peace: a systematic arrangement of commitments and mechanisms to guarantee that aggression by any state against any other would promptly engender the combined resistance of all other states whose help might be needed to deny success to the aggressor. In this effort all necessary means, possibly including force, should be used. All members of the international system were to accept both the negative duty to refrain from aggression—that is, from pursuing any objective or promoting any change by military means—and the positive duty to join in collective actions against any member that might violate that negative duty.

Although both the Covenant of the League of Nations and the United Nations Charter were heavily influenced by the theory of collective security, no such system has ever come into operation. My thesis is that almost no one has ever genuinely accepted the commitment that a collective security system would entail. We have wished for the result promised by the system but have shied away from the burdens, costs, and dangers that participation would involve. Indeed, I have argued for some thirty years that collective security has become a dead issue, that it has been definitely rejected by all, even though it may yet receive occasional lip service.[1] For reasons both good and bad, collective security has proved unacceptable, and those who hope to pro-

mote world order had better look for other methods. So my argument
has run.

In the last few years, certain momentous events have seemed to
challenge that thesis. First, the ending of the Cold War, creating the
expectation of a United Nations Security Council no longer paralyzed
by conflict between the superpowers, has inspired the suggestion that
the Council can now become what it was presumably intended to be,
an agency for the collective enforcement of the ban on aggression. I
have reservations about this proposition, both because it exaggerates
the original commitment of the United Nations to collective security
and because it neglects the fact that the ending of the Cold War does
not eliminate the reasons for the *rejection*, as distinguished from the
frustration, of collective security. In adopting the requirement of unanimity of the Big Five for major decisions of the Security Council,
the founders of the United Nations indicated clearly that they believed
the organization could not and should not attempt to function as a
collective security system in cases involving aggression by the great
powers or their allies or protégés; they envisioned at most a sharply
restricted enforcement agency. The United Nations has not, since
1946, consisted of a mass of states dedicated to making it a full-fledged
collective security system and eager to take part in such a system, but
prevented by the rivalry of the superpowers. Nevertheless, the notion
that the termination of the Cold War changes the prospects for collective security contains a grain of truth: It greatly increases the possibility of Security Council action.

The second development raising doubt about the thesis that collective security's rejection has been total and final is the endorsement of
the ideal of collective security by the leaders of both the Soviet Union
and the United States. President Mikhail Gorbachev announced first,
making statements in 1987 and 1988 that were interpreted by one of
our most eminent Sovietologists, Robert Legvold, as indicating a clear
commitment to participation in what he called "the principle underlying the League of Nations and the United Nations: All nations
banded together against the rogue aggressor state."[2] President George
Bush delayed his endorsement until the Iraqi invasion of Kuwait,
after which he initiated not only the rhetoric calling for world order
by means of collective security but also the policy that culminated in
Iraq's ejection from Kuwait. There are elements of vagueness in President Bush's talk about a new world order, but he has repeatedly and
emphatically insisted, as he did in his address to the United Nations
General Assembly on October 1, 1990, that the organization must be
"a center for international collective security," uniting the collective
strength of the world community to deter and defeat aggression—"to
demonstrate that aggression will not be tolerated or rewarded."[3]

Finally, one can cite as evidence of the revival of the ideal of collective security the extraordinary involvement of the United Nations in the campaign against Iraq's aggression: the promptness, decisiveness, and near-unanimity of the Security Council in the series of resolutions having to do with the case, the emphasis by member states on the necessity and value of UN endorsement and authorization of action against Iraq, and the successful functioning of a coalition of nearly thirty member states, acting ostensibly to enforce the declared will of the international community.[4] Surely, one might argue, all these efforts suggest that the idea of collective security has not been finally discarded but has now been revived, and that the project of making the United Nations an operating agency of collective security has finally gotten under way, launched by a brilliantly successful case!

Let me now turn to a critical examination of this newly optimistic view of the present and future of collective security. I maintain a rather stubborn skepticism about all rhetoric in support of collective security, including that of current political leaders. My contention is not so much that champions of collective security are hypocritical or deceitful, although that is, of course, a possibility, as that they speak without having thought through, faced up to, and genuinely accepted the implications of commitment to carrying the burdens of a collective security system. I suspect that this was true even of President Wilson, and I see no reason to suppose that our latter-day converts to the Wilsonian creed are the first to have determined, with clear understanding and resolute acceptance, what is involved in effectuating such a system. One need not impugn their sincerity, but one may well retain doubt about the depth of the commitment underlying the rhetoric.

Even if we presume that President Bush has made a carefully considered commitment to the collective security method of promoting world order, the question remains as to the adequacy of support, domestic and international, for that approach. On the face of it, the Persian Gulf case reflected widespread support for collective security, deftly mobilized by the Bush administration. The United Nations Security Council put the organization clearly on record as condemning Iraq's aggression, demanding the restoration of Kuwait's sovereignty, requiring member states to join in economic sanctions, and authorizing military measures. With varying degrees of enthusiasm, members of the North Atlantic Treaty Organization, many Arab states, and numerous other members of the United Nations participated in some way or at least endorsed the collective venture. The U.S. Congress gave its approval, and public support was strong. In summary, President Bush succeeded in creating and maintaining a remarkable political consensus and military coalition to defeat Iraq.

This success does not, however, hide the thinness and fragility of support for the vision of a world order to be enforced by collective arrangements. Between active support and clear opposition, there were evident gradations of lip service, qualified approval, and covert opposition. In conformity with traditional attitudes toward collective security, consensus on the end did not translate into consensus on means. It is clear that agreement did not fully extend to the decision on whether and when to resort to force.

Moreover, the support generated for a collective response in this instance carried no necessary implication of support for systematic arrangements for collective suppression of aggression in all cases. Iraq's invasion of Kuwait was, after all, a nearly perfect case for the application of collective security doctrine. The aggression was blatant and there was no uncertainty about the identities of the perpetrator and the victim. The possibility that an unchecked Iraq might gain control over a major portion of the world's oil resources seemed to many states, throughout the world, to threaten their own vital interests, given the fact that activities as diverse as maintaining national defense and distributing food supplies are dependent upon reliable supplies of oil. This situation suggests that, for most states, the objective of curbing aggression coincided with a clear perception of national interests. The Soviet Union withdrew its long-standing support of Iraq, making this situation clearly a post–Cold War episode, an instance in which states could act against the aggressor without fear of encountering opposition from a superpower. In the end, the campaign against Iraq achieved success quickly, easily, and at unexpectedly low cost for coalition forces. This was the collective security theorist's dream case: the flagrant and lonely aggressor, overwhelmed by a substantially united community.

Even so, support for Operation Desert Storm was uneasy and tentative. In the United States, Congress was divided and approval was granted by some members with obvious reluctance. Association of the U.S. Democratic Party with the action was quite tenuous; a majority of Democrats in Congress opposed at least the timing of the resort to arms. Dissent was expressed by prominent clergymen, and a peace movement sprang up, producing protest demonstrations from the very beginning of the coalition's military actions. Among the European states, only Great Britain and, to a lesser degree, France were actively supportive. Japan remained aloof from the coalition. States of the Third World exhibited marked ambivalence. The Soviet Union endorsed the action without participating and showed more misgiving than enthusiasm. In general, members of the United Nations appeared more acquiescent than genuinely supportive. What if the issue of aggression had been fuzzy rather than clear-cut, and the world's sympathies and interests had been sharply divided between the two parties, as is more typical of international conflicts? What if the struggle against the aggressor had been long, costly, and indecisive? These are inescapably rhetorical questions; it seems evident that the modesty of the support for collective action in this case negates any expectation that the world is likely to be united in determination to act against aggression in all future cases.

In my view, Iraq, like Korea, is likely to prove an aberration rather than a prelude to the establishment of a working system of collective security. Iraq differs from Korea in that it did not stimulate—or, at least, has not yet stimulated—a "never again" reaction, but it resembles the earlier case in the failure to encourage the conviction that the collective venture should or can become the model for reaction to future cases of aggression. The Iraqi case, it seems to me, confirms, demonstrates, and emphasizes most of the problems, uncertainties, and difficulties that have previously been associated with collective security and have contributed to its rejection. I now turn to these perennial difficulties, as illustrated by this case.

The first difficulties are posed by what I shall label *quasi-pacifism*: extreme reluctance to use force, inspired by moral or prudential considerations, or both. The quasi-pacifist does not, in principle, reject the use of force under any and all circumstances, but has great difficulty in finding any occasion that seems to warrant military actions. Understandably, quasi-pacifism is an increasingly significant factor in modern society, and particularly in the liberal democracies of the West.

Collective security, by contrast, is a hard-line approach to world order. While it does not necessarily entail a military response to every violation of order, it does require readiness and willingness to resort to arms in every case. Its stock in trade is intimidation; it calls for confrontation. Moreover, it suffers the disadvantage of being a do-it-yourself scheme for world order, offering no alternative to states themselves as the order-keeping agents of the system. In a world that has long yearned for a *Great Somebody* to bestow upon it the blessings of peace and security—a world court that would settle all disputes through legal processes, or a world government that would infallibly restrain all wrongdoers—collective security uncompromisingly insists that there can be no check upon states that resort to violence in pursuit of their objectives save that provided by the combined efforts of other states, acting in recognition of their own interest in maintaining the order of the system. Clearly, such an arrangement is unlikely to appeal to quasi-pacifists.

The enforcement action sometimes required by commitment to collective security always has the appearance of gratuitous, unnecessary,

and non-defensive resort to arms. States, without having themselves
been attacked, choose to fight against the designated aggressor. Thus,
in the Iraqi case, the United States and other members of its coalition
decided to engage Iraq. States loyally performing their duties as members of a collective security system thereby risk seeming to be aggressors themselves. This is especially true when the response to
aggression is, for whatever reason, delayed. Ironically, the longer one
waits to respond to aggression—that is, the more disposition one
shows to give peace a chance, to search for a nonmilitary solution—
the more vulnerable is the ultimate military response to characteri-
zation as the initiation of a war. This was true in the case at hand,
when resort to arms to force Iraq out of Kuwait was postponed for
some five and one-half months, while persuasion, condemnation, and
economic sanctions were put to the test. As the UN deadline of January 15, 1991, approached without evidence that Iraq would give up
its conquest of Kuwait, the American press began to paint President
Bush as the saber-rattler, the one intent on having a war, and Saddam
Hussein as one who wanted peace (as he clearly did; no aggressor
desires to be opposed!). When the delayed campaign in opposition to
Iraq's aggression began, Coretta Scott King declared: "I strongly de-
plore and was deeply saddened by the White House decision to launch
a war against Iraq."[5] Pope John Paul II reacted to the American-led
campaign by declaring that this outbreak of war signaled "a grave
defeat for international law and the international community."[6] To
these high-minded moralists, collective security actions, delayed in the
hope that aggression might be reversed by nonmilitary pressures,
amounted to the unwarranted launching of a war—that is, to aggression. Note how the anti-military bias of the quasi-pacifist, the disposition to assume that war can have no profitable outcome and to argue
that no problem is genuinely amenable to military solution, tends to
defeat any inclination to approve the liberation of a state from ruthless invaders, the upholding of the international law against aggression, and the enforcement of the proclaimed will and intent of the
international community.

Acting in conformity with the obligations entailed by membership
in a collective security system violates the rule of prudence and the
requirements set by the norms of modern democratic societies: Avoid
war if possible; treat war as an absolutely last resort; fight only when
there is no alternative. Collective security requires states to choose to
enter wars that have not been thrust upon them and that they might
avoid. A major obstacle to collective security has always been the excessive reluctance of states to use force, to get involved in messy and
dangerous situations. By some standards, including those of quasi-
pacifists, President Bush was excessively impatient and bellicose in

his reaction to Iraq's aggression; by the standards of a collective security system, a delay of several months in the military response to armed aggression might be regarded as excessively long. At any rate, this case emphasizes the difficulty that would confront efforts to mobilize opinion, in the United States and elsewhere, in support of the prompt and virtually automatic collective resistance to aggression that is envisaged in the doctrine of collective security. It contributes little to convincing aggressors that the organized community will certainly act to defeat their moves, or to assuring potential victims of aggression that the combined strength of fellow members of the United Nations will assist them in timely fashion.

Collective security does not, of course, represent the insistence that military response to aggression should be treated as the exclusive means of maintaining world order, even though it does require that such response not be excluded. The idea of collective security has consistently been associated with arrangements for pacific settlement of disputes, and with obligations to confront aggressors with diplomatic and economic, as well as military, sanctions. Problems pertaining to collective security have persistently included issues of choice, sequence, and timing: What kind of response should be made to a given crisis? In what order should other responses be tried if the first does not avail? When and under what circumstances should diplomatic, economic, or military responses be supplanted or supplemented by one of the others? Our recent case illustrates the continuing difficulty of answering these questions.

Procedures for pacific settlement are not an integral part of, but are a preliminary alternative to, a collective security system. Pacific settlement is intended to reduce the need for an enforcement system by preventing disputes from degenerating into instances of aggression. Thus, in theory, pacific settlement and collective security have distinct areas of applicability—disputes for the former and military conflicts for the latter. In the real world, situations do not always fall clearly into one category or the other, and there is often room for disagreement as to whether the situation at hand calls for the effort to reach a negotiated solution associated with the idea of pacific settlement or for the firm, confrontational stance associated with collective security. When is it appropriate for diplomats to assist the parties in working out a compromise that will save face for both sides; and when is it in order to adopt a judgmental approach, condemning one party as an aggressor and using community pressures to face him down?

The champion of collective security might argue that, in the Persian Gulf case, Saddam Hussein's invasion of Kuwait took the matter out of the domain of pacific settlement and into that of collective security. Indeed, this position was taken by the United Nations, which from the start pointedly invoked the Charter's provisions concerning enforcement rather than those concerning pacific settlement: Chapter VII rather than Chapter VI. This view of the case was not universally held, however, and a major basis of the criticism that Operation Desert Storm engendered was the conviction that the diplomatic approach had been neglected or inadequately tested; one heard much of the contention that Saddam Hussein should have been offered concessions sufficient to enable him to pull back without loss of face.

A distinction should be made between diplomatic negotiations, in search of a pacific settlement for a dispute, and diplomatic pressures or boycott, a type of sanction identified with the operation of a collective security system—that is, intended to contribute to the restraint of the aggressor. The standard doctrine of collective security views diplomatic, economic, and military sanctions, in that order, as the increasingly severe reactions prescribed for dealing with aggression. In practice, international organizations have typically reacted to aggression only by adopting such diplomatic sanctions as formal protest and multilateral condemnation, but such limited measures generally deserve to be interpreted less as real efforts to implement collective security than as mere lip service, indicative of the actual rejection of that approach. Only when diplomatic pressures are joined with economic or military sanctions is it plausible to suggest that the idea of collective security is being taken seriously, and the economic or military half of the combination should be regarded as the major element.

Should economic sanctions be considered merely a prelude or preparation for military sanctions and perhaps an accompaniment of the latter, or should they be treated as an alternative to military action? Twentieth-century students of international organization developed the conventional wisdom that economic sanctions require at least the backing of a military threat; after all, the notion of the economic weapon derived from the historical experience of wartime blockades, which supplemented rather than substituted for military operations. Nevertheless, it is true that President Wilson and other early champions of collective security entertained and encouraged the hope that the goals of that system might be reached by nonmilitary means; that economic sanctions might provide a cheaper, more humane, less morally suspect way of stopping aggressors than military action. Collective security is more palatable if the job can be done without warlike measures, and quasi-pacifists will always be tempted to assume that economic sanctions will suffice. It should be noted, however, that the assumption of the moral superiority of economic to military sanctions may be open to challenge if and when economic boycotts become effective enough to begin to raise the possibility of succeeding, for at that point the civilian population of the targeted state will be suffering severe deprivation. It is not self-evident that it is more humane to starve women and children than to shoot soldiers, and the recent economic blockade of Iraq aroused some moral qualms for this very reason.

Even if economic sanctions fail the test of moral impeccability, however, there is much to be said for defeating aggressors without resort to force, if that is possible. Perhaps the most troublesome issue in the Iraqi case was the question of how long to rely on economic sanctions before adding the pressure of military coercion. The hope that force might not be required to reverse Iraq's conquest of Kuwait was by no means exclusively the product of the wishful thinking of quasi-pacifists. Many sober and serious analysts, in the United States and abroad, believed there was at least a strong possibility that, in time, economic sanctions would cause Saddam Hussein either to retreat from Kuwait or to lose his job to a political leader who would do so. There was much to be said for the argument that Iraq was particularly vulnerable to sanctions, and that the organization of the embargo was one of the most effective in history.

On the other hand, there were valid concerns about leaving Kuwait to the brutal occupation of its conquerors for an indeterminate period, questions about whether delay would increase or decrease the military capacity of Iraq's regime, and uncertainty about whether a genuine military option could be maintained during long months of inaction by the coalition led by the United States. For how long should the world have relied exclusively on economic sanctions? President Bush's decision to add military coercion after hardly more than five months was widely criticized as being premature, and we shall never know whether economic measures alone would have done the job, and, if so, after how long. It should be remembered, however, that the military campaign did not end the economic sanctions but vastly intensified them; the destruction visited upon Iraq by the coalition military forces should be expected to accelerate the effects of the economic sanctions, which at this writing (early June 1991) are still in force. In short, even though the economic sanctions have been in operation for an extended period and have been supplemented by enormous military devastation, Saddam Hussein remains in power in Iraq. This situation might suggest that President Bush's pessimistic estimate of the power of economic sanctions to reverse Iraq's aggression was valid, and it might tend to justify his decision to launch the military response in mid-January. In any event, this case makes it clear that the enterprise of collective security is likely always to be bedeviled by uncertainty and contention as to the appropriateness and necessity of the various types of measures for effectuating the anti-aggression mission. The question of whether and when to move beyond economic pressure to military coercion is a particularly hardy perennial issue that will continue to incite bitter division.

Multilateral moves against aggression, whether or not undertaken by an organized collective security system, pose a number of other questions for which there are no answers likely to produce easy agreement. What constitutes victory for the collective force? When and where should that force stop? Is its proper mission merely to push the aggressor back to his own frontier, or should it invade the aggressor's territory to decimate his military capability and perhaps even to unseat the offending regime? Because theorists of collective security have provided no guidance beyond the proposition that, if deterrence should fail, the aggressive act must be frustrated and the victim of aggression defended, a further question arises: Who should decide these issues? Should the decisions invariably rest with the multilateral body under whose auspices the collective action presumably takes place, or should such issues be settled by the states actively engaged in the venture? Should there be some connection between bearing the burdens and making the decisions?

These matters proved troublesome in the Korean case, when the goals of the coalition resisting North Korea were subjected to expansion and contraction, and there was widespread anxiety as to the good judgment and prudence of the predominant member of that group, the United States. The potential for difficulty about these questions was equally great in the case of Iraq. The United States was perceived in some quarters as something of a loose cannon, and as the triumph of the coalition unfolded the apprehension was widely expressed that President Bush was intent on exceeding the mandate to undo the aggression by liberating Kuwait, going on to destroy Iraq's military establishment and to overthrow and perhaps capture Saddam Hussein. President Bush disarmed his critics, actual and potential, by stopping the military campaign promptly with the ouster of Iraq's forces from Kuwait. This action was clearly a politically prudent decision; whether it was a genuinely wise and proper decision seems, in retrospect, uncertain. President Bush avoided criticism by declining to exceed the UN mandate—but he encountered criticism when the consequences of leaving Iraq's dictator in place, with substantial military power at his disposal, became evident. The terrible events that have occurred in post-war Iraq raise a legitimate question about the appropriateness of limiting the collective enterprise to the objective of removing the invaders from Kuwait.

The question of who decides what the collective force should do and where and when it should stop is only one instance of the larger issue of the relationship between unilateralism and multilateralism in resistance to aggression, which involves difficult questions about leadership, burden-sharing, authority, direction, and control. The theory of collective security essentially ignores this entire range of issues. It seems to assume a kind of spontaneous and universal joining together of states in reaction to aggression; an attack occurs and the whole world rallies to the defense of its target state. Needless to say, the world does not work that way!

The twentieth century has seen the rise of what we may call the multilateral syndrome. This syndrome begins with the recognition that all states are intricately interconnected and that many problems are manageable only by the combined or coordinated efforts of many states. However, this approach tends to go beyond these realistic premises to the dogmatic propositions that unilateral decisions and actions are inevitably selfish and ill-advised, while multilateralism is the reliable font of justice and wisdom in the international system. Collective security is a manifestation of this syndrome. Emphasizing the virtues of multilateralism, its champions have not adequately taken into account the free rider problem: the tendency of those who will automatically enjoy the benefits of public goods to leave the production of those goods to others. The case of Iraq illustrates the vulnerability of the multistate system to this problem, for most states exhibited not so much the resolve to do their part in the maintenance of world order as the willingness to permit and authorize other states to do the job. This case suggests that a collective security system might turn out to be not a "do it yourself" but a "let them do it" scheme. Even in the United States, reaction against the burden we were carrying and worry about our worthiness to run the show tended to produce a "let the United Nations do it" attitude.

Collective security's idealization of multilateralism is matched by its denigration of unilateralism. Herein lies a major dilemma of collective security: While it deplores and discourages unilateralism, it is utterly dependent upon it, for unilateralism is the essential basis of leadership. The recent case, like the Korean case, demonstrates beyond a doubt that there will be no multilateral resistance to aggression without the determined leadership of a great power, a state that does not defer to and wait for the multilateral flock but unilaterally moves out from and pulls as many of that flock as possible along with it. The decisive leader must serve as the instigator and organizer of collective response to aggression and the dominant contributor to it, displaying the willingness to carry a disproportionate share of the burden, pay the fares of numerous free riders, and take the brunt of the inevitable criticism that its leadership constitutes unseemly unilateralism.

There is, in today's world, only one state equipped to play this role: the United States. It clearly did so in the Korean and Iraqi cases, and it conceived its role in Vietnam in that vein. President Bush's vision of a new world order, while not fully articulated, seems to entail U.S. leadership of the United Nations in the systematic enforcement of the rule against aggression. This vision is countered by the broadly held conviction of Americans that we cannot and must not serve as the world's policeman, which is precisely what such leadership of a collective security system would mean. It is challenged by the world's bias against the unilateralism that is, in fact, indispensable to effective multilateralism. U.S. leadership regularly runs afoul, as it did in the recent case, of the charge that the United States is too arrogantly insistent on running the show itself, without adequate authorization, consultation, or direction from without. It should be noted that in the Iraqi case the United States displayed an unaccustomed deference to the United Nations, following the advice that it obtain the blessing and authorization of the Security Council in advance of each step in the progressive mobilization of pressure against Iraq. It is remarkable how little credit the United States gained for this adherence to the multilateral creed, this tempering of its leadership style. If the United States had not invoked and followed the United Nations, it would undoubtedly have been more severely castigated. However, by choosing this course it exposed itself to the charge of abusing and exploiting the United Nations, of putting undue pressure on the organization to endorse U.S. policy. The notion that the United States served the United Nations, in Korea or in Iraq, is rarely to be heard. Realistically, however, the collective enforcement of the ban on aggression is dependent on unilateral initiative in moving multilateral agencies, the kind of leadership that the United States is reluctant to give and that the world is reluctant to accept. The world wants a Great Somebody to maintain order. The Great Somebody turns out, to our chagrin, to be us. "Let the United Nations do it" means, in translation, "let the United States do it, with authorization from the United Nations and with such support and assistance as it can muster."

Finally, I would argue that the decisive difficulty about collective security, one illustrated by the Iraqi case, is the unacceptability of aggression as the exclusive object of collective condemnation and enforcement action. Collective security has been conceived solely as a device to enforce rules against aggression, not as a general law enforcement mechanism. This conception reflects the assumption that war is the central problem of the international system and is produced largely by aggression, the pursuit of objectives by military means. If aggression can be prevented, the world can enjoy peace; if peace prevails, other major problems can be successfully solved. So runs the argument.

From the premise that the world simply cannot afford war, that every state's most vital interest is the maintenance of global order, flows the proposition that aggression, whatever its cause or its purpose, is always intolerable; aggressors must consistently be opposed, and victims of aggression defended. The theory of collective security requires and assumes such a consensus, but, in fact, it has never existed. To establish an absolute prohibition of aggression is to limit changes in the status quo to those that can be peacefully achieved, which all too often comes uncomfortably close to meaning that change is prohibited. It is closer to the truth to say that there is a global consensus that some changes are warranted and required (although there may not be agreement on which changes fall into that category) and that they should be achieved, by force if necessary. The United Nations may have been conceived as an agency for preserving the existing international order against violent challenge, but in the course of its development it has become an instrument for the support of revolutionary demands for justice in the global system; more an anti–status quo than a pro–status quo organization. Furthermore, it is not clear that this orientation either can or should be changed. Virtually everyone and every state considers some objective—the elimination of some injustice, or the promotion of some value—as so compelling that its achievement justifies resort to military aggression. If the United Nations were today a functioning system of collective security, reliably effective against every act of aggression, most of the world would denounce it as a nefarious scheme for shoring up a flagrantly unjust status quo.

Uncertainty about whether aggressors should always be restrained and whether their victims always deserve support is compounded by the conviction that there are other international evils at least as deserving of collective remonstrance and coercive repression. Collective security's preoccupation with aggression is anathema to those whose attention tends to be concentrated on tyranny, colonialism, apartheid, or general disrespect for human rights, and who, in truth, may sympathize with aggression directed against states in which such evils are ensconced. Responding for the Democratic Party to President Bush's 1991 State of the Union message, devoted largely to the Persian Gulf war, Senator George J. Mitchell criticized the administration's failure to respond to such events as the massacre of students in China, the killing of priests in Central America, and the use of violence against demonstrators in Lithuania, arguing that these acts "are as wrong as Iraqi soldiers killing civilians" and that "We cannot oppose repression in one place and overlook it in another."[7] Moreover, many who were critical of U.S. resort to arms to reverse Iraq's conquest of Kuwait have been equally critical of its subsequent refusal to use force to protect Iraq's Kurdish population from persecution and to squelch other domestic abuses by the regime of Saddam Hussein. The world is by no means unanimous in approving collective security's proposition that multilateral coercion should always be brought to bear against aggression and never against any other form of malfeasance.

In conclusion, let me reiterate my belief that the Persian Gulf war does not presage the establishment of an arrangement for the systematic suppression by multilateral means of all acts of aggression, the creation of a collective security system. Rather, I think it points to the existence and probable continuation of a consensus in favor of *selective anti-aggression*, entailing the authorization by the United Nations of collective pressure, to be exercised by an ad hoc coalition under U.S. leadership, and to include military means only if other measures seem ineffective. The theme of this approach is that aggression will perhaps, sometimes—not always—engender collective opposition.

Although President Bush's rhetoric has clearly championed the comprehensive anti-aggression orientation associated with the theory of collective security, there is reason to believe that his real commitment is to a policy of selective anti-aggression. The best evidence of this is perhaps a statement attributed to Secretary of Defense Richard Cheney, with reference to the Gulf War:

This happens to be one of those times when it is justified to . . . send American forces into combat to achieve important national objectives. But they are very rare. Just because we do it successfully this once, it doesn't mean we should therefore assume that it is something we ought to fall back on automatically as the easy answer to international problems in the future. We have to remember that we don't have a dog in every fight, that we don't want to get involved in every single conflict.[8]

In the absence of repudiation by President Bush, this endorsement of selectivity appears to express the policy of his administration. Is this substitution of an option to oppose aggression for the comprehensive commitment demanded by collective security to be deplored, or welcomed? Let us examine the pros and cons, starting with the latter.

On the negative side, it is true that discrimination is likely always to appear invidious, inviting the charge of the double standard, hypocrisy, and inconsistency. Why oppose this aggressor, and not that one? How to justify defending this state against attack while ignoring another's plight? To be selective is to spoil one's moral case, to give up the claim to upholding the principle that the integrity of all states must be respected. More pragmatically, the selective approach sacrifices the possibility of providing a strong deterrent against aggression and offering clear assurance of protection to potential targets of aggression. To pick and choose among cases of aggression is to perpetuate the unpredictability of international relations and the resultant insecurity, rather than to move toward a stable world order.

The case for selectivity derives from the implausibility—indeed, the falsity—of collective security theory's equating all instances of aggression. The theory asserts that every act of aggression, by threatening to destroy international order, violates the national interest of every state. The system requires that statesmen and their peoples believe and act upon that premise, treating all acts of aggression, regardless of time, place, parties, and circumstances, as necessary occasions for fulfillment of the responsibilities of collective resistance. Nobody believes this premise, nor should anyone. In fact, there are great variations in the significance of cases for world order, and for the security of states not immediately under attack. An attack by China upon the Soviet Union would have a greater impact on world order than an attack by Kenya upon Uganda; U.S. interests would be more seriously affected by aggression against Canada than by aggression against Burma. When the League of Nations abandoned Ethiopia to Italian conquest, the eloquent warning, "Never forget that you may someday be somebody's Ethiopia," was sounded, and in retrospect the argument was often made that British and French acquiescence in the violation of Ethiopia, which seemed far away and unimportant, paved the way for German invasion of Czechoslovakia and Poland, which Britain and France regarded as a drastic challenge to their own security. The contention that any act of aggression that is permitted to succeed initiates the general collapse of international order and stability provides the basis for the view that there are no trivial cases and no remote areas; a case that seems unimportant in itself can have consequences of fundamental importance for the entire world. Plausible as this position may be, it does not disturb the conviction of most statesmen, and most of the rest of us, that there are key cases and cases of lesser importance, and that political leaders have the solemn obligation to be discriminating in their reactions, calculating as well as they can the consequences of standing aside, of trying to promote a negotiated settlement, and of joining in the support of one side or the other. The United States and other members of the coalition did not protect Saudi Arabia and liberate Kuwait because of adherence to the principle that any aggression by any state against any other must be defeated. They judged that Kuwait and Saudi Arabia were very important, that Iraq was very dangerous, and in response to that judgment they adopted a policy in accord with that principle.

The case for selective anti-aggression instead of collective security is, at bottom, the realistic proposition that statesmen will not, and the normative view that they should not, abandon discretion and discrimination, adopt a formula rather than formulate judgments, and put

4

Great Power Rivalry and the Persian Gulf

Bruce R. Kuniholm

The influence of the great powers on the peoples and political systems of the Persian Gulf[1] has been longstanding and profound. This chapter examines the interplay between external and internal forces in the region, focusing in particular on the rise and decline of Britain's trucial system. It also delineates how the historical rivalry between Britain and Russia in the Persian Gulf and Southwest Asia[2] provided the context—just as the gradual decline of the British Empire set the stage—for the emergence of the United States as an important factor in the Middle East, and for its eventual involvement in the Persian Gulf crisis.

HISTORICAL BACKGROUND

The policies and imperial aspirations of the world's great powers in the Persian Gulf and Southwest Asia have been repeatedly influenced over the centuries by geopolitical considerations. In the sixth century B.C., Cyrus the Great and his successors subjected the civilizations along the region's great river systems—the Tigris, the Euphrates, and the Indus—to the dominion of a Persian empire that stretched across the Near East from Greece to the frontier of India. Two centuries later the Achaemenid dynasty was conquered by Alexander the Great, who in turn extended his empire from the Balkans to the Indus Valley.

As kingdoms and empires vied for hegemony, indigenous cultures adapted to and, in turn, were transformed by the various influences to which they were subjected. After Alexander's conquests, the Near East was exposed to Greek and subsequently Roman influence, while the brilliant Sassanid dynasty emerged from its Iranian homeland to overthrow its Parthian overlords and extend its rule to the Arabian Peninsula and the Indus Valley.

Throughout, the Persian Gulf served as a line of communications and a natural channel for trade between the Mediterranean and East Asia. Its mercantile cities rose and fell, contesting among themselves for supremacy in the Gulf, competing with others on the littoral of the Red Sea for trade between East and West, and with them serving as the western termini for trade originating in the Far East.[3]

The Advent of Islam

In the seventh century A.D., the Prophet Muhammad and his followers united the Arabian Peninsula. Within a century, Islam radiated westward across the northern shores of Africa to the Iberian Peninsula and eastward across Persia, which Arab armies defeated at the battles of Qaddisya and Nahavand. Islam eventually reached Central Asia and the subcontinent, where Turks, Afghans, and then Mongols swept through the northwest passes previously traversed by Alexander, carrying a new faith and dominating India. By the early eighteenth century, the Mughul empire, founded two centuries earlier by Babur, a descendant of Genghis Khan and Timur (Tamerlane), encompassed all but some coastal enclaves and the southern tip of the Indian subcontinent.

Islamic civilization, meanwhile, centered first in Damascus and then in Baghdad, flourished under the Umayyad and Abbasid dynasties. After the accession of the Abbasids to the caliphate in 750 and the removal of the capital from Damascus to Baghdad, commerce flourished between the Persian Gulf and China, and the sea route between them became the longest in regular use by mankind before European expansion began; by following the monsoons, one could make the round trip in a year and a half.[4]

The Abbasid dynasty gave way, in time, to invaders from the north: first Seljuks; then Mongols under Hulagu, the grandson of Genghis Khan, who captured Baghdad in 1258; and finally the Seljuks' successors, the Ottomans, whose forces, converted to Islam, captured Constantinople in 1453 and brought about the fall of the Byzantine Empire. By the seventeenth century, the Ottoman Empire extended from North Africa and Eastern Europe to the western shores of the Persian Gulf, while the Gulf's eastern shores came under the jurisdiction of the Safavid dynasty, the founders of modern Iran, whose subjects, weathering both Arab and Mongol invasions, had preserved their separate identity. From this time until the present century, the states of greatest significance to the great powers in the region would be Turkey and Iran.[5]

The Coming of the Europeans

The Portuguese, meanwhile, embarking on the voyages of discovery and conquest, rounded the Cape of Good Hope and established trading settlements along the western coast of the Mughul empire in South Asia; with the capture in 1515 of Hormuz, the chief commercial emporium in the Persian Gulf, they inaugurated a century of Portuguese supremacy in the Indian Ocean. Through control of the Red Sea, the Persian Gulf, and the Straits of Malacca, the Portuguese hoped to outflank their competitors and force European trade with the Indies to route itself via the Cape of Good Hope, where they could levy customs and port dues and harass the shipping of rival powers.[6]

Within a century, however, the British acquired increasing confidence in their maritime power and successfully contested the Portuguese monopoly in the region. The result was the establishment of the English East India Company in 1600, and the capture of Hormuz in 1622. Surviving a fierce challenge for mercantile supremacy by the Dutch and subsequently the French, the British by 1765 had become the dominant European power in India and the East India Company became a territorial power whose transformation had important implications for the Gulf.[7]

In 1798, the East India Company negotiated an agreement with Sayyid Sultan, head of the Al Bu Said dynasty and ruler of Muscat (Oman). It was the first of an elaborate web of treaties and agreements with the principalities of the Arabian Peninsula littoral that, in time, would define British hegemony over the first major Gulf system in modern times.[8] The agreement followed Napoleon's occupation of Egypt and resulted from British fear of a French assault on India: launched either from the Suez isthmus with ships from the Ile de France (Mauritius) and the Red Sea; or from the Eastern Mediterranean, overland to the head of the Gulf and then along the coast to India. Complementing the treaty with Oman was another with Persia in 1801 that had two objectives: to threaten the western frontier of Afghanistan, so restraining Zaman Shah, the amir of Kabul, who had invaded India several times; and to create an Iranian buffer against the possibility of an overload attack by Napoleon.[9]

The "Great Game" and Its Consequences for the Gulf

While these threats had disappeared by the time the treaties were concluded, they raised for the first time the problem of how to ensure

the security of British India.[10] After French operations in the Indian
Ocean were brought to an end by the capture of the Ile de France in
1810, and following Napoleon's defeat at Waterloo in 1815, perceptions
of the threat posed by France gradually gave way to that posed by
Russia, which was expanding eastward by land as Europe's maritime
states had by sea. By 1818, the British had destroyed the power of the
principal Indian states, replaced the Mughul empire as the paramount
power in India, and secured a continuous land frontier.[11] As a result,
when Russia acquired valuable land from northwest Persia and eastern Turkey in the treaties of Turkmanchay and Adrianople (1828 and
1829), the British became anxious about their new frontiers. Having
failed to create protectorates in either Persia or Turkey, they sought
to devise a counterweight to Russian influence. This enterprise, the
so-called "Great Game" in Asia, derived from a fact of geography and
a fact of politics: The British had a frontier to defend and they could
find no one to defend it for them. Lacking a geographical equivalent
of the English Channel, they looked for a political equivalent and
eventually attempted to construct a zone of buffer states from Turkey
through Persia to Khiva and Bokhara. The zone was recognized by
both Russia and Britain as independent, possessing recognized boundaries, and preserved by equal British and Russian pressures.[12]

Over time, the Great Game of advancing and protecting great power
interests resulted in modi vivendi whose rules included the implicit
assumption that there should be an equilibrium of forces in the region
and that vital interests should not be threatened. When observed,
these arrangements maintained the balance of power in the region
and (if they were deficient in dealing with the region's emerging nationalist forces) were capable of mitigating tensions between the great
powers. This they did in 1907, 1915–1916, and 1944. The emerging
countries in the buffer zone that separated the imperial powers and
that were subject to imperial understandings, meanwhile, did what
they could to survive. In the period between World War I and World
War II, for example, they allied among themselves against threats
from without. The Balkan Pact of 1934 and the Sa'adabad Pact of 1937
constituted attempts to escape from traditional rivalries to which they
were being subjected. The only alternative to forming alliances was
playing one power off against the other, balancing them in one form
or another, or looking to third powers for assistance. After World War
II, as their survival was threatened by the relative disparity between
Soviet and British power, they turned to the United States for assistance. But this line of analysis is getting ahead of the story in the
Persian Gulf.

While the Great Game was in its infancy, the imperatives of territorial dominion in India were leading the British to obtain and hold command of the Persian Gulf.[13] Implicit in their thinking was the notion that British seapower in the Gulf and Eastern Mediterranean could balance that of Russia in the Black and the Caspian seas. The immediate target of British seapower, the Qawasim of Ras al-Khaimah and Sharjah, controlled several ports on both sides of the Persian Gulf and were renowned for their sailing skills. Deprived of considerable trade by the Cape passage and possessing few natural resources (oil was not discovered until the twentieth century), the tribal chiefs of the Gulf's small city-states were locked in a fierce maritime rivalry with the Al Bu Said dynasty of Muscat (which was also embroiled in a civil war with the conservative religious leaders of Oman's interior) over what little the Persian Gulf itself had to offer: pearl fisheries and trade with India and Africa.[14]

The Qasimi naval confederacy, which was much larger than the 80–100 dhows of its Qawasim core, boasted a fleet of 63 large and 810 small vessels, many of which were faster and more easily handled than European ships. The largest, used for both trading and raiding, were between 200 and 500 tons, had crews of 150 men and carried enormous sails that one British observer considered equal to those of a 36-gun frigate. The Saidi opponents of the Qawasim had 3 brigs and 15 ships of between 400 and 700 tons, in addition to a smaller fleet of 100 seagoing vessels. Although the British were suspicious of Muscat's links with the French on Mauritius, developing ties with the Al Bu Said were reinforced by a desire to prevent Napoleon's acquisition of a base in the Gulf and resulted in assistance to the Al Bu Said in their war with the Qawasim.[15]

While the Qawasim did not usually harm European crews, they were nonetheless responsible for numerous attacks on British vessels. They also attacked Indian merchant ships flying British colors, whose crews they sometimes put to death. As the war with the Al Bu Said continued, the Qawasim, encouraged in their actions by a moral imperative to proclaim a jihad (holy war) that derived from the Wahhabi religious revival in the heartland of the Arabian Peninsula, were emboldened to step up their attacks on merchant vessels—twenty in November 1808 alone—and demand tribute for safe passage.

Britain, its imperial consciousness stimulated by a petition from the merchants of Bombay, in 1809 launched an expeditionary force to rid the Persian Gulf of "piracy." Piracy, as one historian has observed, like treason, is a relative term; however, regardless of how one characterizes the maritime war between the Gulf states, and between the Qawasim and the British, it is clear that Britain intended to look out for its interests in Oman and preserve its prestige at sea. A brief occupation of Ras al-Khaimah coupled with the destruction there and across the Persian Gulf of some seventy dhows allowed for a respite that was only temporary since most of the Qasimi fleet escaped.

Within a few years, East India Company vessels again were attacked, some were captured, and as the small city-states around the Persian Gulf joined in, convoys of merchant ships from India were forced to run a gauntlet of Qasimi dhows in the Strait of Hormuz. Making use of a growing sea power to enforce their will, the British in 1819 mounted another expedition to the Persian Gulf to break the power of the Qawasim. With 11 ships carrying 200 guns, and a force of 1,453 Europeans, 2,094 Indian sepoys, and 600 Omanis, the British expeditionary force destroyed fortifications, vessels, and military stores at Ras al-Khaimah and other sites on both sides of the Gulf, forcing the leading sheiks of the Pirate Coast (subsequently the Trucial Coast) to submit to the British commander and proffer friendship.[16]

BRITAIN'S TRUCIAL SYSTEM, 1820–1971

Judging that peace would depend on cooperation within the Persian Gulf as well as on the vigilance of Britain's naval and military forces, the British commander opted against a punitive settlement. The General Treaty for the Cessation of Plunder and Piracy by Land and Sea, signed by the sheiks of the Trucial Coast and Bahrain between January and March 1820, ended coastal attacks against British shipping and served as the cornerstone of British policy in the region for the next 151 years. While the treaty avoided harsh treatment of the sheikhdoms and protected British shipping, it did not prevent maritime war between the tribes. A subsequent treaty in 1835 established a maritime truce during the six-month pearling season and was renewed periodically until the Perpetual Maritime Truce in 1853 made permanent a complete cessation of hostilities at sea.[17]

In 1879, another agreement provided for the maritime extradition of debtors and was crucial to the stability of the pearling business, which by the 1870s employed a considerable number of Gulf workers—including 1,500 vessels and 42,000 men from Oman, and 713 vessels and 13,500 men from Bahrain. Other agreements attempted to prohibit slave trade, which annually brought ten to fifteen thousand slaves into the region in the first half of the nineteenth century. The slave trade was reduced to a trickle by the 1870s; but because it provided divers for the pearling industry, it continued well into the twentieth century, ending only after the Gulf pearl industry foundered in the face of competition from the cultured pearl industry in Japan. Further agreements with the British addressed communications issues and the prohibition of arms.[18]

As the nineteenth century wore on, Britain, in addition to initiating the complex of treaties and agreements just described, assumed increasing responsibility for the defense of the sheikhdoms. In 1892 it consolidated previous arrangements in the Exclusive Agreement, under which the coastal states promised not to enter into any agreement or correspondence with any power other than Great Britain. Britain, in turn, agreed to provide for the external defense of the trucial states and look after their foreign relations. By the end of World War I, in spite of challenges—both real and perceived—from France, Turkey, Russia, and Germany, Britain clearly was the dominant power in the Persian Gulf. Germany, Russia, and the Ottoman Empire had been defeated; Iran and Iraq, apparently, were at Britain's mercy; Bahrain and Qatar had been brought into the trucial system; and Kuwait was guar anteed independence under a British protectorate.[19]

British policy toward the Gulf throughout this period does not seem to have been consistently informed by any one strategic theme except, perhaps, a general belief, held since 1798, that India's defense must be as far away from India and as cheap as possible. A corollary was that bases in the Persian Gulf must be denied to other foreign powers and that a foreign presence in the region could excite unrest in India. While the defense of India, the defense of lines of communication, and eco nomic interest all played a part in British attitudes toward the Persian Gulf, these objectives rationalized a general and more fundamental perception that peace in the region was required. Since regional powers had failed to keep the peace, Britain assumed the responsibility. British policy, whether formulated primarily by the East India Company, the Government of Bombay (after 1858), the British India Government (after 1878), or the Foreign Office in London (which after the British withdrawal from India in 1947 had sole jurisdiction), was carried out through an economy of force: a political resident in Bushire (in Bahrain after World War II); a few agents in various towns; a British squadron of six cruisers that patrolled the waters of the region; and the Indian army. All were meant not to fight but to exist. As with British India, "judicious coercion" in conjunction with the appearance of unassailable British power was expected to effect British ends. In the Persian Gulf, this strategy meant preservation of the status quo as long as the effort did not become too costly.[20]

The Era of British "Predominance"

A British historian, writing of the Persian Gulf during the nineteenth and twentieth centuries, has characterized its history as a product of the relationships among the geographically isolated local powers of the Gulf coast; regional powers centered in Baghdad, Riyadh and Teheran; and international powers such as the Ottoman Empire, Egypt, France, Germany, Russia, the United States, and Britain.[21] Central to an understanding of the dynamics of these relationships is the fact that British predominance, more limited than many supposed, to a great extent was confined to the lesser powers of the lower Gulf region. Regional powers such as Iran, Iraq, and Saudi Arabia had sufficient geographical advantages, resources, and energies to avoid complete domination. But until these countries were able to assert themselves, as they did later in the twentieth century, they were otherwise preoccupied; first with the problem of survival and, subsequently, with the need to provide security for their oil, as well as with the difficulties that accompanied internal modernization. Under these circumstances, the status quo prevailed and the illusion of British supremacy was perpetuated by the framework of consent within which the British exercised their influence.[22]

On the local level, the stability created by British control reinforced the paternalistic and authoritarian leadership of the coastal states. It also helped to preserve the region's traditional sociopolitical organization, which was characterized by a complicated and delicate balance of power among tribal dynasties. Saidi and Qasimi commercial activities, meanwhile, declined with the loss of their respective advantages in controlling the Gulf's trade routes. The Bani Yas tribal confederation of Abu Dhabi and Dubai correspondingly benefited from its relatively greater power on land; by the 1870s the ruling sheik of Abu Dhabi was the most powerful sheik in the region, and Dubai had begun to rival Sharjah as the principal port on the coast. Regardless of relative losses and benefits, the ruling factions of the small city-states were protected by the British from absorption by their neighbors and collectively enhanced their prestige. While engaged in a confusing complex of feuds, intrigues, raids, and wars, the tribal chiefs, most of whom in the early nineteenth century could hardly be called rulers, gradually came to acquire the authority sufficient to merit the title.[23]

Following World War I and the breakup of the Ottoman Empire, although most peoples of the Middle East gradually achieved independence, the trucial states, under British protection, remained isolated from events in the region. Oil had been discovered in commercial quantities in Persia in 1908, and the British government in 1914 had acquired a controlling interest in the Anglo-Persian Oil Company. These events presaged the development of the region's oil resources and pointed to the Gulf's new strategic significance, but they did not immediately affect the smaller Persian Gulf states. With the exception of Bahrain (1932) and Kuwait (1938), oil was not discovered in commercial quantities in these smaller states until after World War II.

As a result, the evolution of the sheikhdoms continued at a small pace until the 1960s.[24]

Gradual Demise of the Trucial System

British withdrawal from India in 1947, meanwhile, eliminated the basis of Britain's responsibility as an imperial power and transferred responsibility for British policy from the government in India to the Foreign Office. While the Persian Gulf provided 85 percent of Britain's crude petroleum imports by the end of the decade, and protection of the Gulf oil fields had begun to emerge as an important concern, Whitehall was preoccupied with events elsewhere. As a result, Britain's unchallenged position in the Gulf left its purposes "east of Suez" undefined and its military presence unquestioned. In place of an integrated strategic doctrine, Whitehall simply assumed that Britain could remain in a position to influence developments in the Indian Ocean.[25]

Britain's decision in 1954 to withdraw its 80,000 troops from Egypt and the Suez crisis in 1956, however, challenged this assumption and significantly affected the Foreign Office's strategic thinking. The Suez crisis, like the Iranian crisis for the United States a quarter of a century later, provided a reference point for those advocating improvements in Britain's military capabilities: increased airlift capabilities, larger strategic reserves, and development of amphibious forces. More important, however, was the fact that restrictions on staging and overflight rights during the 1956 crisis called into question the reliability of any air route passing over the Middle East. As a consequence, military strategists began to focus on the desirability of stationing reserve elements at foreign bases to avoid dependence on precarious sea and air links. In the interim, public clamor for defense retrenchment and concomitant pressures to reduce manpower were resolved by a decision to abolish National Service (discussed subsequently); an increased emphasis on smaller, better equipped, more mobile conventional forces; and a greater reliance on nuclear deterrence.

The result of these developments was the creation of a more elaborate defense establishment "east of Suez." The British increased expenditures on their three major bases in Kenya, Singapore, and Aden; they also undertook smaller expansion projects, creating permanent accommodations for British troops and forward facilities for operations at Bahrain and Sharjah. In addition, the British established elements of a strategic reserve in Kenya and Singapore. They also based a balanced fleet at Singapore. They prepositioned heavy equipment and supplies at selected points; and they stationed an amphibious warfare

squadron at Aden, which became headquarters of a separate integrated command responsible directly to London. By 1964, the Middle
East Command had 8,000 members of the British armed forces, not
counting dependents, in its garrison.[26]

Behind the arguments about commitments, alliances, peacekeeping,
and economic interest that explained Britain's role east of Suez, two
considerations appear to have been central: British troops were already in the region and the Foreign Office continued to think of Britain as a world power. The armed services were also committed to this
line of thinking, and as they were continually engaged in military
campaigns east of Suez, they were not inclined to question it. As a
result, Britain supported the independence of the oil-producing states
during renewed violence and unrest in 1958; it also supported Kuwait
(from which it received half of its oil needs in the late 1950s) against
Iraqi threats in 1961. The forty-five ships Britain deployed to the region on ten days' notice during the recent Persian Gulf crisis, whether
or not they were crucial in deterring Iraqi designs, appeared to justify
the overseas deployment of British power.[27]

By this time, however, doubts about overseas bases in an era of
decolonization had begun to surface. As Britain's military burdens in
Malaysia, Indonesia, and Aden became more costly, severe strains
within the defense establishment provided evidence that those burdens would overtake the resources available. To make matters worse,
the rising tide of nationalist opposition, initially thought to be decades
away, proved closer than many had realized. The Labour Party, determined not to relinquish Britain's peacekeeping role and committed
to cuts in defense spending, began to discover after its return to office
in October 1964 that the two were incompatible. Throughout the next
four years, British defense policy east of Suez was driven by economic
issues. The military demands and political ineffectiveness of U.S. involvement in Vietnam, together with a growing conviction within the
British government that Britain's interests were primarily European,
encouraged a reassessment of Britain's overseas role. The catalyst was
Britain's deteriorating balance of payments position and the government's consequent determination to reduce overseas defense expenditures.[28]

A decision in 1957 to abolish National Service—implemented in
1962—resulted in a 50 percent reduction of manpower in the British
Army. The growing cost of new weapons systems was compounded by
a growing reluctance in the country to bear the burden of empire.
Britain's increasing loss of influence over the Persian Gulf's regional
powers in the 1950s, while not paralleled in its relations with the
smaller Gulf states, indicated a trend in Britain's relations with the
world east of Suez. In 1961, the British gave up their protectorate in

Kuwait, and their control in the Persian Gulf was reduced to Bahrain, Qatar, Oman, and the trucial states. As well-armed guerrillas in Yemen rendered old methods of control increasingly ineffective, and the base in Aden increasingly provoked the unrest it was intended to prevent, the government decided to withdraw from Aden. By this time, a retreat from a world role had become an accepted aim within the British government; debate focused not on whether withdrawal should occur but on how it should take place and at what rate. On November 29, 1967, the last British troops departed from Aden, and the stage was set for the end of the last important vestige of the nineteenth century's Pax Britannica.[29]

Britain's Departure from the Gulf

On January 16, 1968 ("Black Tuesday" to the British Ministry of Defense), Prime Minister Harold Wilson announced that British forces would be withdrawn from east of Suez before the end of 1971. Thereafter, he noted, Britain would retain no special capability for use in the area, relying instead on a general capability, based in Europe, to be deployed overseas as circumstances required.[30]

The political maneuvering that took place over the next three years was intense and deserves brief attention if only to convey a sense of the complex interplay between external and internal forces in the Persian Gulf.[31] While the smaller oil-producing sheikhdoms under British protection (Qatar, Bahrain, Abu Dhabi, and Dubai) wanted Britain to stay and were willing to pay the $35 to $40 million estimated annual cost of retaining British forces in the region, the Persian Gulf's major powers (Iran, Iraq, and Saudi Arabia) insisted that Britain honor its commitment to withdraw. The Conservative Party in Britain, meanwhile, hoped to put a stop to the decision and, after its return to power in June 1970, attempted to see if it was either practicable or desirable to reverse Labourite policy. In the interim, the Foreign Office suggested that the Gulf rulers form a federation to ensure at least a measure of mutual protection. As a result, the rulers of Bahrain, Qatar, and the trucial states in February 1968 duly signed an agreement to establish a Federation of Arab Emirates.[32]

Negotiations toward federation, however, were impeded by several factors. The Shah opposed the move because he saw it as a guise for the retention of British influence; he also claimed sovereignty over Bahrain (primarily as a bargaining chip for other interests in the Gulf) and saw British influence as an impediment to realization of his ambitions.[33] The trucial states and Qatar, in turn, were unwilling to put themselves in a position of having to support Bahrain against Iranian claims and hence were wary of any federation that included Bahrain.

They were also concerned that Bahrain's relatively large population (200,000) and thriving economy would dominate the federation. To make matters worse, the Al Thani dynasty of Qatar had a longstanding territorial dispute with the ruling Al Khalifa of Bahrain over the Hawar Islands and Zubarah (a village on the northwest coast of the Qatari peninsula).

Qatar and Bahrain, on the other hand, had good relations with Saudi Arabia; Bahrain, in particular, counted on Saudi support against Iran. Since federation with Abu Dhabi (the wealthiest of the trucial states) would put Qatar and Bahrain in the position of having to support Abu Dhabi in an ongoing territorial dispute with Saudi Arabia, the sheikhdoms were reluctant to join. The Saudis, for their part, insisted on satisfaction of territorial claims in eastern Arabia before acquiescing in the creation of the federation. There were other complications, but these give a fair sample of the difficulties involved.

Conservative opposition to Labourite policies in Britain, meanwhile, gave hope to the rulers of the smaller Persian Gulf states that they might yet retain British protection. This hope, given new life by Conservative support for the palace coup in Oman in July 1970, caused the rulers to drag their feet in negotiations toward federation. The British-supported coup in Oman, however, was intended primarily to stabilize the unraveling political situation there prior to Britain's departure from the region. Ultimately, the Conservatives realized that the decision to depart from the Persian Gulf could not be reversed. As the eminent journalist David Holden noted at the time, "to retain British forces in the Gulf once their withdrawal had been promised would have done more than any other single thing to promote the disorder which their continued presence would have been designed to prevent."[34]

With British encouragement, Abu Dhabi eventually was induced to concede some of the Saudi claims. Iranian claims were a more difficult matter. The Shah, in return for giving up his claim to Bahrain, insisted on sovereignty over three small islands in the Gulf—Abu Musa (administered by Sharjah) and the Greater and Lesser Tunbs (administered by Ras al-Khaimah). He coveted these islands because they were strategically located and would increase Iran's share of oil exploration rights on the continental shelf; as a consequence, the Iranian government informed Britain that it would not recognize the proposed federation of smaller Arab states unless its demands for the islands were met. After indications that the ruler of Sharjah would accommodate the Shah and a compromise on Abu Musa could be reached, the way was paved for the creation of the United Arab Emirates (UAE), which was proclaimed on July 17, 1971 (albeit without the participation of Ras al-Khaimah, which would not compromise on the

Tunbs). Bahrain, which refused to be part of the federation, declared its independence on August 14, 1971, and Qatar followed suit on September 11, 1971.[35]

A tacit agreement between Iran and Britain, meanwhile, provided that Britain would not oppose Iranian occupation of Abu Musa and the Tunbs, and that Iran would not attempt to occupy the islands until December 1, 1971; *after* the British treaties with the trucial states were abrogated and Britain's obligations to protect them had ceased. The UAE, scheduled to be inaugurated on December 2, would have no obligation to support Ras al-Khaimah's claims on the Tunbs because the latter was not part of the federation. As it turned out, Iran occupied the three islands on November 30, 1971, while British protection was still in force, but it made no difference. Aside from a few casualties among a police detachment from Ras al-Khaimah (which eventually joined the UAE in February 1972) and rhetorical protests from most of the Arab states, the main consequences were Libya's nationalization of the British Petroleum Company's assets and concessions and Iraq's break in relations with Britain and Iran (to which Iraq expelled 60,000 Iranians). With the departure of Britain's 6,000 ground troops from Bahrain and Sharjah, and the emergence of the Gulf sheikhdoms as states, the question that now posed itself was how the Persian Gulf's pluralistic power system would work and what system of security would replace the apparent vacuum in the region.[36]

NOTES

1. Use of the term "Persian Gulf" is best explained by Ambassador Hermann Eilts:

> The Arab-Iranian nomenclature controversy over the Gulf, which was so bitter in the late 50s and early 60s, was a by-product of the late President Nasser of Egypt's brand of Arab nationalism. It has in recent years been abated by quiet usage of the neutral term "Gulf" both inside and outside of the Middle East area. Though reluctant to become involved in the dispute, the United States as early as 1960 formally opted for the use of the term "Persian Gulf" on grounds of long established global usage and without any hegemonial connotation. "Arabian Gulf" is in fact a recent Arab appellation for that body of water. Some Arab charts of the late 18th–early 19th century refer to it as the "Gulf of Basra," a designation drawn from the Arab (Iraqi) port on the Shatt Al-Arab at the head of the Gulf. The term "Arab Gulf" (not Arabian) was used by the late 18th–early 19th century English and American ship masters to designate the southern reaches of the Red Sea, roughly from Jidda southwards to the Bab Al-Mandab. ("Security Considerations in the Persian Gulf," *International Security* 5, no. 2 (1980): 79)

2. The term "Southwest Asia" has been used within the U.S. government since 1979, when, according to former Assistant Secretary of State for Near Eastern and South Asian Affairs Harold Saunders, "it was no longer possible to allow continued use of 'the Middle East problem' as synonymous with 'the Arab-Israeli problem.' 'Southwest Asia' was introduced to broaden the focus to include the problems of the Persian Gulf and those stemming from the Soviet thrust into Afghanistan." Saunders observes that no sharp lines can be drawn and that relations of the states in the region with neighbors such as Turkey and India are on occasion important parts of the picture. *The Middle East Problem in the 1980s* (Washington, DC: American Enterprise Institute for Public Policy Research, 1981), 83.

3. George Hourani, *Arab Seafaring in the Indian Ocean in Ancient and Medieval Times* (Princeton: Princeton University Press, 1951), 4; and Roger Savory, "The History of the Persian Gulf: The Ancient Period," in *The Persian Gulf States: A General Survey*, eds. Alvin Cottrell et al. (Baltimore: Johns Hopkins University Press, 1980), 3–13.

4. Hourani, 53, 61, 64, 70–75.

5. Savory, 3–13; and Bernard Lewis, ed., *Islam and the Arab World: Faith, People, Culture* (New York: Alfred A. Knopf, 1976), 16.

6. Roger Savory, "The History of the Persian Gulf: A.D. 600–1800," in Cottrell et al., eds., 14–40.

7. Malcolm Yapp, "The History of the Persian Gulf: British Policy in the Persian Gulf," in Cottrell et al., eds., 71.

8. Rouhollah Ramazani, *The Persian Gulf and the Strait of Hormuz* (Alphenaan den Rijn, The Netherlands: Sijthoff & Noordhoff, 1979), 25.

9. J. B. Kelly, *Britain and the Persian Gulf, 1795–1880* (Oxford: Clarendon Press, 1968), 62–68, 96; and Yapp, 72–73.

10. Edward Ingram, *The Beginning of the Great Game in Asia, 1828–1834* (Oxford: Clarendon Press, 1979), 4; Kelly, 73.

11. Malcolm Yapp, *Strategies of British India: Britain, Iran and Afghanistan, 1798–1850* (Oxford: Clarendon Press, 1980), 584; Kelly, 73, 96–97.

12. Ingram, 5, 13, 14, 17, 50, 328, 337–339. David Fromkin points out that tsarist expansion against the Islamic Asian regimes on the Russian frontier was not undertaken for the purpose of thwarting Britain: "It had begun before the British came to Asia, and would have continued whether the British had arrived or not." In this sense, he observes, it was similar to U.S. expansion westward in the nineteenth century, which was regarded as a national destiny that seemed manifest. Fromkin argues that Russian expansion, while not directed against Britain, without British opposition might have led to the incorporation of Persia and so would have endangered Britain's international interests. British expansion therefore was directed at Russia, for whom the British threat was equally real. As a result, he concludes, the Great Game in Asia "was played for real stakes, and not merely imaginary ones—the unjustified fears and mutual misunderstandings upon which historians tend to focus." David Fromkin, "The Great Game in Asia," *Foreign Affairs* 58, no. 4 (1980): 936–951.

13. Kelly, 1–2.

14. Ingram, 326. For a brief discussion of trade in the Gulf, see Donald Hawley, *The Trucial States* (London: Allen & Unwin, 1970), 118–120. While the feuding between these tribes is too complicated by and intertwined with tribal migrations and splits to go into here, suffice it to observe that the Al Bu Said was descended from the Hinawiyah, a southwest Arabian stock (also designated as Qahtani or Yemeni) originating in Yemen and generally considered to be among the first wave of settlers on the Gulf littoral in the first millennium B.C. The Qawasim were descended from or allied with the Ghafiriyah (also designated as Adnani or Nizari), who originated in central and eastern Arabia and migrated to the Omani hinterland and the Trucial Coast in the fourth and fifth centuries A.D. In the eighteenth century, tribes in the area from the Trucial Coast to Oman aligned themselves with one or another tribal faction. Tribes in the interior of Oman tended to align themselves with the Ghafiri faction, the Al Bu Said with the Hinawi faction. Along the Trucial Coast, the Qawasim in Ras al-Khaimah and Sharjah aligned themselves with the Ghafiri faction (against the Al Bu Said), while their rivals the Bani Yas (in Abu Dhabi and Dubai) aligned themselves with the Hinawi. For insight into the tribal alignments in the Arabian Peninsula, see Robert G. Landen, *Oman since 1856: Disruptive Modernization in a Traditional Arab Society* (Princeton: Princeton University Press, 1967), 34–37, 58–60; Christine Helms, *The Cohesion of Saudi Arabia: Evolution of Political Identity* (Baltimore: Johns Hopkins University Press, 1981), 51–60; Hawley, 42–43, 80–84, 97, 147, 150, 179; J. B. Kelly, *Arabia, the Gulf and the West: A Critical View of the Arabs and Their Oil Policy* (New York: Basic Books, 1980), 107–108.

15. Hawley, 90–102, 121–122; Kelly, *Britain and the Persian Gulf*, 109–111, 134.

16. Kelly, *Britain and the Persian Gulf*, 65–66, 99–154; Hawley, 90, 102–129. See Kelly, 363 n., for the origins of the term "Trucial Coast."

17. Kelly, *Britain and the Persian Gulf*, 159; Hawley, 126–141, 314–318; Rosemarie Said Zahlan, *The Origins of the United Arab Emirates: A Political and Social History of the Trucial States* (New York: St. Martin's Press, 1978), xii. In 1839 the British occupation of Aden blocked Mehmet Ali's army in Yemen and precluded his obtaining command over passage through the Red Sea and the "overland" route to the East. British intervention in Syria also helped to deny him command of the "direct" route from the Eastern Mediterranean to the head of the Persian Gulf in 1840. J. B. Kelly notes the similarity between Mehmet Ali's tactics and those of Nasser in the 1960s. J. B. Kelly, *Arabia, the Gulf and the West*, 240–241.

18. Hawley, 316–321; Kelly, *Britain and the Persian Gulf*, 414–417, 831, 834; Zahlan, 8, 180.

19. Briton Cooper Busch, *Britain and the Persian Gulf, 1894–1914* (Berkeley: University of California Press, 1967), 384–386; Kelly, *Britain and the Persian Gulf*, 407–409; Hawley, 138, 159, 181, 320–321; Zahlan, 17; Malcolm Yapp, "The History of the Persian Gulf: The Nineteenth and Twentieth Centuries," in Cottrell et al., eds., 59.

20. Yapp, "British Policy in the Persian Gulf," 98; Yapp, *Strategies of British India*, 13, 585; Ingram, 332, 334; Zahlan, xiii, 21; Hawley, 164–166.

21. Yapp, "The Nineteenth and Twentieth Centuries," 41–42.

22. Ibid., 58–61; Yapp, "British Policy in the Persian Gulf," 82, 88–89, 98; Zahlan, 19, 21.

23. John Duke Anthony, *Arab States of the Lower Gulf: People, Politics, Petroleum* (Washington, DC: The Middle East Institute, 1975), 4; Hawley, 142–146; Zahlan, xi-xiii, 1, 9–11, 196–199; Yapp, "The Nineteenth and Twentieth Centuries," 66.

24. Zahlan, 18, 190–204; Anthony, 4; Hawley, 146; Keith McLachlan, "Oil in the Persian Gulf," in Cottrell et al., eds., 202–205.

25. Phillip Darby, *British Defense Policy East of Suez, 1947–1968* (London: Oxford University Press, 1973), 5, 22–26; Hawley, 168. Kelly notes the "considerable difference in outlook between the British foreign and colonial services, the guiding spirit of the one being accommodation [diplomacy and reconciliation of opposing interests], and that of the other, consolidation [a sense of responsibility and a habit of authority]." Kelly argues that when the Foreign Office assumed the duties of the India Office, it inherited neither the spirit nor the outlook of the Indian Civil Service. Kelly, *Arabia, the Gulf and the West*, 37, 97–99.

26. Darby, 94–95, 101–108, 118–126, 175, 280–281; R. J. Gavin, *Aden under British Rule, 1839–1967* (London: Hurst, 1975), 344.

27. Darby, 154–156, 219–221, 331.

28. Ibid., 209–216, 241–242, 283–284, 309, 328–329. For a critical account of the Labour Party's perceptions and political judgments of South Arabia, see Kelly, *Arabia, the Gulf and the West*, 1–46.

29. Darby, 103–108, 115–116, 162, 201, 297–298, 309, 328–330; Gavin, 347–348; David Holden, *Farewell to Arabia* (London: Faber & Faber, 1966), 17–68; Yapp, "British Policy in the Persian Gulf," 95–98; David Holden, "The Persian Gulf: After the British Raj," *Foreign Affairs* 49, no. 4 (1971): 721.

30. Darby, 325.

31. The family and tribal feuding that is characteristic of the Gulf as a whole (personalities are more important than abstract ideas) has been aptly characterized by John Duke Anthony, who notes that characteristically, owing to their territorial claims, the rulers of the sheikhdoms "have had poor relations with their immediate neighbors and good relations with the Ruler just beyond. This leapfrog pattern of good and bad relations has resulted in a sense of mutual animosity permeating both sides of nearly every frontier" within the emirates. Anthony, *Arab States of the Lower Gulf*, 109, 111. See also David Long, *The Persian Gulf: An Introduction to Its Peoples, Politics, and Economics*, rev. ed. (Boulder Colo.: Westview Press, 1978), 45–46.

32. David Holden, "The Persian Gulf: After the British Raj," *Foreign Affairs* 49, no. 4 (1971), 721–735; J. B. Kelly, *Arabia, the Gulf and the West*, 53.

33. Rouhollah Ramazani notes that Iran used the claim to Bahrain from the very start as a bargaining chip for Abu Musa and the Tunbs. Rouhollah Ramazani, *Iran's Foreign Policy, 1941–1973: A Study of Foreign Policy in Modernizing Nations* (Charlottesville: University Press of Virginia, 1975), 411. The Shah pursued a strategy of accommodation with as many Middle Eastern states as possible to avoid condemnation for anticipated acquisition of Abu Musa and the Tunbs, 421–427.

34. Kelly, *Arabia, the Gulf and the West*, 53–59, 81–82, 141–142; Holden, "The Persian Gulf," 724–730. Another factor complicating agreement among the rulers had to do with perceived caste differences. See the discussion of these differences by Anthony, *Arab States of the Lower Gulf*, 69. On the subject of withdrawal, Holden, 729, notes that the value of British troops had proved illusory.

35. Kelly, *Arabia, the Gulf and the West*, 87–94; and Long, *The Persian Gulf*, 48–49.

36. Kelly, *Arabia, the Gulf and the West*, 95–103; and Ramazani, *The Persian Gulf and the Strait of Hormuz*, 26, 28.

5

The U.S. Experience in the Persian Gulf

Bruce R. Kuniholm

This chapter traces the process by which the United States gradually took over Britain's role in maintaining the balance of power along the empire's old lifeline. It underscores the continuity of geopolitical considerations among the great powers. For the West, oil may have replaced trade and empire as a rationale for commitments, but the object of deterrence was still Russia and the lines that were drawn between East and West were more or less the same as those that existed during the imperial rivalries of the past.

The Persian Gulf, meanwhile, at least initially, played only a marginal role in U.S. strategic thinking. In spite of oil interests in Saudi Arabia, the region assumed importance in U.S. policy councils only in the late 1960s when, as in the 1940s and 1950s, Britain's continuing withdrawal from the Middle East forced another reassessment of U.S. interests. Reassessment, in turn, precipitated the search for a policy that would allow the United States once again to fill the vacuum created by Britain's departure: a search that led the United States at first to support Iran as a surrogate for its interests, and then to make a commitment to the defense of the region.

The administration of President Lyndon B. Johnson, it should be noted, took strong exception to Britain's decision to withdraw from the Persian Gulf, although not necessarily for the reasons that many suppose. Secretary of Defense Robert McNamara opposed a U.S. presence in the Indian Ocean on the grounds that the U.S. Navy did not need commitments in another ocean. Secretary of State Dean Rusk wanted Britain to maintain its presence in the region because he believed the United States needed the help of a major ally in carrying out its global responsibilities. The Persian Gulf itself, however, played a relatively insignificant role in U.S. strategic thinking up to that time. In January 1968, it appeared that the United States was seeking to *avoid* having to fill the vacuum created by Britain's departure. Instead, it contemplated a security arrangement among the region's larger states: Iran, Turkey, Pakistan, Saudi Arabia, and Kuwait.[1] By 1971, when the British withdrawal took place, the states among which a security arrangement was contemplated had been narrowed to Iran and Saudi Arabia.

HISTORICAL BACKGROUND

The Truman Doctrine

From World War II, when the Persian Corridor played an important part in the supply of lend-lease goods to Russia, to 1971, when the British withdrew from the Gulf, the United States generally regarded the Persian Gulf (with the important exception of Saudi Arabia) as primarily a British preserve. Nevertheless, the steady decline of Britain's position in the Middle East gradually led the United States to assume Britain's role in maintaining the balance of power along the empire's old lifeline. Thus, in the 1940s, as Britain was forced to contemplate withdrawal from its empire, including Palestine, India, and Burma, Whitehall's decision to cease supporting Greece and Turkey (in conjunction with Soviet threats against Iran and Turkey that exceeded wartime understandings) led President Truman to enunciate the Truman Doctrine. In doing so, he implicitly committed the United States to maintaining the balance of power in a region that previously had been virtually outside its cognizance and within the British empire's sphere of influence. By the early 1950s, the U.S. government had come to view the balance of power in the Near East as directly related to the balance of power in Europe and considered Turkey as the linchpin of its policies. As a result, President Truman supported incorporation of Greece and Turkey into the North Atlantic Treaty Organization (NATO) alliance.[2]

The Eisenhower Doctrine

In the 1950s, Britain's decision to leave Egypt and to look instead to Iraq as a secure alternative for maintaining a political-military presence in the Middle East led Secretary of State John Foster Dulles to encourage development of a regional defense arrangement in the Middle East's "northern tier" states. While Turkey, Iraq, Pakistan, Iran, and Britain became members of the Baghdad Pact in 1955, the

United States did not. To do so, it was felt, might have limited U.S. influence with Arab states other than Iraq; it also would have allied the United States with Iraq, which was officially at war with Israel. Following the debacle over Suez in 1956, President Eisenhower promulgated the Eisenhower Doctrine to fill the void created by Britain's withdrawal and to serve notice that the United States would defend the Middle East against a perceived Soviet threat.

The Eisenhower Doctrine extended the containment policy from the northern tier states to the Middle East in general: Congress subsequently authorized use of armed force to assist non-Communist Middle Eastern nations threatened by armed aggression from any country controlled by international communism. Rooted in a misperception of regional problems and a mistaken assumption of the preeminence of the Communist threat, the Eisenhower Doctrine ultimately foundered on the fact that instabilities in the region were neither caused by the Soviet Union nor capable of being deterred by the application of power. This realization was brought home by the revolution in Iraq in 1958 and Iraq's formal withdrawal from the Baghdad Pact in 1959. The U.S. response was to restructure the northern tier concept of buffer states by negotiating executive agreements with Turkey, Pakistan, and Iran in what was now called the Central Treaty Organization (CENTO). The obligations of the United States were to take such action, including the use of armed forces, as mutually agreed upon and as envisaged in the Eisenhower Doctrine. While not constituting a formal guarantee of their security, the bilateral agreements effectively institutionalized U.S. military support to the CENTO countries.[3]

However ineffective U.S. commitments to the Middle East were in the 1950s, they presented few problems relative to those posed by the British decision to leave the area east of Suez a decade later. By then, global commitments and the war in progress in Vietnam precluded the kind of substantial U.S. commitment that had been possible in the past. U.S. presence in the region at the time was minimal. The deployment of MIDEASTFOR (a flagship and two destroyers operating out of Bahrain) in the Persian Gulf was acknowledged to be symbolic. The U.S. lease of an airfield in Dhahran, Saudi Arabia, had been terminated in the early 1960s by mutual agreement. Aside from oil, which was selling for less than $1.50 a barrel when President Nixon took office, the primary U.S. interest seems to have been the communications and intelligence-gathering sites that were established in the late 1950s. The Navy, however, had been seeking military facilities in the Indian Ocean at least since 1960, and this objective gained currency after India requested emergency air defense assistance during its brief war with China in 1962. The end result was an executive agreement between Britain and the United States in December 1966 that made the islands in the British Indian Ocean Territory available for joint defense. U.S. interest in the island of Diego Garcia stems from this period. According to one official familiar with policy during this time, however, U.S. interests in and strategic plans for the region were perceived by commentators as more expansive than they in fact were.[4]

THE NIXON DOCTRINE AND THE TWIN-PILLAR POLICY, 1969–1979

Shortly after taking office, the administration of President Richard M. Nixon, burdened by the war in Vietnam, initiated a major review of policy in the Gulf. The focus of the review was the question of how the Nixon Doctrine, first enunciated in June 1969, could best be applied to the region. As subsequently elaborated, the Nixon Doctrine specified that the United States would furnish military and economic assistance to nations whose freedom was threatened but would look to those nations to assume primary responsibility for their own defense.[5] The result of the policy review was the president's endorsement in November 1970 of what became known as the "twin-pillar" policy. Its rationale was that the United States had strategic interests in Iran and Saudi Arabia, which meant that support for either would alienate the other. Despite their mutual distrust, cooperation between the two nations was felt to be essential in the face of growing Arab radicalism, most recently evidenced during the Jordan crisis two months before. Britain, U.S. officials believed, would retain much of its political presence and influence in the Gulf. As a result, there would not be a power vacuum per se but realignments of the region's power balance were expected to occur. The United States, for its part, could ensure stability through cooperation with Iran (which U.S. officials recognized as the region's predominate power) and Saudi Arabia. MIDEASTFOR, of course, would be maintained. The United States could not withdraw when the British were departing; the Russians, moreover, had begun to deploy military forces in the region and might get the wrong signal. U.S. diplomatic representation in the Persian Gulf, meanwhile, would be expanded and an austere communications station, along with an 8,000-foot supporting runway, would be built on Diego Garcia. The Lower Gulf states, however, would be encouraged to look to Britain for their security needs.[6]

This framework, in conjunction with the Nixon administration's increasing emphasis on the Iranian "pillar," served as the basis for U.S. policy until 1979, when the Iranian revolution and the Soviet invasion of Afghanistan forced the United States, once again, to reexamine its priorities and reformulate its policies. Until then, evolution of the twin-pillar policy was most affected by several other important factors: the Shah's world view; the Nixon administration's decision in May 1972 to leave decisions over the acquisition of military equipment to the Iranian government; and the consequences of the oil embargo that followed the 1973 Arab-Israeli war.

The Shah's View of the World

Iran's emergence as a key pillar in U.S. policy was due as much to the Shah's vision of Iran's role in the world as it was to circumstance. His goal was to transform Iran into the region's paramount power to protect Iran's resources and acquire the military capability to counter threats to the regional status quo.[7] Informing his vision, and his long-standing desire to obtain a security commitment from the United States, was the history of his own weakness dating back to World War II, the Azerbaijan crisis in 1945–1946, and the nationalization crisis in the early 1950s when, with U.S. and British assistance, the Mossadeq government was overthrown and Pahlavi rule restored. U.S. policies during the Indo-Pakistani wars of 1965 and 1970–1971, however, led the Shah to conclude that allies and their security commitments were unreliable, and to dismiss the value of CENTO as having "never been really serious." The Indo-Pakistani wars also reinforced a desire for self-reliance and confirmed the Shah's belief that military might was its most important component.[8]

The Shah's unlimited appetite for weapons and his overruling concern for security were fed by a myriad of threats to the regional status quo. These threats had been accentuated, in his view, by the 1958 revolution in Iraq. They were made more dangerous after 1968 when a new regime in Baghdad challenged Iranian interests in the Shatt al-Arab and Khuzistan (which a conference of Arab journalists in 1964 had declared to be "an integral part of the Arab homeland"). And that was not all. Following Britain's withdrawal from Aden in 1967, a Marxist-oriented government had been formed in the People's Democratic Republic of Yemen (PDRY). The PDRY and Iraq were supporting an ongoing rebellion in Oman's Dhofar province; Iraq was also supporting Kurdish and Baluch movements for autonomy in Kurdistan (which includes the western part of northwest Iran) and Baluchistan (which includes the eastern part of southeast Iran). Saudi Arabia, finally, had suffered a coup attempt by Air Force officers in 1969. These developments, in conjunction with the changing balance of power in the region, made the Nixon administration receptive to the Shah's concerns; they also led the United States and Britain to underwrite a $1 billion Iranian defense program before Britain's military forces had withdrawn from the Gulf.[9]

The May 1972 Agreement

By the time President Nixon and National Security Advisor Henry Kissinger arrived in Teheran in May 1972 (on their return from the Moscow summit), Britain's forces had departed from the Persian Gulf. Kissinger now judged that the balance of power in the region was in grave jeopardy. Syria had invaded Jordan in 1970, and its relationship with the Soviet Union was well established. Egypt had signed a friendship treaty with the Soviets in 1971, and over 15,000 Soviet troops remained in Egypt. The Soviets had concluded a similar treaty with Iraq only seven weeks before the Nixon visit, and two days after the ceremony a squadron of Soviet warships had arrived at the Iraqi port of Umm Qasr. The Soviets had then begun massive deliveries of advanced modern weapons to Iraq. Britain's military forces had been gone from the Gulf for less than half a year, and already the situation appeared to be getting worse. In Kissinger's view, it was imperative that the regional balance of power be maintained. Iraq would achieve hegemony unless local forces were strengthened or U.S. power built up. Neither Congress nor the American public, however, would support the deployment of U.S. forces in the region.[10]

Since Iran was willing to fill the vacuum left by Britain and was willing to pay for the necessary equipment out of its own revenues, President Nixon acquiesced in the Shah's desire to obtain advanced U.S. aircraft and insisted that future Iranian requests not be second-guessed. In short, the decision on what military equipment Iran could acquire would be left to Iran, and review procedures would be eliminated. The controversy over whether this U.S. commitment was "open-ended" or not began after the policy was called into question by Secretary of Defense James Schlesinger in August 1975, and it continued in the aftermath of the Iranian revolution when critics cited it as one of the revolution's causes. Henry Kissinger argues that the commitment was not open-ended and that the substantial quantities of arms that were sold were needed to maintain the regional balance of power.[11] In retrospect, it seems clear that expenditures on high-tech equipment were excessive, and that the exposed profile of the many technical and advisory personnel necessary to make sophisticated equipment operational were a fundamental part of the Shah's burgeoning domestic problems.[12] "In Iranian eyes," Barry Rubin observes, "it was the arms-sale program, more than any other aspect of the alliance between the United States and Iran, that compromised the

Shah's image with Iranians and led them to believe that the Shah was America's 'man.' "[13]

The 1973 Arab-Israeli War and Its Consequences

The effect of the 1973 Arab-Israeli war on U.S. policy in the Persian Gulf and Indian Ocean was profound. U.S. and Western economic vulnerability to the oil embargo underscored the strategic importance of the region, which was recognized as vital. A comprehensive reevaluation of strategy in the Indian Ocean, moreover, concluded that the United States could not place heavy emphasis on allied support. This judgment, along with heightened suspicions of a growing Soviet military presence in the region (reinforced by a Soviet treaty of friendship with Somalia in July 1974), had two important consequences: the U.S. Pacific Fleet's periodic deployment in the Indian Ocean as a contingency naval presence; and, after considerable debate, the expansion of Diego Garcia from a communications station to a naval facility capable of supporting major air and naval deployments.[14]

From Kissinger's perspective, the 1973 war also underscored the value of Iran as an ally. It was the only country bordering the Soviet Union that did not permit the Soviets to use its air space. The Shah refueled U.S. fleets, did not use his oil to bring political pressure on the United States, and absorbed the energies of his radical neighbors (e.g., Iraq), thus preventing them from threatening the region's moderate regimes. President Nixon's encouragement of the Shah's support for the Kurds in Iraq also prevented Iraq from making more than one division available to participate in the 1973 war.[15]

The Shah's ability and inclination to make large weapons purchases, meanwhile, increased greatly following the war. Iran had ceased receiving direct economic assistance from the United States in 1967, partly because of changing realities in the international petroleum market and partly because of massive U.S. expenditures in Vietnam. Now, following the 1973 Arab-Israeli war, the Shah's already rapidly increasing revenues quadrupled. The difference in earnings that increased oil production and higher prices made in the space of a decade is extraordinary: Where 1.7 million barrels a day (MBD) brought in $482 million in 1964, 6 MBD brought in $21.4 billion in 1974. As a consequence, the level of expenditures on arms increased exponentially. Where the value of purchase agreements between 1950 and 1972 amounted to slightly over $1.6 billion, purchase agreements in the next four years totaled over $11.6 billion. The value of arms transactions in 1974 alone ($3.9 billion) was twice the value of all arms contracted during the twenty-two years prior to the Arab oil embargo.[16]

The Iranian Pillar Crumbles

The Shah's massive expenditures, coupled with Iran's lack of a developed infrastructure and its shortage of trained manpower, magnified the opportunities for and disposition toward corruption, waste, and inefficiency.[17] Fluctuations in the international oil market, meanwhile, wreaked havoc with Iran's overheated economy, loosened the existential underpinnings of its burgeoning urban population, and contributed to a contempt for authority that was accentuated by the progressive breakdown of the economic and social systems. In the absence of any meaningful structures for political participation in Iran, the only person who could be held accountable when things went badly was the one who took the credit when things went well: the Shah. His inability to reach out to his people, or to mobilize their energies, and his association with foreign and non-Islamic forces became a serious liability.

If there is a consensus among the scholars who have investigated the Iranian revolution's complex causes, it is that support for the Ayatollah Khomeini derived less from what he stood for than from what he opposed: the Pahlavi regime, the monarchy itself, foreign control, and cultural domination. Thanks to Khomeini, the dislocations and identity concerns that accompanied Iran's uneven development were given a focus; economic grievances, existential need, and political frustration among the lower and middle classes coalesced into a common opposition to the Shah. Beyond that, none of the sociopolitical groups who supported the revolution could agree on even basic conceptions of legitimacy and authority. The Shia religious establishment, meanwhile, which was independent of the state, provided a framework (if not the motive) for the revolutionary movement as a whole. After the revolution, this framework, in conjunction with the charismatic figure of Khomeini, would facilitate the *ulama*'s control of the government.[18]

The causes of the Iranian revolution and an analysis of U.S. policy toward Iran during the hostage crisis are beyond the scope of this chapter. What is pertinent is the fact that the revolution undermined the two-pillar policy, which had been followed with little change by the administrations of President Ford and President Carter, and raised serious questions about its central premise: that regional states could assume primary responsibility for their own defense. A Marxist coup in Afghanistan in April 1978 had been followed by a Soviet-Ethiopian treaty in November 1978; by early 1979 the PDRY was creating problems in Yemen, and in March, following the crumbling of the Iranian "pillar" and the reorientation of Iran's geopolitical posture, Turkey and Pakistan withdrew from CENTO. In the course of these adverse regional developments, U.S. officials were left without a strategic conception of how to protect regional interests.[19]

In this conceptual vacuum, President Jimmy Carter's National Security Advisor Zbigniew Brzezinski first broached the concept of a security framework for the region. The essence of the concept, as it developed, was an increased naval presence in the region, an improved capability to introduce rapidly deployed forces into the area, and access to facilities in the area (as well as coordination with NATO allies) to support an expanded presence and broadened contingency capability. The hostage crisis that began in November 1979, meanwhile, pointed to the limitations on U.S. capabilities to project military power into the region.[20]

THE SOVIET INVASION OF AFGHANISTAN AND THE CARTER DOCTRINE

The Soviet invasion of Afghanistan in December 1979 underscored the limitations on U.S. capabilities. It also revolutionized the geopolitical picture in the region. The most plausible explanation for the Soviet invasion of Afghanistan is that the Soviets went in to prevent the certain collapse of the Marxist government in Kabul and to replace a recalcitrant leader with one who was more responsive to Moscow's bidding. In so doing, the Soviets may well have been concerned about their own security interests, the effects on their own Muslim population of a failure to move, and the international implications of perceived Soviet weakness. But if, in the short term, the invasion had a defensive quality, in the long term it presented possibilities that were offensive. As such, the invasion was clearly opportunistic: The United States could not prevent it; it put the Soviets in a position to provoke and exploit the region's instabilities; and, ultimately, it provided them with strategic advantages; even if those advantages had not been part of the original calculation.[21]

Afghanistan made more urgent the development of the strategic framework that had been under discussion since the fall of the Shah. That framework was now fleshed out and expanded after its rationale was described in President Carter's State of the Union message on January 23, 1980: "Let our position be absolutely clear: an attempt by any outside force to gain control of the Persian Gulf region will be regarded as an assault on the vital interests of the United States of America, and such an assault will be repelled by any means necessary, including military force."

In spite of assertions to the contrary, the so-called Carter Doctrine was carefully considered. Its intent was to put the Soviets on notice that the region was of vital importance to the United States and, in a departure from the Nixon Doctrine, to make clear that the United States assumed ultimate responsibility for regional defense. Less clear was the extent of the area included in "the Persian Gulf region." Pakistan, for example, sought but received no clarification as to whether it was included in the region to which the Carter Doctrine applied. The president's lack of precision, however, was not ill considered. It *was* advisable to be wary of undertaking a commitment that could not be met. Legitimate questions were raised about the matter of vagueness, but if the region was vital there was no escaping the logic of the statement, which regional insecurity appeared to require. Until the security framework was broadened, the Carter Doctrine served a useful deterrent function. It did not write off countries whose loss was less than vital, and it kept options open with respect to contingencies in others. If something like the Carter Doctrine was required, however, there was no reason for being too specific about U.S. commitments and, by implication, spelling out (as Secretary of State Dean Acheson did in 1950 with regard to East Asia) what the United States would not do; particularly since the nature of many contingencies (such as the invasion of South Korea in 1950) made it virtually impossible to know ahead of time how vital a particular area was and what an appropriate response to a particular contingency might be.[22]

Whatever its merits and shortcomings, the Carter Doctrine defined a U.S. stake in the Persian Gulf region. During the rest of 1980, the Special Coordinating Committee of the National Security Council met over twenty times to develop the administration's regional security framework: Defense capabilities in the regional states were improved; access to facilities was acquired in Oman, Kenya, Somalia, and Egypt; force capabilities were enhanced; and the NATO allies were pressed to specify shared responsibilities. In spite of more ambitious goals and a change in rhetoric ("strategic consensus" for a time replaced "security framework" until it was recognized that there was no consensus on strategy), President Reagan's administration essentially continued and consolidated the security framework initiated by the Carter administration. By the end of the 1980s, the United States had undertaken a number of initiatives that contributed substantially to the Department of Defense's ability to deploy over 500,000 U.S. troops to the Gulf in the aftermath of Saddam Hussein's invasion of Kuwait in August 1990. By the end of the 1980s, the United States had prepositioned a thirty-day supply of ammunition, fuel, and spare parts for a Marine Corps division aboard thirteen maritime prepositioning ships in the Indian Ocean. It also had located support equipment at Diego Garcia, Masirah (Oman), and Ras Banas (Egypt), as well as overbuilt runways and overstocked maintenance sets at selected sites such as Dhahran and King Khalid Military City in Saudi Arabia.

The intentions of the United States to protect its interests in the Persian Gulf were further increased with the acquisition of additional strategic lift capabilities. These capabilities included eight SL-7 fast deployment logistics container ships capable of moving a mechanized division to the Gulf via the Cape of Good Hope from ports in the United States in fifteen to nineteen days. They also included improved strategic air lift, extension of the service life of the C-5A, an increase in the cargo capacity of the C-141, and procurement of fifty-six additional KC-10 tanker aircraft and fifty C-5Bs. By the end of the 1980s the United States had the military capabilities to support its commitment in the region and the stage was set for its rapid military response to the Iraqi invasion of Kuwait.

NOTES

1. Phillip Darby, *British Defense Policy East of Suez, 1947–1968* (London: Oxford University Press, 1973), 294–295, 325; Rouhollah Ramazani, *Iran's Foreign Policy, 1941–1973: A Study of Foreign Policy in Modernizing Nations* (Charlottesville: University Press of Virginia, 1975), 409. For a contemporary examination of the possibility that serious conflict would result from Britain's 1971 military withdrawal from the Gulf, see *The Gulf: Implications of British Withdrawal*, Special Report Series, No. 8 (Washington, DC: Center for Strategic and International Studies, Georgetown University, February 1969).

2. See Bruce Kuniholm, *The Near East Connection: Greece and Turkey in the Reconstruction and Security of Europe, 1946–1952* (Brookline, MA: Hellenic Press, 1984).

3. See Kennett Love, *Suez: The Twice Fought War* (New York: McGraw-Hill, 1969); Townsend Hoopes, *The Devil and John Foster Dulles* (Boston: Little, Brown, 1973); and Stephen J. Genco, "The Eisenhower Doctrine: Deterrence in the Middle East, 1957–1958," in *Deterrence in American Foreign Policy: Theory and Practice*, eds. Alexander George and Richard Smoke (New York: Columbia University Press, 1974), 309–362.

4. Gary Sick, "The Evolution of U.S. Strategy toward the Indian Ocean and Persian Gulf Regions," n.d., manuscript in the author's possession. Gary Sick served on the National Security Council staff during the Carter administration and part of the Reagan administration.

5. Henry Kissinger, *White House Years* (Boston: Little, Brown, 1979), 223–225.

6. Sick, "The Evolution of U.S. Strategy"; Barry Rubin, *Paved with Good Intentions: The American Experience and Iran* (New York: Oxford, 1980), 125–126; U.S. Congress, House, Committee on Foreign Affairs, *New Perspectives on the Persian Gulf*, Hearings before the Subcommittee on the Near East and South Asia (Washington, DC: G.P.O., 1973); and U.S. Congress, House, Com-

mittee on Foreign Affairs, *U.S. Interests in and Policy toward the Persian Gulf*, Hearings before the Subcommittee on the Near East (Washington, DC: G.P.O., 1972). For Soviet naval deployments in the Indian Ocean see Bruce Watson, *Red Navy at Sea: Soviet Naval Operations on the High Seas, 1956–1980* (Boulder, CO: Westview, 1982).

7. Amin Saikal, *The Rise and Fall of the Shah* (Princeton: Princeton University Press, 1980), 137–147.

8. Rouhollah Ramazani, *The United States and Iran: The Patterns of Influence* (New York: Praeger, 1982), 39–41; Alvin Rubinstein, *Soviet Policy toward Turkey, Iran, and Afghanistan: The Dynamics of Influence* (New York: Praeger, 1982), 74.

9. Rubin, 142, 204–205; Ramazani, *Iran's Foreign Policy*, 405, 416–418, 428; Selig Harrison, *In Afghanistan's Shadow: Baluch Nationalism and Soviet Temptations* (Washington, DC: Carnegie Endowment for International Peace, 1981), 35, 106–108; Kelly, *Arabia, the Gulf and the West*, 134.

10. Kissinger, 1258–1265; Kissinger, *Years of Upheaval* (Boston: Little, Brown, 1982), 669; see also Ramazani, *The Persian Gulf*, 46, for the visit of the Soviet squadron.

11. Kissinger, *White House Years*, 1258–1265; *Years of Upheaval*, 668–670; U.S. Congress, Senate, Committee on Foreign Relations, *U.S. Military Sales to Iran*, A Staff Report to the Subcommittee on Foreign Assistance (Washington, DC: G.P.O., 1976); Ramazani, *The United States and Iran*, 44–45; Rubin, 162, 170–171. For Kissinger's deflection of Schlesinger's concern over arms sales to the Shah, see Rubin, 170–171.

12. Robert Graham, *Iran: The Illusion of Power* (New York: St. Martin's, 1979), 168–189.

13. Rubin, 260.

14. Sick, "The Evolution of U.S. Strategy." See also David Long, "The United States and the Persian Gulf," *Current History*, January (1979): 27–30, 37–38, esp. 29. Maxwell Johnson notes that the Pentagon first realized the significance of Diego Garcia after the contingency deployment of a carrier strike force to the Indian Ocean during the 1971 Indo-Pakistani war. *The Military as an Instrument of U.S. Policy in Southwest Asia: The Rapid Deployment Joint Task Force, 1979–1982* (Boulder, CO: Westview, 1983), 31. Kissinger's response to a question as to whether he would consider using military action against oil prices set off a furor. "I am not saying that there is no circumstance where we would not use force," he observed. "But it is one thing to use it in the case of a dispute over price, it's another whether there is some actual strangulation of the industrialized world." *Business Week*, January 1975.

15. Kissinger, *White House Years*, 1262, 1265.

16. Rubin, 130; Ramazani, *The United States and Iran*, 40–42, 47–48.

17. Nikki Keddie, "The Iranian Revolution in Comparative Perspective," *American Historical Review* 88, no. 3 (1983): 579–598; Ramazani, *The United States and Iran*, 122–123; James Bill and Carl Leider, *Politics in the Middle East*, 2d ed. (Boston: Little, Brown, 1984), 382; Edward Mortimer, *Faith and Power: The Politics of Islam* (New York: Vintage, 1982), 296–376, esp. 300–303; and Rubin, 252–272, who discusses over twenty factors that con-

tribute to an explanation of the Iranian revolution. A number of former U.S. officials such as Henry Kissinger (*Years of Upheaval*, 672–673) and Jack Miklos (*The Iranian Revolution and Modernization: Way Stations to Anarchy*, Washington, DC: National Defense University Press, 1983, 64) question the argument that broader political participation would have made a difference in the situation in Iran or that anyone has a coherent idea of how to channel the forces let loose by the process of development. While the problem clearly deserves much more extensive examination, the Shah's record on the issue was abysmal and deserves most of the criticism that has been heaped on it.

18. Sick, "The Evolution of U.S. Strategy."

19. Ibid.; Cyrus Vance, *Hard Choices: Critical Years in America's Foreign Policy* (New York: Simon & Schuster, 1983), 369–370; Zbigniew Brzezinski, *Power and Principle: Memoirs of the National Security Adviser, 1977–1981* (New York: Farrar, Straus, Giroux, 1983), 444–450; and the statement by Matthew Nimetz, Under Secretary of State for Security, Science and Technology, U.S. Department of State, *U.S. Security Framework*, Current Policy No. 221 (Washington, DC: Bureau of Public Affairs, September 16, 1980). For a detailed analysis of the genesis of the Carter Doctrine and its reinterpretation under the Reagan administration, see Maxwell O. Johnson, Chapter 2.

20. Nancy Newell and Richard Newell, *The Struggle for Afghanistan* (Ithaca: Cornell University Press, 1981), 108; Henry Bradsher, *Afghanistan and the Soviet Union* (Durham, NC: Duke University Press, 1983), especially Chapter 8, "The View from the Kremlin," 149–168; Raju Thomas, "The Afghanistan Crisis and South Asian Security," *Journal of Strategic Studies* 4, no. 4 (1981): 415–434; Rubinstein, 170; and the comments by Joseph Sisco in U.S. Congress, Senate, *U.S. Security Interests and Policies in Southwest Asia*, Hearings before the Committee on Foreign Relations (Washington, DC: G.P.O., 1980), 42–50.

21. Jimmy Carter, *Keeping Faith: Memoirs of a President* (New York: Bantam: 1982), 483; Brzezinski, 445–450. See also David Newsom, "America Engulfed," *Foreign Policy* 43 (Summer 1981): 17–32. For a discussion of Secretary of State Acheson's exclusion of Korea from the U.S. defense perimeter in January 1950, see Robert Donovan, *Tumultuous Years: The Presidency of Harry S. Truman, 1949–1953* (New York: Norton, 1982), 136–138.

22. Brzezinski, 446–450; and Sick, "The Evolution of U.S. Strategy."

PART II
THE ARAB DIMENSION

6

Arab Perspectives of the Gulf Crisis

Christine M. Helms

This chapter examines the factors that influenced Iraq's decision to invade Kuwait; perceptions by Arabs of the Iraqi invasion; the subsequent arrival of a large American-led military force; Iraqi president Saddam Hussein's regional and international strategies during the crisis; and the impact of the war upon Iraq. Finally, it examines the perceptions in the Arab and Islamic worlds of the American-led coalition goals, their impact on interregional and intraregional affairs, and the challenges that are ahead.

FACTORS INFLUENCING IRAQ'S DECISION TO INVADE KUWAIT

Four primary factors influenced the Iraqi regime's policy formulation prior to its invasion of Kuwait and its subsequent behavior during the Persian Gulf crisis. First, Iraq, relative to the majority of Arab states, had been isolated from many regional and international contacts since the revolution of 1958, which overthrew the Western-oriented Hashemite monarchy. The Iraqis' experience, with few exceptions, of the language, processes, and institutions of international forums was accordingly constrained. For example, they did not fully appreciate either the direction or the binding nature of President Bush's step-by-step process initiating UN resolutions. Second, the Iraqi decision-making process was increasingly controlled after the Iran-Iraq cease-fire in 1988 by Saddam Hussein. This control was to the detriment of the Ba'ath Party, Saddam Hussein's original base of support, which had ruled Iraq since 1968. Formerly important Ba'ath Party bureaucrats were marginalized while several of Saddam Hussein's relatives and in-laws were promoted to important positions. Third, Iraq and, indeed, many other Arab countries had been more preoccupied with the consequences for the Middle East of European union slated for 1992 than they were with the increasing Soviet and U.S. coordination and the evolving realignments of the so called post–Cold War period. Iraqi statements during the crisis, for example, indicate that they had expected the Soviets to delay or, at a minimum, dilute American-led resolutions at the United Nations. Finally, Iraq expected Arab and non-Arab Islamic states—governments and populations—to reaffirm their historical loyalties. Yet many regimes—notably Egypt, Syria, and Turkey—clearly believed that membership in the coalition would auger greater economic and political rewards than previous rhetorical commitments to Arabism and Islam.

In short, Iraq's misunderstanding of international commitments and the U.S. resolve to maintain the coalition despite the political and monetary cost, as well as assumptions about previously accepted regional caveats regarding unity, left the regime vulnerable at the outset. While Saddam Hussein frequently took opportunistic decisions to undermine the coalition, such as when he offered free oil to any country willing to break the economic blockade or when he released the hostages as a "humanitarian" gesture, his behavior was reactive.

Iraqi motivations for the invasion of Kuwait remain speculative and less well understood. In part, this situation is because of the increasingly centralized nature of the regime and the inaccessibility of its leadership once the crisis was initiated. There is anecdotal information that some high-ranking Ba'ath members, perhaps even within the Revolutionary Command Council, may not have been told of Saddam Hussein's intent to invade Kuwait in advance. There were also reports of Iraqi soldiers apologizing to Kuwaitis during the early days of the invasion. Yet it is undeniable that there was a palpable euphoria among the general Iraqi population. All Iraqi governments, including the pro-West Hashemites of pre-1958 and the subsequent military regimes that ruled until 1968, regarded Kuwait as a natural geopolitical and economic extension of their country that had been severed by the European mandate powers in the post–World War I period. All had made statements (and some had made military moves) to infringe on Kuwait's sovereign rights. Furthermore, virtually landlocked by six countries with only 15 kilometers fronting the Gulf region, Iraq had felt increasing vulnerability since at least the 1970s as its strategic interests were increasingly directed toward the Persian Gulf. This vulnerability was because of its plans to ship oil from off-shore facilities through the Strait of Hormuz and what were viewed as Iranian hegemonic ambitions.

Unless or until members of Saddam Hussein's inner circle discuss their decision-making process, the primary motivation for the invasion appears to have been economic. Iraq, quite simply, was cash strapped. At the beginning of the Iran-Iraq war, Iraq had some $36 billion in reserves. Reliable estimates of its debt to non-Arab lenders at the cease-fire in 1988 was $50 billion at a minimum. Since 1988, that debt had reportedly increased despite selective repayment of loans and the restructuring and elimination of nonessential contracts. The government essentially mortgaged existing and future oil reserves to develop and repair the basic infrastructure of the country. Reflecting these pressures, Iraq encouraged privatization, controlled black marketeering, and duplication of technology.

In order to service its debt, Iraq was paying $10 to 18 billion per annum. Foreign companies offered financing, but at rates high as 20 percent. Estimates regarding Iraq's finances are revealing. Iraq's OPEC (Organization of Petroleum Exporting Countries) quota in mid-1989 was 2.73 million barrels per day (mbpd). At $16 per barrel, Iraqi earnings would be $14 billion, insufficient even to service debt. Iraq had to have an increase in oil prices or seek a larger export quota. At a production rate of 3.85 mbpd at the same price, Iraq would theoretically break its cycle of accumulated debt. By 1990, Iraq's quota had risen only to 3.14 mbpd, including a domestic consumption rate of 400,000 mbpd. Therein lay one of Iraq's grievances against Kuwait and the United Arab Emirates, since both were allegedly exceeding their OPEC quotas.

Iraqi officials repeatedly aired their frustrations in many intra-Arab forums, most notably at the Arab summit in Baghdad in April 1990. Iraq also complained that it should not have to repay its debt to Kuwait incurred during the Iran-Iraq war and that Kuwait was reportedly overproducing an oil field that was shared by the two countries. In addition, Iraq wanted to exercise some form of control over the Kuwaiti islands of Warba and Bubiyan for strategic reasons relating to its off-shore oil facilities and a proposed deep water port. Iraqi grievances culminated in a detailed letter presented to the Arab League and released publicly by Iraq's foreign minister in July 1990. A hurriedly arranged Saudi-sponsored talk between Iraq and Kuwait that failed was immediately followed by the Iraqi invasion.

EVOLVING ARAB PERCEPTIONS OF THE CRISIS

There were essentially three stages in which Middle Easterners viewed Iraq's invasion. During the first, the invasion itself, there was unanimity of opinion. All Arab and non-Arab Muslim states condemned it without exception. The reasons for this condemnation can be found in the early formation of the Arab League in 1945. National independence was stressed as a criterion of membership, implicit in which was recognition of the territorial integrity of fellow members. There have been only two egregious violations of this since the formation of the League: Syrian military involvement in Lebanon, and Iraq's outright invasion of Kuwait.

The crisis entered a new calculus when a large, American-led military force arrived whose posture shifted within several months from defense of Saudi Arabia to offense if Iraq did not voluntarily withdraw. However, the historical memory of foreign colonial influences has left a bitter, enduring legacy both in the Arab and non-Arab Islamic worlds. During this period, President Bush's strategy and objectives came under critical scrutiny by many in the region. Among his stated aims were the ejection of Iraqi troops from Kuwait, return of the legitimate Kuwaiti government, and protection of Saudi Arabia and access to oil. Later, the safe return of foreign nationals was included. There were additional statements by high-ranking U.S. officials about protecting democracy and even American jobs. It became increasingly clear that there were as well two unstated, perhaps more important, objectives: toppling Saddam Hussein and destroying Iraqi military capabilities, including both exotic weapon facilities and ground capabilities.

There were several key issues elucidated by Middle Easterners. One had to do with official U.S. references to *legitimate* governments and the protection of *democracies*. There has been an increasingly virulent debate in Arab societies since the mid-1970s about what constitutes legitimacy. Regimes might be benign, but were they democracies? This line of reasoning was one of Ayatollah Khomeini's challenges to entrenched leaderships during the 1980s when he opposed hereditary governments.

Arabs were quick to identify other anomalies in President Bush's stated objectives. Some noted that Kuwait was not a democracy as much as a family-run oil company. Its parliament had been dissolved in 1986. An active pro-democracy movement was severely quashed and its press censored in the spring of 1990. The U.S. administration had also sought the aid of Hafiz al-Asad, a man who many Arabs felt had a much worse reputation than Saddam Hussein. Moreover, while the West talked about the sovereignty of nations, the modern Middle Eastern nation-state system was a product of the European mandate powers during the post–World War I period. Almost every state in the region has had some boundary dispute with its neighbors. The Saudis themselves had created their own state through territorial conquest. The legitimacy of regimes never ceased to be questioned because many had either been installed or were given the backing of mandate powers.

Another issue that was raised was whether Saddam Hussein really had threatened Western access to oil. It was noted that Iraq had been selling increasingly larger quantities of oil to the Western world over the past decade, including the United States. Iraq wanted a higher price for oil, some $25, but that was not far off prices advocated by some Western analysts to promote conservation and alternative energy research. Most significant, Iraq was the only oil producer during the 1980s that increased the capacity both of production facilities and export terminals. It sought a larger share of the OPEC production quota because, like Iran, it needed revenue for reconstruction after the Iran-Iraq war. In fact, Iraqi oil production capacity was believed to be nearing 6 to 7 mbpd. Saudi production capacity, for comparison, is 10 mpbd, but 2.5 mpbd was "mothballed" when the crisis began.

SADDAM HUSSEIN'S REGIONAL STRATEGY

Saddam Hussein's strategy throughout the crisis was to buy time in the hope that the international coalition would dissolve. He pursued this objective in a variety of ways. Within the Middle East, he expounded on popular Arab themes that, more often than not, were extremely sensitive subjects for Arab regimes that feared domestic unrest within their own states. As an Arab, Saddam Hussein extolled the masses to remember colonialism and the earlier control by the West of their resources. As a Muslim, he aroused virulent anti-foreign sentiment by recalling concepts embedded in Islam about sacred space, which has political connotations. U.S. forces were literally in the heartland of the Islamic world where God first delivered the Islamic message to Arabs in Arabic. As a secularist, he addressed a hitherto taboo topic: the difference between "have" and "have-not" Arab states.

It was this last issue that enabled Saddam Hussein to garner popular support by bringing into doubt the goals of President Bush's new world order. In the Western media, the "haves" are regarded as the oil-rich states: the lower Arabian Gulf states, Oman, and Saudi Arabia. The "have-nots" are the states of north Africa, Yemen, Jordan, Syria, Lebanon, Somalia, Djibouti, Sudan, and Egypt. President Bush tried to diffuse this issue by labeling Iraq a "have" state. In truth, however, Iraq is the only Arab state that does not fit either category because, in the Middle East, the distinguishing characteristics of these two groups go much deeper than wealth. The "haves" are also the countries with small populations, totaling only some 12 million. Their governments are without exception hereditary: the kingship of Saudi Arabia, sultanate of Oman, emir of Kuwait, and sheikhdoms of the lower Arabian Gulf. Stories abound in the region about how these leaderships squander their oil wealth.

By contrast, the population of the "have-not" states is some 250 million. Before the exploitation of oil, these states possessed the greater cultural clout. These states constitute the Fertile Crescent region of history. It is the region around which Britain organized its linchpin policy centered on Iraq and Egypt to protect their sea routes to India. This area is where the only three major, permanent Middle Eastern rivers—the Nile, Tigris, and Euphrates—are found. Here, the concept of Arabism was refined in its present political form during this century; here, notably, the notion of Palestine has been most fervently embraced. Governments of the "have-not" states have been almost entirely overthrown and are now dictatorships and republics, excepting only the kingships of Morocco and Jordan. Although a few of these states have oil and gas resources, many are or will become energy importers within the near future. Many suffer from high unemployment, staggering inflation, competition for scarce resources, inefficient and corrupt administration, and one of the highest birthrates in the world.

During this stage of the crisis, Saddam Hussein began to wave the identical banner lofted by Khomeini during the 1980s. He called for regional economic development, redistribution of wealth, opposition to hereditary governments and to foreign interference. He found a ready audience. Some 70 percent of the Middle East's population is under twenty years of age and getting younger, with the region's high population growth rate of 3.2 to 3.5 percent. In cities like Tehran, Iran, it is as high as 4 percent. Within the next two decades, the population of the Arab "have" states, which control the region's vast oil reserves, will double to 20 million and that of the "have-nots" to 500 million. Iran's current population of 55 million will double by the year 2006. Unfulfilled expectations will make many states vulnerable to domestic unrest.

When some nineteen Palestinians were killed on the Temple Mount by Israeli police and soldiers in October 1990, popular feelings in support of Saddam Hussein intensified. Harsh criticism began to be leveled in many parts of the Arab world at America's "double-standard," an inability to conceive of a linkage between implementation of UN resolutions against Iraq and those concerning Israel.

Young Arabs began to refrain from criticizing Saddam Hussein's invasion of Kuwait because, from their perspective, the greater evil was the large foreign presence. The fact that the blockade also prohibited food shipments was an especially sore point. That Saddam Hussein counted on Arab masses to pressure their governments was most evident in his call for a jihad against the Saudi regime prior to hostilities and, eventually, his continued Scud missile attacks into Israel after the war began.

Arab coalition allies indicated their sensitivity to this. Although President Bush claimed he had the overwhelming support of Arab states, that was an exaggeration. In the Arab League vote taken to condemn Iraq, Tunisia did not attend; Jordan, Sudan, and Mauritania voted against Iraq, but with reservations; and Algeria and Yemen abstained. When Algerian President Chadli Benjadid toured the Middle East in late 1990 to find an Arab resolution to the crisis, he was greeted in all Arab countries with the exception of Saudi Arabia. This situation was not true for an earlier Algerian initiative. Even though Syria and Egypt, key Arab coalition states, announced they would help liberate Kuwait, they refused to engage in offensive actions against Iraq. There were also popular calls in Morocco for the government to withdraw its forces. Feelings continued to intensify as the blockade began to hurt Jordan more than Iraq and when the Saudis expelled Palestinian and Yemeni workers and stopped the remaining 20 percent of Jordan's oil shipments.

Sentiment against the American-led military presence and doubts about President Bush's new world order had resonance even in non-Arab Muslim countries. There were clashes in Pakistan between civilians and police as the public decried Pakistani participation in the coalition. Even the influential Army Chief-of-Staff Mirza Aslam Beg called openly for the return of Pakistani troops. In Turkey, the dispute over Ozal's support led to the resignation of his defense and foreign ministers and, later, his military chief-of-staff. Saddam Hussein also announced the settlement of Iraq's long-standing conflict with Iran to the astonishment of the West. There was a flurry of visits between officials of the two countries, especially when Iran agreed to offer safe haven to Iraqi planes once the war began.

IMPACT OF THE WAR ON REGIONAL ATTITUDES

The crisis entered yet another phase once hostilities ensued. American euphoria that Iraqi troops were routed from Kuwait with so few coalition forces killed was not shared by the majority of those in Arab and non-Arab Islamic states. Many in the region thought the crisis was a game of nerves. President Bush, it was believed, would never use force or Hussein would withdraw at the eleventh hour. When the air strikes began, the response can be characterized as stunned silence. The fact that there was no visual documentation of the destruction inside Iraq at first lent events an unrealistic quality. Arab coalition members, in particular Saudi Arabia, attempted to censor media reports about the extent of the destruction of Iraq's infrastructure. Thus, a negative reaction was slow to gather momentum. Only when the U.S. military began to release daily the number of bombing sorties, bomb tonnage dropped, and videos of precision bombing did news travel more quickly and a negative reaction begin to gather momentum. Even without television, no one needed to be told the long-term ramifications for Iraq when international radio broadcasts reported that 3 out of 6 bridges in Baghdad and some 27 out of 35 bridges over the Euphrates had been destroyed. However, by then events had gone beyond the ability of the Arab and Islamic states to contain or redress.

The general reaction in the region in the immediate aftermath of the war was one of psychological devastation and shock at the level of destruction wrecked upon Iraq's infrastructure and the news that more than 100,000 Iraqi soldiers had died. A UN report released in March referred to the "apocalyptic" conditions inside Iraq, which had been returned to a pre-industrial period. Its population of 18 million was without water and electricity and risked famine and epidemics. At the same time, the frustrations of Iraq's northern Kurdish and southern Shi'ite communities was vented in uprisings against the government and thousands, if not tens of thousands, more were killed.

Kuwait's so-called legitimate government was returned, but here too doubts remain about the future. The country may emerge truly democratic after its trials or become repressive as entrenched forces attempt to maintain power.

IRAQI RESPONSE TO THE AFTERMATH OF THE WAR

Within Iraq itself Saddam Hussein is reviled, but at the same time it is unlikely that the United States will be embraced as anything other than a colonial power or the lesser of two evils. The United States was perceived to be the driving force behind the UN resolutions and the instrument of Iraq's destruction. Following the Shi'ite and Kurdish uprisings, President Bush was accused of having urged the Iraqi people to rise up and topple Saddam Hussein and then ignoring their pleas.

While it was unlikely that President Bush had in mind the events that ensued, the result of the war has been the initiation of a period of protracted, low-intensity conflict. A Pandora's Box of racial, religious, and linguistic differences has been opened that will be difficult to close and that affects all states on the Arab, Persian, and Turkish frontiers. Of the combined Kurdish population, Iraq only has some 18 percent while Iran has some 25 percent and Turkey more than 50 percent. Not surprisingly, Turkey's President Ozal has been reluctant to admit Iraqi Kurds when the nation has problems with its own Kurdish population.

The difficulties of reestablishing stability within Iraq itself or containing dissent are formidable. Iraq is one of the most pluralistic countries in the region. Kurds, primarily Sunnis who are concentrated in the north, comprise some 20 percent of the population. However, there are also Christian Kurds, different Kurdish dialects, and competing claims by Kurdish leaders for power. The majority of Sunni Arabs, some 20 percent or more, are found in central Iraq. Shi'a, 55 percent of the population, are concentrated in the south where two of the most important Shi'a cities are found—al-Nakjaf and Karbala. Iraq also has scattered pockets of Turks in northern Iraq; some 500,000 or more Christians (who, incidentally, roughly equal estimates of the Kuwaiti population); and other groups, such as the Yazidis, who reportedly practice a combination of Jewish, Christian, and Islamic rites.

POLITICAL POSSIBILITIES

There are only five groups who are or will be the most viable players in Iraqi domestic politics. The first is obviously Saddam Hussein himself, but even if he remains in power, his hold on Iraq will be tenuous. There will be many factors pressuring his removal; primary among them is that his survival seems likely to ensure Iraq's isolation in regional and international affairs. Saddam Hussein's ouster may give Iraq more leverage with regard to the implementation of UN resolutions, a better chance of economic assistance from outside sources, and eventual entrée to other regional security groupings that may evolve.

Be that as it may, alternative leadership choices are limited. It is plausible that someone in Saddam Hussein's close, inner circle could eliminate him or that some other member of his family would claim leadership. In either case, they would be likely targets for other groups. They have no reputation within the Ba'ath Party. The military has long resented the assumption of military titles by a select few of Saddam Hussein's appointees.

There is the ever-present Ba'ath Party, particularly other members of the Revolutionary Command Council, who were increasingly sidelined since 1988; these individuals might claim they were isolated during these years and, therefore, not responsible for recent events.

Despite the role of the Iraqi military in putting down the uprisings in Iraq, they remain the most likely successor at present to the Ba'ath Party and Saddam Hussein. Whether they supported Saddam Hussein or not, the Iraqi military, in the aftermath of the war, had to turn and fight for the territorial integrity of the Iraqi state. Toppling Saddam Hussein became a secondary concern. It seems certain that the processes of instability are likely to continue within and, perhaps, outside Iraq for the foreseeable future.

It is doubtful that many of the outside opposition groups have broad credibility. A few of them have a membership of only one or two individuals, such as exiled army colonels and former Ba'athists. A number have been absent from the country for a decade or, in a few cases, several decades. They have little understanding of what has transpired in Iraq since they left. Because the groups have divergent means and ends, their alliance must be seen as temporary at best. When Kurdish guerrilla leader Jalal Talabani went to Baghdad for negotiations with Saddam Hussein after the war, for example, he was immediately accused by Iraqi opposition groups in Syria of selling out on an earlier agreement. Furthermore, Iraqi Communists are disliked by devout Muslims; and extreme Islamic radicals, such as the Da'wa Party that has advocated and used terrorism, are unlikely to have broad popular support. Some prominent Shi'a families actually are of Persian origin. Some groups have received foreign funding, notably from Iran and Syria. During the Iran-Iraq war, some openly sided with Iran. The danger exists that if any isolated group takes power, they would use the opportunity to carry out retribution and advance their own interests against other minorities.

The most effective Iraqi governments have been those who have been able to appeal across the country's ethnic, religious, and linguistic divisions. In retrospect, it is worth noting that the Ba'ath attempted to do just this during the 1970s and 1980s. The party was civilian and directed membership to Iraqi youth. It emphasized the notion of Iraqi identity versus communal affiliations. Saddam Hussein has once again attempted to address this issue by renewing promises of a Kurdish autonomous zone and announcing the eventual elimination of the Revolutionary Command Council and free elections. Yet the prospects for stability on the Persian, Arab, and Turkish frontiers remain slim unless the Kurdish population can be reintegrated into the national structure politically and socially.

THE FINAL DENOUEMENT?

While it remains, as always, difficult to make absolute statements about the future, certain long-term political trends are already discernable. War did not bring peace and stability to the Middle East. Indeed, it may auger a new period of domestic national unrest and regional dissension since the consequences of the war cannot be contained territorially to Iraq and Kuwait. The Middle East will become increasingly intractable if President Bush's new world order is seen to be selectively applied to a few, if no progress is made in the Arab-

Israeli problem, and as continued demographic trends exacerbate social problems.

There almost certainly will be increasing polarization between the
"have" and "have-not" Arab states, Arabs and non-Arabs, and Muslims
and non-Muslims. Many Arab regimes joined the coalition not out of
any rightly guided notion of world peace but because they envisioned
financial and political benefit. President Bush's next dilemma is
whether he can meet those expectations. If not, Western allies today
may not be there tomorrow. Signs of fragmentation in the coalition
itself were evident as early as May 1991 when Egypt summarily announced the withdrawal of its 40,000 troops from Saudi Arabia. The
peace process itself has been protracted with few results to date.

By waging a punishing air war, President Bush minimized coalition
losses. Yet the strategy of using such devastating force may ultimately
be counterproductive. Within the Middle East as a whole, President
Bush has left a legacy that may go far beyond that of any other foreign
power. Anti-American sentiment, now diffuse, may become more organized and focused over time.

7

Political Currents in the Arab World before the Iraqi Invasion of Kuwait

Alan R. Taylor

Political currents in the Arab world are in a constant state of flux, influenced in various directions by the drift of regional and global politics. Dramatic change in the local arena is often the result of a charismatic leader's attempt to challenge the status quo through a platform that appeals to a large segment of the commonality. These platforms invariably take issue with some aspect of U.S. Middle East policy, frequently in connection with the sensitive Palestinian question. Saddam Hussein's invasion of Kuwait was an example of such a turn of events in the Middle East. The scenario began with the restructuring of inter-Arab politics following the 1979 treaty between Egypt and Israel, and it was encouraged by the shifting mood in the increasingly powerful Arab "street."

The rise of Gamal Abdul Nasser in Egypt in the early 1950s and of the Ba'ath Party in Syria and Iraq in the early 1960s reoriented inter-Arab politics in terms of a progressive-conservative power struggle. It was a time of high expectations and extravagant rhetoric, and of bitter rivalries between the contending protagonists. But it came to a dramatic end with the Six-Day War in June 1967. After the devastating defeat at the hands of Israel's superior military establishment, the Arabs began to distance themselves from utopian ideologies and to adopt a pragmatic way of defining and achieving finite goals.

Anwar Sadat of Egypt became the principal architect of the new pragmatism in inter-Arab politics, which dominated the 1970s. He formed a tacit alliance with Syria and Saudi Arabia that, in essence, accepted the existence of the Jewish state but sought to initiate a process of Israeli withdrawal from the occupied territories. He achieved an important political victory when this succeeded in dislodging Israel from the east bank of the Suez canal in the October 1973 war. This event seemed to guarantee the permanent ascendancy of Sadat's approach to the resolution of Arab problems. Because he interpreted his success as a license to assign priority to Egyptian interests in formulating his policies, however, he was soon embarked on a course that brought him into sharp conflict with the majority of Arab states. When this course led him to Camp David in September 1978 and the treaty with Israel in March 1979, Egypt was suspended from the Arab League and the Arab system entered a new phase.

Saddam Hussein was consolidating his political power in Iraq just at this time. Seeing an opportunity to lead his country out of its traditional isolation, he assumed a leadership role in inter-Arab politics after Camp David. At the 9th Arab Summit Conference conducted in Baghdad in early November 1978, Saddam Hussein enhanced his own image by adopting a centrist position between Egypt's allies and critics. At a meeting of Arab foreign and economic ministers in Baghdad in late March 1979, he was even more effective in keeping the divided Arab system together and in engineering the passage of a resolution imposing punitive measures on Egypt for signing a treaty with Israel that was not adequately linked to the Palestinian issue in the West Bank and Gaza. In effect, he was able to bring most of the Arab states into support of his own relatively radical position on Sadat's policies.

Saddam Hussein also formed a tacit working alliance with Jordan and Saudi Arabia in 1979. Despite the very different political systems in the three countries, their common interest in containing the attempts of the new Islamic government in Iran from exporting its revolution to the neighboring Arab states made such an alliance possible. Following diplomatic preliminaries, it was operative by the end of the year.

In this context, the Iraqi leader began to qualify the kind of role he wanted to play in the Arab system. On February 8, 1980, he issued a National Covenant, referred to by some as a pan-Arab charter. Its ostensible purpose was to suggest the principles on which inter-Arab cooperation should be based. But it also conveyed a message to the Arab masses that Saddam Hussein was emerging as the champion of Arab unity, a new Nasser who was willing to address the grievances of the underprivileged and the disenchanted.

These accomplishments on the diplomatic level and in building a charismatic image that could tap the latent power in the Arab street vanished with the onset of the Iran-Iraq war in September 1980. Though provoked by Iran, the decision to go to war was a devastating miscalculation by Saddam Hussein. It dragged on for eight years, depleted Iraq's resources, and diverted attention away from the more important goal of leading the Arab world in an innovative new direction under Saddam Hussein's leadership. It was not until the war was over in the late 1980s that he was able to resume his original political course within the Arab system.

The 1980s were in many respects as disappointing as the previous decade with respect to the long-range aspirations of many Arabs. The Iraqi-Saudi-Jordanian alignment was so engrossed in the Iran-Iraq war that no headway was made in developing a more viable system of inter-Arab cooperation, especially in terms of addressing the vast discrepancy in wealth between the oil-producing states and the poorer countries. Saddam Hussein's pan-Arab charter was all but forgotten, and nothing pointed to any improvement in the quality of life for the underprivileged throughout the Arab world.

Another problem was the lack of progress in the Arab-Israeli peace process. Though the Palestinian issue does not directly affect all Arabs, the failure to resolve it has become a symbol of all that was wrong in the Middle East. President Reagan took less interest in promoting peace than President Carter; even though he eventually tried to launch a U.S. initiative, he and Secretary of State Shultz were never able to assign the Palestinian question sufficient priority to get significantly close to a settlement. President Bush seemed more likely to make headway, but his efforts had only started when the decade ended.

As many in the Arab world looked back at the 1970s and 1980s, what they saw was an initial attempt to achieve finite goals by replacing the ideological approach of the 1960s with a new pragmatism. This approach produced a degree of political success following the October 1973 war, but it failed to bring about an Israeli withdrawal from the occupied territories, leaving the status quo essentially unaltered. President Carter's interest in promoting Arab-Israeli peace seemed to offer some hope, but Camp David produced a separate peace between Egypt and Israel without resolving the Palestinian question in the West Bank and Gaza. This peace led to Egypt's suspension from the Arab League and the polarization of the Arab system.

Though the 1980s began with the formation of a tacit alliance by Iraq, Jordan, and Saudi Arabia, and the prospect of greater cooperation among the Arab states through the implementation of Saddam Hussein's pan-Arab charter, the Iran-Iraq war blocked progress toward this end. During the same period, the Reagan administration failed to bring about any real change in the Arab-Israeli stalemate. Against this background, there was a growing sense in the Arab world during the 1980s that the most important problem confronting the Arabs was the failure of the majority of their states to move in the direction of greater democratization. This growing sense had the effect of galvanizing the drift of politics to the street, a process that had been going on since the early 1970s and that had been profoundly encouraged by the overthrow of the Shah's regime in neighboring Iran in 1979.

The conservative establishment in Iran had been toppled by Islamic resurgence, a movement that conceived of itself as a "counterculture" pitted against the status quo and all the pretenses and inequities it represented. Though the ideology of replacing the existing order with an Islamic state may have remained a questionable alternative, the idea of a counterculture revolution rubbed off on many and became a prominent feature in the political psychology of the Arab street.

By 1989, there were a number of important question marks about the portents of the 1990s. President Bush's clear interest in reviving the peace process, combined with the Soviet-American rapprochement, created a climate of rising expectations. The Arabs watched the peace initiative launched by President Bush and Secretary of State Baker, and the increasingly cordial relations between the United States and the Soviet Union, with intense interest. The world seemed on the brink of a major diplomatic revolution, suggesting a possible change for the better in the Arab world.

With the ending of the Iran-Iraq war in 1988, Saddam Hussein began to consider returning to his earlier attempt to establish himself as the new hero of Arab nationalism. Such a leadership image had a potential appeal to the counterculture mentality as the ultimate solution to the seeming inability of the existing regimes to deal effectively with the many problems facing the Arab world, both internal and external. Given the less accommodating Soviet policy toward radical Arab states like Iraq, Saddam Hussein's aspiration to revive a charismatic role for himself depended largely on the outcome of President Bush's peace initiative.

After months of intensive effort to lay the groundwork for Israeli-Palestinian negotiations designed to be the foundation of a comprehensive settlement of the Arab-Israeli conflict, President Bush and Secretary of State Baker reached a dead end in the spring of 1990. The principal obstacle to the success of the endeavor was the non-cooperative position of Israeli Prime Minister Shamir. President Bush and Secretary of State Baker were annoyed at Shamir but did not take measures to pressure him into compliance. Though there was no awareness of it at the time, this situation was the opportunity for which Saddam Hussein had been waiting.

Deeply disappointed by the derailing of the peace process and by President Bush's declared intention to suspend the dialogue with the Palestine Liberation Organization (PLO) following a terrorist raid in Tel Aviv at the end of May, the PLO announced in early June 1990 that it was shifting the focus of its diplomatic activity from Egypt to Iraq. This shift was more than a switch from a moderate to a radical state for support. It was the opening through which Saddam Hussein could resume his quest for the backing of the Arab street and all the agitated forces of discontent throughout the Arab world.

The gambit on which he embarked was relatively simple. With the PLO in his pocket, he had the most important credential for the intended audience. What he needed to convert this position into an activist policy was some kind of assault on the established Arab order that had come to be seen by the Arab masses as the barrier to a more promising future. Kuwait was the obvious choice. Iraq had long held irredentist claims to Kuwait, which it considered a legitimate part of its own territory. The ruling Sabbah family was anathema to those Arabs who wanted to change the status quo, and there had been recent disputes between Iraq and Kuwait over the production and pricing of oil. Furthermore, the U.S. ambassador in Baghdad, April Glaspie, reportedly told Saddam Hussein on July 25, 1990, that the United States had no position on such disputes between Arab states.

These developments set the stage for a dramatic Iraqi move to accomplish several aims all at once: the annexation of Kuwait, an assault on the conservative-moderate Arab order, the emergence of Saddam Hussein as the hero of Arab aspirations, and the establishment of a strong Arab position on the Palestinian issue. With a view to gaining these advantages in one stroke, Saddam Hussein decided to attack Kuwait and carried out the operation on August 2, 1990.

As logical as Saddam Hussein's agenda may have seemed to him at the time, it was based on several serious miscalculations. The first was that President Bush would reject the action and set up an international coalition that would challenge and ultimately end the annexation. The reality of this miscalculation began to become clear soon after the invasion.

The second was that although Saddam Hussein appealed to the alienated segments of the Arab populace, there were even more powerful elements in the Arab world that considered him a dangerous despot. Indeed, a fact that Saddam Hussein never took into consideration was that his own brutal authoritarianism was an important part of the very problem for which he was presenting himself as the solution. The charismatic image, though it carried some weight with the Palestinians and the Arab street, was considerably minimized by the participation of Egypt, Syria, and other Arab countries in the coalition. The undisguised aggression against an Arab neighbor, one that had helped Iraq during the war against Iran, also played an important role in the opposition of most Arab states and their constituencies to the invasion of Kuwait.

A third miscalculation was Saddam Hussein's failure to recognize that his own strategy to thrust himself into the forefront of Arab politics ran directly counter to the new trend in international relations. The termination of the Cold War and the Soviet-American endorsement of the "new world order" concept ruled out the kind of aggressive action Iraq undertook in marching into Kuwait and devastating the country. There was a global consensus against it, reflected in the various UN resolutions and the determination with which the coalition forces ejected Saddam Hussein's troops from Kuwait.

The building of a new world order will necessarily involve a reconstruction of the Middle East in the aftermath of the Persian Gulf war. While Saddam Hussein's influence has been greatly diminished, the currents in Arab politics that led to the crisis have not disappeared. The Arab street is still there and it is a powerful force. The counterculture mentality is still there and it shapes the thinking of many. The Palestinian issue is still there and will only be exacerbated by a continuing impasse in the peace process. The lack of democratization in the Arab world is still there and will remain a source of discontent until some way is found to encourage a diffusion of institutionalized power downward in the political processes of the area. The unsettling discrepancy between rich and poor nations in the Arab world is still there and will be an ongoing source of disharmony if some system of diminishing need through the expenditure of excess capital is not implemented.

If the dislocations of the past evolved out of unrecognized and misunderstood sociopolitical forces and the unrest that flowed from their discontent, it should not be expected that stability can be achieved in the future without dealing directly with the indigenous currents that help shape the course of events. Though a degree of power has gravitated to the street and become part of the political equation, the Arab masses are undirected in their frustration and are easily manipulated, as they were to some extent by Saddam Hussein. That is to say, they are capable of becoming a powerful destructive force but not of introducing a corrective program. What is needed, therefore, is a framework for reconstruction that addresses the underlying social, economic, and political problems of the area.

A viable Middle East order cannot be imposed. If it represents an attempt to set up a regional system geared primarily to the needs of external powers, it will evoke a negative indigenous reaction that will preclude any progress toward stabilization. The guiding principle should be to meet the legitimate needs of the populace; not to pander to them, but to help the regional states establish the institutional structures that will allow their constituents to live in dignity and security.

The task is certainly not easy and will require careful thought and planning. An important starting point would be to implement the necessary requirements of an Arab-Israeli peace process, including an international conference and serious consideration of a two-state solution. If the Israeli government cannot accept such an agenda, it must simply be brought into compliance whether it likes it or not. Failure to address this issue would be highly counterproductive. It has to be recognized that the unresolved Arab-Israeli conflict has been the most disruptive force in the Arab world since the end of World War II.

The Arab states, acting collectively, should play a leading role in the reconstruction process. They are the natural agents of change and the implementation of programs designed to share the vast petroleum resources of the area, to guarantee a basic respect for human rights, and to promote democratization and popular self-determination without imposing one political system or another on any particular society. The lessons of the Persian Gulf crisis and the war against Saddam Hussein will not be forgotten. There is an awareness that things cannot remain the same; that fundamental alterations are necessary.

Working with the world community to build a new world order in the 1990s, the leadership of the Arab world has an opportunity to convert the Arab system into what it was originally intended to be; an instrument of constructive cooperation among interdependent states. But these leaders must also acquire a new sensitivity to the needs and aspirations of the commonality of their respective countries. The political structure of the Arab world has been in a process of transformation since the Six-Day War. The street has been activated; Islamic resurgence has become a part of the equation; and a volatile climate engendered by inequities, monopolization of power, and the unresolved Palestinian issue has led to tensions, dislocations, and war. Recognition of these problems should be the starting point of any attempt by the local states to construct a better regional order.

Stabilization in the Middle East in the 1990s and the twenty-first century depends on the degree to which the forthcoming system of regional interaction represents the actual social forces operative within the area. Political systems on all levels cannot survive indefinitely if they fail to meet the needs of their constituents. Especially at a time when the people have come to play a greater role in the shaping of their destiny than ever before, this principle will be the decisive factor. The success of the new world order and of the regional Middle Eastern order that accompanies it depends on a clear perception of this reality.

PART III

RESPONSES TO THE IRAQI INVASION OF KUWAIT

8

U.S. Responses to the Persian Gulf Crisis: Grappling for a Policy

Bruce R. Kuniholm

The historical forces explored in the earlier chapters, conditioned by changing international circumstances, have proved increasingly inadequate as a framework within which to view the momentous developments of the last twelve years: the fall of the Shah and the advent of revolutionary Iran; the Soviet invasion of Afghanistan; the Iran-Iraq war; the increasing collapse of the Soviet empire and the end of the Cold War, the Iraqi invasion of Kuwait (made possible, one might argue, by the end of the Cold War); and the Gulf War of 1990–1991. These developments have changed the geopolitical environment of the Persian Gulf and have created the need for a new attempt at constructing a viable U.S. policy for the Persian Gulf—a subject discussed in this chapter.

In the early 1980s, President Reagan underscored Saudi Arabia's importance by his "corollary" to the Carter Doctrine: The United States would not permit Saudi Arabia "to be an Iran." If it was unclear which countries in the Persian Gulf region other than Saudi Arabia were vital to the United States and if a political strategy for the region was still lacking, it was in part because of the Reagan administration's ideological predisposition to focus on East-West issues and in part because of conceptual inertia. Strategic thinking about the region ignored regional priorities. It also continued to consist of what Gary Sick, an official who served on the National Security Council staffs of both the Carter and Reagan administrations, had characterized as "post-hoc adjustments to unanticipated and largely unwelcome developments." Once such adjustments were made, they tended to become mired in the status quo. Administrations that understood the inadequacy of military power alone to influence political events in the region nonetheless tended to rely on arms sales, military deployments, and (occasionally) economic assistance as the bedrock for their policies.

THE IRAN-IRAQ WAR

In this atmosphere, little creative thinking was done. In the course of the eight-year-long Iran-Iraq war, for example, when Iraq ran into serious difficulties, both the United States and the Soviet Union—which shared an interest in the equilibrium of the Persian Gulf—tilted toward Iraq. The United States was concerned with access to the Gulf's resources and with preventing any one country from dominating the region. The Soviets, for their part, desired good relations with all the Persian Gulf states. From a Soviet point of view, an Iranian victory would have resulted in the defeat of an ally, given Iran hegemony over the Persian Gulf, and created instabilities on the Soviet-Iranian border that it did not need—particularly as ethnic/religious tensions played themselves out in the Transcaucasus. These reasons, in addition to U.S.–Soviet competition (and, for the United States, a serious credibility problem in the Middle East resulting from the Iran-Contra affair), also explain why both countries offered to reflag Kuwaiti tankers.

Iran for a long time was unwilling to agree to a formal cease-fire until its war aims were met. Although these aims varied, they generally included international acknowledgement of Iraq's responsibility for starting the war (or an international arbitration committee to determine the aggressor), reparations, and the overthrow of Saddam Hussein and his Ba'athist regime. Saddam Hussein, however, was not willing to step down and the Ba'athists believed that even if he did, no Ba'athist would be acceptable to the Iranians anyway. Under these circumstances, Saddam Hussein sought to influence the outcome by perpetuating the tanker war. Since its inception in 1984, the tanker war had damaged well over 400 ships and resulted in a total damage write-off estimated as equal to half the total tonnage sunk in World War II. The purpose of hitting Iranian tankers was to cut Iran's economic lifeline, internationalize the war, and so bring pressure to bear on Iran. Other means of bringing pressure on Iran included the use of poison gas and terrorizing Iran's urban population with Scud-B missiles.

Given the stalemate at the front, Iran's options were few and the success of the Iranian revolution eventually was threatened. Iran was unable to isolate the war from the Persian Gulf, its offensive was stalled, and it had a relatively small air force. It could not retaliate at sea because, with the completion of the oil pipeline connecting Iraq to the Saudi pipeline at Yanbu, Iraq shipped all of its oil exports by pipeline through Turkey and Saudi Arabia. As a result, Iran attacked ships from Kuwait, which supported Iraq, and attempted to disrupt trade in the region.

Iraq, meanwhile, needed peace. Faced with a war of attrition it could not win and' the prospect of a continued mobilization it could not afford, it insisted on a formal cease-fire and resorted to drastic measures whose purpose was to internationalize the war. The problem for those attempting to mediate the war was that it was virtually impossible to be neutral. To support freedom of the seas or a cease-fire at sea supported Iran, since it kept Iran's economy going and allowed it to continue the war. To protect Kuwaiti tankers as nonbelligerents in fact supported the Iraqi war effort. To support a general cease-fire (as did United Nations Resolution 598) also supported Iraq, since it prevented Iran from delivering the final blow to Iraq and forced it to the peace table short of its aims.

Although Iran may have had legitimate grievances against Iraq for starting the war and a legitimate grievance against the United Nations Security Council for adopting, at the beginning of the war, Resolution 479 (which did not link a cease-fire to a withdrawal of forces to recognized international boundaries), there was little U.S. or Soviet sympathy for its point of view. Its willingness to sacrifice so many lives (most of which were lost while on the offensive) was seen as unnecessary and excessively vengeful.

From the U.S. government's point of view, the situation required that Iran be contained by Iraq and the Gulf Cooperation Council (GCC). As a result, U.S. policy sought mandatory enforcement measures against the side that was not willing to accept a cease-fire, negotiations, and a withdrawal to international borders. The United States did not believe it would be advantageous for either side to win. This perception (which made sense if one looked to a viable resolution of the conflict) was consistent with the U.S. position during the October 1973 Arab-Israeli war when it opposed Israel's attempt to capture Egypt's Third Army after Israel crossed the Suez canal. The United States, by supporting the sovereignty and territorial integrity of both Iraq and Iran, in effect supported the containment of Iran by Iraq and the GCC.

Ultimately, developments within Iran, coupled perhaps with a rapprochement between the United States and the Soviet Union (which inhibited Iran's ability to play one power off against the other), led the ailing Ayatollah Khomeini to accept a cease-fire—a step that he characterized as "more deadly than taking poison" but that made possible (if not easy) an end to one of the bloodiest wars of the century. In Afghanistan, meanwhile, a decentralized tribal system (along with outside support such as Stinger anti-aircraft missiles) enabled the Afghan guerrillas to thwart the Soviets—lacking a single head, one observer has noted, they could not be defeated by a single stroke. That very strength, however, has also impeded their capacity to organize themselves following the Soviet withdrawal—the many heads have not been able to speak with one voice.

THE IRAQI INVASION OF KUWAIT AND
THE ALLIED RESPONSE

In looking at the problems that confront us in the aftermath of the Persian Gulf war, it might be useful (1) to examine briefly what brought on the war, and (2) to explore the reasons why the United States became involved in the Persian Gulf crisis. Once we have understood what is at stake, we can turn to the difficulties that lie ahead and review briefly some of the preliminary concerns that already are being discussed in government circles.

Saddam Hussein invaded Kuwait for a number of reasons. He had long been extraordinarily ambitious and had aspired to be the leader of the Arab world. That in part explains his disastrous invasion of Iran ten years before. The eight-year war caused him to incur a debt of $70 billion; he needed money to rebuild his economy and subsidize the large army and police state that ensured his continuation in power. He felt the Arab countries were ungrateful for his role in containing revolutionary Iran and he wanted to cancel his debt to the Kuwaitis (who angered him by overproducing their OPEC quotas). He also saw the end of the Cold War as removing any Soviet restraints on his ambitions and, indeed, legitimizing them (because there was no one left to restrain what he saw as an Israeli-American alliance).

Iraq's claim to Kuwait was largely specious. It is true that the boundaries of every country in the Middle East from the Mediterranean to India have been defined in one way or another by imperial powers (this fact constitutes, in part, the root of the Palestinian problem, which I will discuss later) and that those boundaries have generally followed imperial rather than indigenous interests. But Iraq's claims on Kuwait are based on earlier, Ottoman claims, which were also imperial. Neither the Ottomans nor the Iraqis ever had any real control over the area.

It is ironic that Iraq's incorporation of the oil-rich province of Mosul, an area inhabited largely by Kurds and previously under the Turkish governor of Diyarbakir, was insisted upon in 1926 by the British, who wanted an Iraqi state to be militarily and economically viable, and whose arbitrary boundaries the Iraqis can thank for their oil reserves. In any event, if the Iraqi claim to Kuwait *had* had merit and Saddam

Hussein had wanted to pursue it, there were appropriate forums for the adjudication of international territorial disputes.

Iraq, apparently, had other objectives. In all probability Saddam Hussein, after incorporating Kuwait (and doubling his 10 percent share of the world's oil reserves), hoped to intimidate, if not invade, Saudi Arabia and thereby control over half of the world's crude oil reserves. This gain would have given him the capacity to control the international price of oil, to periodically undercut attempts to seek alternative sources of energy by making massive investments cost-ineffective, to disrupt the international economy, to become a dominant regional power, and to continue playing on the alleged threat of Zionism and imperialism to justify using his expanding arsenal. His ultimate aim, as evidenced by his public speeches, was to become the leader of the Arab world. As such he would have posed a serious threat to every country in the region that opposed him—and, ultimately, to the United States. There are a host of scenarios one could play out to underscore the threat to international peace that Saddam Hussein would have become.

Iraq, meanwhile, apparently felt that the United States—which alone had the capacity to react immediately and in force—would not do so, given our performance in Iran in 1979–1980, in Lebanon in 1983–1984, and our initial reluctance (changed only by Kuwaiti willingness to look to the Soviets as an alternative) to reflag Kuwaiti tankers in 1986–1987. The fact that the United States had tilted toward Iraq during the Iran-Iraq war (which Iraq had started but which Saddam Hussein appeared to be losing at the time) may have encouraged Saddam Hussein's cynicism and led him to believe that the international community in general would do little to oppose him.

The United States responded to Iraqi aggression, however, and it did so because of a combination of interests. Most concrete is the fact that over half of the world's trillion barrels of oil reserves is located in the Persian Gulf. To focus only on oil, however, and to treat it as a commodity that one might or might not choose to buy, instead of a resource whose possession has extremely important international implications, is to trivialize what was at stake in the Persian Gulf, a trivialization most vividly exemplified by those who opposed U.S. involvement with the slogan "No blood for oil." If Iraq had been allowed to get away with occupying Kuwait and intimidating Saudi Arabia, it would have controlled their oil resources. Saddam Hussein is an assassin, a torturer, and a very ruthless dictator who does not respect the norms followed by the international community. He has proved that time and time again over the past two decades. He has acquired chemical and biological weapons (as well as systems that could deliver them), he has attempted to build nuclear weapons, and he has shown a willingness to use those weapons that he possesses. In the last ten years, he spent an estimated $50 billion on armaments. One doesn't have to be a prophet to predict what Saddam Hussein would have done with his control of Persian Gulf oil. He needed to be stopped sooner or later, and it is better that it was sooner rather than later.

The United States, one should remember, had made clear commitments to defend its vital interests in the region as far back as the Carter Doctrine in 1980. If we had not honored those commitments, our credibility would have been worthless. Many of us may react somewhat derisively when the term "credibility" is used because it was so often misused as a justification for further commitments in Vietnam, but there is no doubt that it was at stake here. If we were not willing to honor our commitments in a region where there was no question that our vital interests were at stake (and this is one of many factors that clearly differentiate the Gulf crisis from the war in Vietnam), it would have raised serious questions about our trustworthiness as an ally. Countries surrounding Iraq would have drawn the appropriate conclusions, to the detriment of our long-term interests.

Beyond the issue of commitment was the fact that the world was entering a new, post–Cold War era where the traditional balance of power in the region could no longer be relied upon to stabilize crises once they developed; if the Soviets had not had serious internal problems at this time and had still been a world power, Iraq likely would never have invaded Kuwait. The future of a new international order, whose sanctity was being tested in the face of Iraq's unilateral use of force, hung in the balance. Even if one were skeptical about the feasibility of a new international order (and many are), the combination of principle, commitment, vital interest, and capability—the United States had spent the ten years since the Carter Doctrine gearing up for such contingencies—all suggested that if the United States and the international community did not respond to this situation, it was not clear when they would ever respond to any contingency and what destabilizing behavior they would invite. It also would soon have become much more costly to confront the threat posed by Saddam Hussein, and we would all have been wringing our hands.

Most Americans, I think, and for reasons discussed above, supported the initial deployment of U.S. troops to the Persian Gulf. Once Saddam Hussein had been deterred from intimidating or attacking Saudi Arabia, we were faced with the problem of getting him to withdraw from Kuwait. The UN resolutions were totally appropriate. The question then was whether or not—and if so, when—we would have to use force to facilitate his withdrawal. It was at this point that a substantial minority of Americans (and Congress) had differences with the administration. The embargo was working and would continue to work. Virtually half of Iraq's gross national product came from the export of oil, and the spigot had been turned off. But with the additional U.S. deployment in November and the shift to an offensive force posture, the United States began to limit its options. We had so many troops in place that we almost had to act. At the time—and without the benefit of hindsight—it was difficult for many to imagine realistic scenarios in which our interests would have been served by the use of force against Iraq because the political variables were too unpredictable and difficult to control.

Subsequent events made clear that Saddam Hussein would not have withdrawn from Kuwait that easily, and it is possible that over time the embargo would have run into serious political difficulties. Forced to allocate scarce resources, he might have chosen to starve his civilian population first. Public opinion in the West would have reacted divisively, the coalition might have come apart, Saddam Hussein might have become a hero (and the coalition might have been vilified) in an Arab world that admired him for toughing it out, and he might have proceeded to develop even further his weapons of mass destruction— he might, for example, have developed a capacity to carry chemical or even nuclear weapons in the Scuds whose range he had increased. Such weapons used against Israel almost certainly would have provoked an Israeli retaliation; retaliation, in turn, might well have torn apart the coalition, and the United States would have been in a very difficult fix when it came to its policies in the Middle East in the aftermath of the war.

There is no control group in history to prove President Bush's decision right or wrong—a point that congressmen flushed with victory and bent on vilifying those who disagreed with them should keep in mind. The difficult choices the president confronted caused most decision-makers to be ambivalent about whichever position they took (one needs only to have listened to the thoughtful debate in Congress), whether they wanted him to pursue the embargo (and leave attack as a later choice) or to give him authorization to use force immediately. Whatever position they initially supported, most Americans (and Congress) also rallied around the majority and supported the president's subsequent military efforts to oust Iraq from Kuwait.

In spite of the successful expulsion of Iraq from Kuwait and the success of "Operation Desert Storm," President Bush's decision not to pursue Saddam Hussein's forces and destroy his power base in Baghdad allowed Saddam to mobilize his remaining forces and crush a Kurdish rebellion in the north and a Shiite rebellion in the south, causing as many as two million refugees to flee to the Iranian and Turkish borders. Following the Security Council's condemnation of Iraq's repression of its civilian population and an appeal for humanitarian relief efforts, the United States, in conjunction with a number of coalition forces, launched an enormous relief effort to assist the refugees. By the end of June 1991, a terrible refugee situation had improved somewhat, and allied forces pursuing relief efforts in the safe havens of northern Iraq began to turn over some of their protection and relief activities to the United Nations. Almost a year later, Saddam Hussein was still in power, negotiating with the Kurds once more on their status within Iraq. The embargo, meanwhile, was still in effect, and the allied coalition was strongly critical of Iraq's failure to comply with the conditions of the cease-fire.

THE CHALLENGES AHEAD

In the wake of the Persian Gulf war, the United States must once again assess the nature of the threats to its vital interests in the region and the best means by which to protect them. The experience of the 1970s and 1980s was an instructive one for both the United States and the Soviet Union on the rules of the Great Game of imperial rivalry; the failure of the United States to abide by those rules in Iran may have encouraged the Soviets to break them in Afghanistan. In any case, both nations seem to have recognized the limits of their capacities to dominate the region in the modern era—either by themselves or through surrogates; they also seem to have understood that foreswearing domination does not mean the abandonment of their interests since it is a relatively easier task to counter than it is to support successfully those who aspire to regional hegemony. This experience, in conjunction with the end of the Cold War, has changed the nature of perceived threats to the region (which are now seen as coming from regional states such as Iraq or Iran). It has also led to the emergence of what both the United States and whatever replaces the Soviet Union may see as an increasingly appropriate response in the post–Cold War era—an attempt to codify new rules of the game in the Persian Gulf and Southwest Asia, and a collective effort to enforce international law under the auspices of the United Nations, all the while supporting a regional balance of power among Iraq, Iran, and the states of the Gulf Cooperation Council.

In the immediate future, aside from addressing the plight of the Kurds, the United States will probably want to maintain the embargo on Iraq until Saddam Hussein has complied with *all* UN resolutions— a practical impossibility given the enormous debt Iraq would have to pay. The resolution on reparations could, of course, be modified in the interest of the coalition's desire to see Iraq reconstitute itself as a viable (if unthreatening) state, but not while Saddam Hussein is still in power and his regime poses a danger to his own people and other states. The possibility of qualifying the reparations resolution might very well by used as a carrot by the coalition to give the Ba'athist regime an incentive to remove Saddam Hussein from power. A benevolent Ba'athist regime may be an oxymoron, but it may be possible to find a replacement for Saddam Hussein who can reach a modus vivendi with the rest of the country. Meanwhile, the coalition can continue to beat Iraq with its stick, continuation of the embargo. Speculation about next steps could go on forever. It should not, however, overshadow the need to keep in mind a long-term vision of what our policies should be in the region; and while it is important to recognize the practical difficulty of implementing such policies, it is important to identify components of the vision from which they spring and to encourage public discourse if we want to avoid losing sight of what we are pursuing.

The disintegration of Iraq must be avoided, or there will be chaos in the region. If Iraq were to disintegrate, Syria or Iran would be tempted to prey on Iraq. An autonomous Kurdish area in the north, for example, to the extent that it threatened to become an independent state, would pose serious problems for both of these countries as well as Turkey because of their internal Kurdish populations. As a result, while paying close attention to the treatment of the Kurds, it makes sense to endorse the territorial integrity of Iraq and to support a regional balance of power among Iran, Iraq, and the Gulf Cooperation Council. While U.S. forces are necessary for the time being to safeguard the Kurds, they should be replaced as soon as feasible by coalition and UN forces. It is important to avoid being sucked into the situation in Iraq. The United States has no UN mandate to do so. The ensuing commitments and responsibilities would be endless. The United States would get no credit and all the blame for a situation that has posed problems for centuries. While there has been much second-guessing about what the president should have done at the end of the war—and many believe he should have directed allied forces to destroy all of the Iraqi military and crush Saddam Hussein—there is no control group in history to play out some of the disastrous consequences that could have followed in the aftermath of such a course. Extended U.S. involvement, moreover, would have created unfortunate precedents for responsibilities elsewhere (e.g., the West Bank and Gaza) and raised serious problems for policy in the region—particularly since it would have been seen as corroborating the arguments of those who insisted that the United States was bent on establishing a foothold in the Gulf.

The Persian Gulf states, meanwhile, should be encouraged to undertake a major development scheme that bridges the gap between rich and poor in the region; they should also be encouraged to examine

closely the problem of creating better structures for political participation. In Kuwait, for example, the war will likely inspire a movement
for constitutional reform and greater freedom. The ruling family will
undoubtedly oppose this movement, which the United States should
nevertheless support. There are lessons to be learned from the fall of
the Shah of Iran.

Military forces from countries other than the United States, acceptable to the coalition in general and to the GCC in particular, should
be deployed in the region (to the extent that necessity dictates), where
they will contribute to a security framework that should also include
Turkey and Egypt. Such a framework will include forces that serve as
a trip wire for UN and/or coalition forces that should guarantee the
territorial integrity of every state. If there cannot be a new world order, there is no reason why there cannot be a new regional order. The
United States should encourage other countries to take part in such
an order and should limit its deployment to an air force contingent,
including AWACS, in a supporting role that is "over the horizon" but
that allows for immediate reaction to impede an attack. The maintenance of airstrips and the prepositioning of supplies, equipment, and
maintenance sets will continue to allow for the possibility of rapid
deployment of allied forces to the region in the event that a trip wire
is tripped. The very fact that the coalition forces did what they did in
support of Kuwait should make such a commitment credible, and
therefore less likely to be tested. Burden sharing is a must.

There must also be an internationally supervised mechanism for
controlling the proliferation of conventional and unconventional weapons, and a mechanism for the adjudication of international territorial
disputes in the region. Ultimately, the proliferation of poison gas and
ballistic missiles risks causing far greater damage than the already
enormous loss of life in the Persian Gulf war. There are now at least
seven countries in the Middle East and Southwest Asia—from Israel
to India—that have ballistic missiles. Three countries in the region
(Israel, Pakistan, and India), moreover, are capable of manufacturing
nuclear weapons, and others have ballistic missiles that are capable
of carrying nuclear weapons. These developments, along with the war,
all suggest that we need to give serious thought to arms control in the
region (including intrusive inspection in order to monitor the situation), and to the better management of affairs between states (on both
international and regional levels) if we are to survive. With the Cold
War over, a code of conduct agreement among the world's major sup-
pliers of arms—particularly if it is crafted with the care that is necessary—would not be a bad place to start.

Last but not least, there must be a continuing effort to address the
Arab-Israel/Palestinian problem. The Palestinian problem and the

broader Arab-Israeli question are among the most complicated and difficult problems ever to exist in international politics. This chapter is not the place to outline one's views on such a difficult subject, but it must be addressed briefly. It may not seem to be related to the current situation in the Persian Gulf, but it *is* seen as related to that situation by many Arabs who view Israeli occupation of the West Bank and Gaza as little different from Iraq's occupation of Kuwait, or Syria's occupation of Lebanon, and who believe that U.S. policy reflects a dual standard when it comes to condemnation of Iraq and support for Israel. Now that the war in the Persian Gulf is over, the two problems will be linked by the requirements of a post-crisis security framework in the Persian Gulf. That at least appears to have been the price paid by Secretary of State Baker for regional support for the allied coalition.

9

Nonmilitary Responses to the Iraqi Invasion of Kuwait: Use of Economic Sanctions

Kimberly Ann Elliott

There seems to be a growing consensus among analysts of the Persian Gulf war that while there are lessons to be learned from the experience, there were too many unique features for it to serve as a model for responding to likely future crises. One exception is the UN embargo of Iraq, which could serve as a model—though not a perfect one—for how multilateral sanctions in the cause of dispute settlement should be implemented. Unfortunately, the unique factors in this case suggest that the use of economic sanctions in support of collective security is likely to be more an aberration than a precedent. Analysis of the use of sanctions in the twentieth century confirms Inis Claude's thesis presented in Chapter 3 that the quest for collective security has been an illusive one and, despite the end of the Cold War, is likely to remain so. Nevertheless, a few suggestions for improving the implementation of collective economic sanctions and enhancing their effectiveness are offered at the end of this chapter.

ECONOMIC SANCTIONS IN THE TWENTIETH CENTURY

Although there is a rich history of sanctions episodes from ancient Greece through the nineteenth century, the cases on which this discussion is based occurred after World War I; both because earlier episodes are less well documented and because lessons from the distant past may seem less relevant to today's problems. Prior to this century,

most of the documented episodes foreshadowed or accompanied warfare. Even through World War II, the objectives sought with the use
of sanctions retained a distinctively martial flavor. However, the hor-
ror of World War I for the first time prompted serious consideration
of economic sanctions as an alternative to the use of military force.

Unfortunately, neither the League of Nations nor the United Nations historically has been a particularly effective peacekeeping institution, and economic sanctions have become rusty weapons in the
armory of collective dispute settlement. Instead, sanctions have been
wielded unilaterally in the majority of cases, most often by the United
States after World War II as it tried to shape the international system
to its world view. My analysis indicates that the United States, either
alone or in concert with its allies, has deployed sanctions 77 times.
Other significant users have been the United Kingdom (22 instances,
often in cooperation with the League of Nations and later the United
Nations), the Soviet Union (10 uses, usually against recalcitrant satellites), and the Arab League and its members (4 uses of its oil mus-
cle). The League of Nations used sanctions on four occasions in the
1920s and 1930s, and the United Nations has mandated the use of
sanctions only twice—against Rhodesia from 1966 to 1979, and
against South Africa since 1977 (though in the latter case, only arms
and other munitions are affected).

Most of the sanctions between 1914 and 1940 were linked to military action, with sanctions usually imposed to disrupt military adventures or to complement a broader war effort. The League of Nations
efforts to settle disputes using sanctions as an alternative to military
force had varied results: from success in inducing Greece to back down
from its incursion into Bulgaria in 1925 to the celebrated failure to
persuade Italy to withdraw from Abyssinia in the mid-1930s. Although
other foreign policy motives became increasingly common in the period
following World War II, sanctions were still deployed on occasion to
force a target country to withdraw its troops from border skirmishes,
to abandon plans of territorial acquisition, or to desist from other military adventures. In most instances in the post-war period in which
economic pressure was brought to bear against the exercise of military
power, the United States played the role of international policeman.
However, aside from the 1956 Suez incident (when the United States
pressed the French and the British into withdrawing their troops from
Egypt), major powers have never been able to deter the military adventures of other major powers simply through the use of economic
sanctions.

Closely related to the military adventure cases are those episodes
in which sanctions are imposed to impair the economic capability of
the target country, thereby limiting its potential for military activity.

This approach was an important rationale for the broad-based multilateral controls on strategic trade that the United States instituted against the Soviet Union and China in the late 1940s; the same rationale was cited by U.S. officials in defense of sanctions against the Soviet Union following the invasion of Afghanistan and the crisis in Poland in the early 1980s. It is doubtful whether these cases have yielded positive results, not least because it is difficult to hamper the military capabilities of a major power with marginal degrees of economic deprivation.

Sanctions have also been deployed in pursuit of a number of foreign policy goals other than those related to warfare and national security. Especially noteworthy is the frequent resort to sanctions in an effort to destabilize foreign governments, usually in the context of a foreign policy dispute involving other issues. Destabilization episodes have most often found a superpower pitted against a smaller country. The United States has engaged in destabilization efforts fifteen times, usually against other countries in the Western Hemisphere such as Cuba, the Dominican Republic, Nicaragua, Brazil, Chile, and Panama. Sanctions contributed at least modestly to the overthrow of President Trujillo of the Dominican Republic in 1961, of Brazilian dictator João Goulart in 1964, and of Chilean President Salvador Allende in 1973; sanctions played a minor role in the electoral defeat of the Sandinistas in Nicaragua in 1990. On the other hand, Cuba under Fidel Castro has not succumbed to three decades of U.S. economic pressures; in large measure that is because it received compensating aid from the former Soviet Union. Likewise, despite costly U.S. economic sanctions, Manuel Noriega was able to retain power in Panama; it finally took U.S. military intervention to dislodge him.

The Soviet Union has also picked on its neighbors, though less successfully. Each time the Soviets have used sanctions in an effort to topple a rebellious government within the socialist bloc—Yugoslavia in 1948, China in 1960, Albania in 1961—the effort failed. The only Soviet success came in 1958, when Finland was coerced into adopting a more pliant attitude toward Soviet policies. Finally, the United Kingdom also has participated in the destabilization game through the use of economic sanctions to topple hostile or repressive regimes in areas where the British once exercised colonial influence: Iran in 1951–1953, Rhodesia in 1965–1979, and Uganda in 1972–1979.

Since the early 1960s, sanctions have been deployed in support of numerous other foreign policy goals; most of them were relatively modest compared to the pursuit of war, peace, and political destabilization. For example, sanctions have been used (again primarily by the United States) on behalf of efforts to protect human rights, to halt nuclear proliferation, to settle expropriation claims, and to combat international terrorism. In recent years, controlling the proliferation of chemical and biological weapons, as well as ballistic missile technology, has become an important goal for using sanctions among the advanced industrial countries.

Methodology

Economic sanctions for purposes of this chapter are defined as the deliberate, government-inspired withdrawal, or threat of withdrawal, of customary trade or financial relations. "Customary" does not mean "contractual"; it simply means levels of trade and financial activity that would probably have occurred in the absence of sanctions. Foreign policy goals in this analysis encompass changes expressly sought by the sender state in the political behavior of the target. Though sanctions also serve important domestic political purposes, this analysis is confined to evaluating the effectiveness of sanctions in changing the policies, capabilities, or government of the target country.

Since sanctions cannot coerce the surrender of territory as easily as they can free a political prisoner, the first step was to arrange the cases being analyzed into five categories based on the objective sought: (1) modest, including settling expropriation disputes, improving human rights, and inhibiting nuclear proliferation; (2) destabilization of the target government; (3) disruption of relatively minor military adventures; (4) impairment of the military potential of an adversary; and (5) other major goals, for example, ending apartheid in South Africa.

In addition to the objective sought, several political and economic factors are identified that might be expected to affect the outcome of a sanctions effort. The *political variables* include:

- Companion policies used by the sender country, namely, covert maneuvers, quasi-military activity (such as massing troops on the target's border or stationing naval forces off its coast), and regular military activity
- The number of years economic sanctions were in force
- The extent of international cooperation in imposing sanctions
- The presence of international assistance to the target country
- The political stability and economic health of the target country
- The warmth of prior relations (i.e., before the sanctions episode) between sender and target countries

The *economic variables* include:

- The cost imposed on the target country, expressed in absolute terms, in per capita terms, and as a percentage of its gross national product (GNP)

- Commercial relations between sender and target countries, measured by the flow of two-way trade between them expressed as a percentage of the target country's total two-way trade

- The relative economic size of the countries, measured by the ratio of their GNPs

- The type of sanctions used, namely, an interruption of exports from the sender country, an interruption of imports to the sender country, or an interruption of finance

- The cost to the sender country (expressed as a qualitative index because of the lack of hard data)

The success of an economic sanctions episode—as viewed from the perspective of the sender country—has two parts: the extent to which the foreign policy outcome sought by the sender country was in fact achieved, and the contribution made by the sanctions (as opposed to other factors, such as military action). An index system can be used to rank each element on a scale from one (failed outcome; zero or negative sanctions contribution) to four (successful outcome; significant sanctions contribution). By multiplication, the two elements are combined into a *success score* that ranges in value from one to sixteen, with a score of nine or higher being rated as a successful outcome.

Success does not mean that the target country was vanquished by the denial of economic contacts, or even necessarily that the sanctions decisively influenced the outcome. Success is defined against more modest standards. A score of nine means that sanctions made a modest contribution to the goal sought by the sender country and that the goal was in part realized; a score of sixteen would mean that sanctions made a significant contribution to a successful outcome. By contrast, a score of one indicates that the sender country clearly failed to achieve its goals and that sanctions may have left it worse off than before. In some cases, the sender may have achieved some or all of its objectives, but the case will still fall into the failed column if sanctions played only a minor role in the outcome. In fact, this occurred in all of the episodes to which we assigned a score of eight, including the Iraq case, and in about one-third of those to which we assigned a score of six.

General Conclusions

Using this definition, sanctions have been successful in 34 percent of the 116 cases studied. However, the success rate significantly depends on the type of policy or governmental change sought. Episodes involving destabilization succeeded in 52 percent of the cases, usually against target countries that were small and shaky. Cases involving modest goals and attempts to disrupt minor military adventures were successful 33 percent of the time. Efforts to impair a foreign adversary's military potential, or otherwise to change its policies in a major way, succeeded infrequently.

An analysis of the 116 cases indicates that these measures are most effective when:

- The goal is relatively modest, thus lessening the importance of multilateral cooperation, which often is difficult to obtain, and reducing the chances a rival power will bother to step in with offsetting assistance (though if significant international cooperation is achieved—as in the Iraq case—more difficult goals may move within a coalition's reach)
- The target is much smaller than the country imposing sanctions, and it is economically weak and politically unstable (the average sender's economy was 187 times larger than that of the average target)
- The sender and target are friendly toward one another and conduct substantial trade (the sender accounted for 28 percent of the average target's trade in success cases but only 19 percent in failures)
- The sanctions are imposed quickly and decisively to maximize impact (the average cost to the target as a percentage of GNP in success cases was 2.4 percent and 1 percent in failures, while successes averaged 2.9 years in duration and failures 8 years)
- The sender avoids high costs to itself

Of course, some sanctions fail because they were never intended to succeed, in the sense of producing a real change in the target's behavior. As one analyst has noted, when sanctions have been used primarily for domestic political or other rhetorical purposes, " 'effective' sanctions [in an instrumental sense] were not a primary policy goal, and such sanctions were not imposed."[1] Sanctions may also be imposed timidly, and hence ineffectively, if conflicting goals are not weeded out. For example, the administrations of President Reagan and President Bush imposed economic sanctions against Panama in an effort to destabilize the Noriega regime. Simultaneously, however, they wanted to avoid destroying their political allies in the Panamanian business and financial sectors. Sanctions were imposed incrementally and then gradually weakened by a number of exemptions intended to support the second goal: In the end, the sanctions proved inadequate and military force was used to remove Manuel Noriega.

A major caveat to these general conclusions must be mentioned. Success in the use of sanctions has become increasingly elusive in recent years. If one splits the case sample roughly in half, into those initiated before 1973 and those begun after that date, a striking difference emerges. Forty-four percent of the sanctions episodes in the pre-1973 period succeeded, whereas the success rate among the cases begun after 1973 was just under 25 percent. Even more striking is the decline in the effectiveness of sanctions imposed in pursuit of modest goals, from 75 percent to 21 percent.

However, these trends need to be qualified: The increasing use of sanctions despite declining effectiveness can be attributed almost entirely to the U.S. experience. Other senders, including multilateral coalitions in which the United States played a relatively minor role, both reduced their reliance on sanctions and improved their record: from ten successes in twenty-eight attempts prior to 1973, to six out of thirteen since. In contrast, after posting a better than 50 percent average in the earlier period, the U.S. success rate has been less than 20 percent since 1973.

The most obvious and important explanation of the sharp decline in the effectiveness of U.S. sanctions is the relative decline of the U.S. position in the world economy. Unlike the early post-war era, the United States is no longer the major supplier of many goods and services, nor is it the only source of economic assistance for developing countries. Since the 1960s, trade and financial patterns have grown far more diversified, new technology has spread more quickly, and recovery in Europe and Japan has created new, competitive economic centers.

Thus, one by-product of the evolution of the world economy since World War II has been a narrowing of the circumstances in which unilateral economic leverage may be effectively applied. Success for individual sender countries increasingly depends on the subtlety, skill, and creativity with which sanctions are imposed; a test the United States has frequently failed. For multilateral sanctions, increasing economic interdependence is a double-edged sword. It may increase the power of economic sanctions, because countries are more dependent on international trade and financial flows, but it also means more countries may need to be involved in the sanctions effort and there are likely to be more countries capable of undermining the effect of a sanctions effort should they choose to do so.

USE OF SANCTIONS IN THE MIDDLE EAST CRISIS

The United Nation's embargo of Iraq was starkly different from previous sanctions efforts. Never before had sanctions been so comprehensive in their coverage. Never had they imposed such enormous costs on the target country. Although the goals were extremely difficult, the sanctions were imposed quickly, comprehensively, and with an unprecedented degree of support. The economic embargo was agreed to by the United Nations Security Council less than a week after the invasion of Kuwait. Within a month, it approved the use of naval forces to enforce the sanctions. Within two months, the United Nations had added an air embargo and had authorized secondary boycotts of countries violating the resolutions. Finally, Iraq's economy, geographically isolated and skewed as it is toward oil, is far more vulnerable to economic coercion than others that have been the target of sanctions. Because 90 percent of its export revenues come from oil, which is easily monitored and interdicted, smugglers would have had no incentive to evade the sanctions once Saddam Hussein had exhausted his reserves and whatever he was able to plunder from Kuwait.

Though there was inevitably some leakage, the embargo covered virtually all of Iraq's trade and financial relations—three to four times above what has typically been necessary to achieve successful results. Historically, when the sanctioning country or group accounted for 50 percent or more of the target's trade, it had an even chance of achieving its goals. The embargo had enormous impact on the Iraqi economy, perhaps as much as 48 percent of its GNP on an annual basis. Prior to this case, the cost imposed on the target by sanctions never exceeded 16 percent, and the average cost in successful cases was 2.4 percent of GNP, one-twentieth of the impact on Iraq. The cost to the target reached double digits on only three other occasions, and in all three of those, sanctions contributed to a positive outcome. Of eight sanctions episodes where the cost to the target was 5 percent of GNP or more, six resulted in at least partial successes for the sanctioning country or countries.

However, the boycott of Iraqi and Kuwaiti oil also imposed high costs on some members of the sanctioning coalition and could have had severe consequences for the global economy if oil prices had remained at $40 per barrel or more. Sanctions efforts often weaken over time because the high costs to the sender countries themselves erode support for the coercive measures. To counter this tendency, the United States and its allies went to extraordinary lengths to ameliorate those costs, especially to the hardest hit. Saudi Arabia and other oil exporters capable of doing so boosted oil production to offset losses from Iraqi and Kuwaiti production. In addition, the United States took the lead in organizing an economic action plan to recycle the short-term windfall profits gained by the Saudis and other oil producers, and to encourage Japan, Germany, and others to provide grants and low-cost loans to developing countries hurt by higher oil prices and by lost trade and workers' remittances. The International Monetary Fund and World Bank also provided concessional loans to developing countries suffering balance of payments stresses because of the sudden jump in oil prices.

Thus, the sanctions imposed against Iraq followed our recommendations almost to the letter. Although success could not be guaranteed, one thing is clear: Five months was far too early to declare the sanctions a failure. As indicated in testimony by officials of the U.S. Central Intelligence Agency, the impact of the embargo would not have peaked before late spring of 1991. There is also typically a lag before the impact of sanctions is reflected in political actions. Historically, sanctions imposed in pursuit of ambitious goals have taken just under two years to work. Given the draconian impact of the sanctions against Iraq, somewhat less time might have been required. However, President Bush and his advisers apparently concluded that the risks of waiting were too high, that the coalition could not be held together for a year or more. There are several reasons for thinking that the administration's assessment of the sanctions option was overly pessimistic.

First, Iraq's geographic position and heavy dependence on oil eliminate many of the enforcement problems that typically plague sanctions efforts. Just three countries are key in keeping Iraq's oil off world markets: Saudi Arabia and Turkey, which control the pipelines that carry virtually all of Iraq's oil exports; and the United States, whose navy blocked any attempt to ship oil by sea. With no way to get oil out, Iraq had no source of foreign exchange—the Central Intelligence Agency estimated Iraq would run out of money by summer—and smugglers don't take credit. Second, as we have noted, the United States and its allies took unprecedented steps to offset the costs borne by the sanctioning countries themselves. Third, many argue that the coalition was politically too tenuous to hold for a year or more. It was feared that an increase in Israeli-Palestinian tensions or an outbreak of terrorism could fracture the coalition. However, the military option hardly obviated those risks and could have increased them. Israeli restraint in the face of Iraq's missile attacks suggests those fears may have been exaggerated.

Obviously, concern about the fate of Kuwaitis subject to the brutal Iraqi occupation made any decision to prolong the crisis very difficult. However, these concerns and the other risks of waiting had to be balanced against the anticipated costs of undertaking the military option. For example, there was no assurance that many more Kuwaitis would not be killed in the course of an allied military attack. Also, the question must be raised whether the destruction of Kuwait's oil fields might have been avoided had the coalition not used military force. Overall, the analysis suggests that sanctions had a high probability of achieving the United Nations' stated goals, if given a chance.

LESSONS FROM THE UNITED NATIONS EMBARGO OF IRAQ

Although the embargo of Iraq was a stunningly successful example of international cooperation in support of collective security, it also revealed several areas in which the effectiveness of sanctions might be strengthened. These areas involve both issues affecting the choice of sanctions as a tool of multilateral diplomacy and measures to improve the technical effectiveness with which the tool is used.

The first and most fundamental issue to be addressed in responding to a threat to collective security is deciding what policy course is most likely to achieve the goals of the international coalition. A major criticism of sanctions in the Iraq case was that even if they succeeded in forcing withdrawal from Kuwait, they would have left in place Iraq's huge army and its unconventional weapons capability. This criticism may be true. But, ironically, the UN embargo is now being used as leverage to ensure that stockpiles of those weapons and the capability to produce them are completely destroyed, goals that supposedly only military force could attain. It also is not clear that military force served our long-term goals of peace and stability in the region better than sanctions could have.

A second issue is one of time. Economic sanctions do take time to work, though effective implementation can shorten the lag before they achieve maximum physical impact. In addition to the steps recommended in the following discussion for improving the instrumental effectiveness of sanctions, the decision to impose sanctions should be coupled with clear recognition and enunciation of the patience required and the willingness to pay the domestic price of that decision. If that political will to stick with sanctions can be clearly communicated to the leadership in the target country (or to groups that may seek to replace that leadership), the period required before it complies with international demands may be further reduced.

A key conclusion of the general analysis of economic sanctions in the twentieth century is that they tend to be most effective when they are imposed quickly and decisively. Two lessons from the Iraq experience could improve future multilateral sanctions efforts. First, many nations, though approving United Nations Security Council Resolution 661, did not have national legislation for implementing its provisions. The welter of responses and the complications and delays created by the confusion have been documented by the Research Centre for International Law of Cambridge University.[2] International lawyers are now studying the notion of drafting a model law that could be adopted worldwide so that UN resolutions could be quickly and consistently implemented.[3]

Second, though time is of the essence in imposing sanctions, in most cases they will need to be sustained for many months, if not years. Another important finding of the general sanctions analysis is that high costs to sender countries can erode support for sanctions and render them ineffective. Thus, a key to sustaining sanctions will be offsetting these costs, at least to key members of the sanctioning coalition. Article 50 of the United Nations Charter provides for consultation with the Security Council to address the "special economic problems arising from the carrying out" of preventive or enforcement measures adopted by the United Nations. Although the efforts to do this in the Iraq case were unprecedented in their scope, and the efforts of the oil exporters to moderate and reverse the oil price hike surprisingly successful, the costs imposed on countries from enforcing the sanctions were insufficiently compensated and appear to have been largely forgotten once the war was begun. As of late March 1991, twenty-one countries had notified the United Nations of problems under Article 50, claiming total losses of some $30 billion.[4] If these problems are not adequately addressed, many countries may, in the future, decide that the costs of non-compliance are lower than the costs of compliance.

Finally, there is the question of the role of food and medical supplies in a sanctioning effort. Although the United States has from time to time manipulated food aid shipments (and embargoed all grain shipments to the Soviet Union following its invasion of Afghanistan in 1980), it has typically exempted shipments of food and medical supplies from broader sanctions efforts for humanitarian reasons. The United Nations did the same when it imposed comprehensive mandatory sanctions against Rhodesia. The issue became an important one in the Iraq case because of the relatively high dependence of Iraq on imported food and because its geographic position allowed an unusual degree of enforcement, including the naval interdiction of ships suspected of carrying supplies to Iraq.

But a policy that must rely on hunger to achieve its ends quickly loses its moral authority and, just as quickly, its support. Moreover, it is not clear that a food embargo would have had the intended effect. Widespread starvation in Iraq probably could have been staved off for quite some time, if not indefinitely, through substitution and belt-tightening. Moreover, the presence of thousands of Americans, Europeans, Indians, and other non-Iraqis intensified the policy dilemmas in this case. United Nations Security Council Resolution 661 from the beginning exempted "supplies intended strictly for medical purposes." For moral and political reasons, and in the interests of alliance harmony, humanitarian circumstances in which food shipments would be allowed should have been clearly and broadly defined. Rather than undermining the sanctions the exemptions would have intensified the political pressure on Saddam Hussein. While the pain of sanctions would still have been severe, especially for the urban middle class that formed the broad base of Saddam Hussein's political support, humanitarian shipments would have allowed the UN coalition to demonstrate clearly that its fight was with his regime, not the Iraqi people. Had the Iraqi leadership refused such shipments for technical reasons—for example, who should distribute the supplies—unrest would surely have increased; and Saddam Hussein's standing in the Arab world might also have suffered.

However, exemptions do raise enforcement problems. Since the Security Council authorized naval forces in the area to use any means necessary to enforce the sanctions, they could have inspected ships allegedly carrying food and medical supplies to Iraq to confirm that they carried only humanitarian supplies. In addition, the extension of offsetting assistance to countries suffering from enforcement of the sanctions could have been predicated on full compliance with the sanctions. The primary lesson for the future is that starving people is neither an appropriate policy nor is it politically wise; and it is not generally necessary for instrumental effectiveness.

CONCLUSIONS

Just as World War I was not the war to end all wars, so the international response to Iraq's invasion of Kuwait—impressive though it was—will not end aggression in the world. It is unlikely that future breaches of the peace will be so blatant, the aggressor so odious, or the potential consequences for the global economy so serious. Thus, it is unlikely that future efforts to enforce collective security will evoke similar agreement on goals and commitment to enforcement measures.

Nevertheless, it is worth studying the role of economic sanctions in collective security efforts. Adoption of the measures recommended here should encourage cooperation in future efforts and enhance the chances of success. In general, the more cooperation the better the odds of success when ambitious goals are sought; however, multilateral sanctions have achieved at least modest success in the past with far less cooperation than was present in the Iraq case. The military action against Iraq was successful in operational terms, but it entailed enormous economic, political, environmental, and human costs. An effective collective security system needs the threat of military force as its ultimate enforcement tool, but the aftermath of the war in the Middle East should provide more than sufficient incentive to take whatever steps are necessary to make economic sanctions a viable instrument for the enforcement of collective security.

NOTES

This chapter is based in large part on Gary Clyde Hufbauer, Jeffrey J. Schott, and Kimberly Ann Elliott, *Economic Sanctions Reconsidered*, 2d ed., 2 vols. (Washington, D.C.: Institute for International Economics, 1991).

1. See Michael P. Malloy, *Economic Sanctions and U.S. Trade* (Boston: Little, Brown, 1990), 626.

2. See E. Lauterpacht, C. J. Greenwood, Marc Weller, and Daniel Bethlehem, eds., *The Kuwait Crisis*, Vol. 1: *Basic Documents*, and Vol. 2, *Sanctions and Their Economic Consequences* (Cambridge: Grotius Publications, 1991).

3. See Jeremy P. Carver, "The Gulf Crisis: Does Article 41 Have a Future?" Remarks to the International Law Association, British Branch, January 16, 1991, unpublished; and Carver, Remarks on "The Gulf War: The Law of International Sanctions," *Proceedings of the 85th Annual Meeting*, The American Society of International Law, Washington, D.C., April 18, 1991.

4. *Journal of Commerce*, 28 March 1991, p. 5A.

10

U.S. Military Response to the Iraqi Invasion of Kuwait

James Blackwell

HOW WE WON THE WAR

The Iraqi army was well trained, battle tested, and highly skilled at conducting combat operations after eight years of war with Iran and two years of continued building and expansion after the end of the war. It was basically a medium-technology, Third World armed force, the kind anticipated by many of us for mid-intensity conflicts in the post–Cold War era. Its strength was its mass, which, once in motion, developed a powerful momentum.

In the concluding months of the Iran-Iraq war, Iraqi forces outnumbered Iranian defenders sometimes by as much as twelve to one. In the Kuwait Theater of Operations, allied officials contend that Iraqi forces had a numerical advantage in tanks and fighting troops—as opposed to support troops—of as much as three to one. In the end their leaders betrayed them; their experiences against Iran were no preparation for what the allies did to them; and the constant aerial, artillery, and naval gunfire pounding broke the will to fight for more than half of the defending Iraqis. Those who had some fight left in them were swiftly and violently outmaneuvered and destroyed by the most effective armor lightning thrust in the history of warfare.

SUPERIOR PEOPLE

The allies fought with largely volunteer forces, and the all-volunteer U.S. force did not happen by default. It was carefully built and preserved out of the "hollow" force that had been allowed to develop in the 1970s. It capitalized on the natural talents of Americans for self-motivation and self-improvement, which were disciplined and allowed to flourish in a force that encouraged people to be all they can be. These good people had good leaders. To be sure, there were a few exceptions. But the overwhelming majority of the military leaders of the campaign were men and women of character, integrity, skill, and experience.

Professionalism permeates the entire officer and non-commissioned officer corps; that did not happen by accident. Single-mindedness of purpose, vision for the ultimate outcome of the fight, and perseverance in adversity characterized the national leadership behind the force. President Bush hired the right people to lead the effort, gave them the resources to conduct the fight, and provided the national and international leadership to see it through to a successful conclusion. He was helped in this effort by a secretary of state, secretary of defense, and chairman of the joint chiefs of staff who served these efforts well. Special recognition should be made of the fact that the theater commander-in-chief, General H. Norman Schwarzkopf, was uniquely suited to the role called for in an allied commander.

The U.S. Congress was also important in providing the congressional leadership support of the force in the field. Several leaders in the Congress provided key support on a number of votes leading up to the deployment and initiation of hostilities. And during the deployment and fighting, a number of congressional delegations traveled to the theater to visit the troops and find out from commanders what other support the Congress could provide.

U.S. military force structures underwent a fundamental transformation during the 1980s. All the services had shed their post-Vietnam organizations by the mid-1970s, but the conversion to an all-volunteer force had devastated the armed forces. Too many holdover draftees who should have been released hung on far too long. Discontent permeated the ranks, while drug and alcohol abuses were rampant. Pay was miserably low and motivation to work suffered from the lack of a sense of mission. The problems had caused then Army Chief of Staff General Edward C. "Shy" Meyer to testify in 1979 before Congress that the United States had a "hollow" military force.

The build-up and modernization of the 1980s changed all that. New equipment was purchased; pay and allowances were raised substantially; and training conditions improved. More important, U.S. forces were given a new strategic focus. After the Arab-Israeli war of 1973, the concept of combined arms warfare was felt to be the best means to meet the most important threat—the Soviet conventional military machine—that U.S. forces would have to be prepared to fight, especially in what was then the most threatened theater of potential war, the central plains of Europe.

Army divisions, Air Force and Navy fighter wings and ships were reorganized from top to bottom. Battleships were brought out of mothballs and refitted with new high-technology radars and missiles. New frigates were designed and new classes of cruisers capable of managing complex battle campaigns were created. Aircraft organizations became more diverse, integrating ever more advanced technologies into even more sophisticated and complex squadrons and wings for air superiority, defense suppression, close air support, interdiction, and strategic bombing. Ground forces became highly specialized, with the Marines concentrating on amphibious operations while the Army developed eight kinds of infantry, among other kinds of forces.

All of this required investments of time and money in developing the right organizational schemes to exploit both new technology and the steadily increasing quality of people coming into the force. Many experiments were conducted and some organizational ideas were discarded. Innovation was encouraged; the only bad idea was the one not raised for consideration.

One concept that was widely hailed at the time of its inception was that of the "Total Force." This was the notion that some parts of the armed forces could be in the reserves or the National Guard, where costs were lower because the organizations did not train on a full-time basis. For World War II the reserves had been mobilized as a huge new force with each division formed from scratch, trained as basic fighters, and put through the paces of larger unit maneuvers before being shipped off to the war as a whole.

The problem with this approach was that it took so long to get entire divisions and even larger corps ready to go to the war that had the Germans and Japanese been only a little more powerful or more successful on the battlefield, there might not have been sufficient time to wait for their arrival. After the war, military leaders wanted forces that were ready to fight on short notice.

Increasingly, in the 1980s, the Department of Defense could not afford to man all the complete divisions, ships, and wings that it felt were necessary to deter the Soviet threat, so greater reliance was placed on the reserves. The Total Force policy was designed to incorporate greater reliance on the reserves without creating new vulnerabilities from long training requirements after call-up. The design was to have much of the logistics infrastructure of the active forces in the reserves and most of the combat power in the active duty forces. A somewhat delicate balance was maintained between being ready to fight on short notice and building in some reaction time to a developing crisis, for if all potential crises had to be met with forces in being, the country would likely go bankrupt in the attempt to finance such a large standing force.

Eventually, by the mid-1980s, much of the combat power of the force was also in the reserve or National Guard structure. Many air wings required for early deployment contingencies were in the Air National Guard; much of the military airlift capability and all of the air interceptor squadrons for defense of the continental United States went to National Guard or Reserve Components. In Desert Storm, these air units performed their tasks well; conversely, some ground units had difficulties.

The Army and Marine Corps chose different paths to integrating reservists and national guardsmen into their forces. The Army took a two-tiered approach. Individuals and small units were given support roles such as supply, transportation, civil affairs and administration, among others. Combat functions were largely reserved for the active force with the exception of a few "round out" brigades. These brigades were formed and trained within particular geographic regions and were designed to become part of active duty divisions when mobilized.

Those active duty divisions assigned reserve brigades were reduced in strength proportionately; consequently, to get an entire full strength division to the field, its affiliated National Guard brigade was needed. It was assumed by force planners that a certain short amount of train-up time was needed and would be available to get these reserve brigades ready to go with their active duty counterparts.

In Desert Storm, it did not work out that way. The 24th Infantry (Mechanized) Division had only two brigades in peacetime; it was to rely on its round out brigade, the 48th Georgia (Army) National Guard, if it were to be called into action. When Operation Desert Shield was ordered in August 1990, the 48th Army National Guard brigade was not called to active duty initially and the 24th Infantry Mechanized Division went to Saudi Arabia with another, separate brigade from the active force. When the 48th Army National Guard brigade was later called to active service, it was not declared ready for deployment before the war ended.

The U.S. Marine Corps had a different approach to the integration of reservists. The Marine Corps kept its force structure almost entirely in its active components and pursued a "round up" approach. With this idea, a fully combat ready Marine division consisted of three brigades, all in the active forces. Additional combat and support units were in the reserves and were designated to be added to the Marine divisions if they were deployed in combat. Most Marine operations in peacetime are at brigade level or below, and rarely do the Marines expect to operate a full division in the field as a complete force. This expectation is a function of the role the Marines are called on to perform as the nation's primary contingency force around the globe.

Thus, when the Marines were called on to deploy two divisions to Desert Storm, reserve battalions were integrated into division task forces already formed from among the active battalions in the divisions. Virtually all the combat power of the Marines was in Saudi Arabia by December, including substantial portions of the Marine Corps Reserve.

This experience must cause Pentagon force planners to reevaluate the Total Force concept. While the integration of reservists and guardsmen on an individual or small unit basis worked for support forces, the reliance on larger units for combat arms must be reassessed in the light of Desert Storm. If the practice is to be continued, either more time must be provided before deployment or more resources will be needed to keep reserve combat brigades ready to deploy on shorter notice.

The greatest payoff of all from the investments of the 1980s was in training. Huge investments were made in modern training facilities such as the Air Force's Nellis Air Base, where pilots routinely practice their skills in mock aerial combat with a specially trained and equipped "aggressor" squadron that employs Soviet tactics. The Navy's version of this concept was popularized in the hit motion picture *Top Gun*. The Army and Marine Corps have built huge training complexes in the U.S. desert southwest where entire brigades operate in near combat environment, also against a foe that practices Soviet tactics. It is the most realistic peacetime training in the world.

Much of this training was made possible by the development of sophisticated training devices and simulators. Pilots can push the performance of their aircraft to their limits and suffer a "crash" without danger to valuable jets or risk to human life. Low power laser beams replace bullets and missiles, while sensors can detect target hits to let people know when they have been careless or caught off guard. Extensive computer networks keep track of and record each movement and engagement to evaluate the performance of individuals and weapons afterwards from every possible vantage point.

These exercises have immeasurably improved the performance of Americans in battle, giving them great confidence in their abilities and their equipment and permitting rehearsals of battles beforehand. Such confidence provided a crucial element of the miraculously low casualty rates in Operation Desert Storm.

Another element of the way the people of Desert Storm worked together so well was the set of command relationships put in place for the war effort. Whenever large armies are fielded, the sheer size of the force requires the appointment of several generals to command the force. A 700,000-man army is far too much for one general alone to command. Problems can arise when subordinate generals are required to work together under one of their own, especially at the highest levels.

The basic problem is that the self-confidence, aggressiveness, and accomplishment that are the prerequisite for successful command make it a challenge for such a person to also be a team player. Personal rivalries can become institutional rivalries as well. Thus, over the years the U.S. military establishment had developed particular service approaches to warfare in the Army, Navy, Air Force, and Marines that often reduced the effectiveness of U.S. forces operating together or jointly.

In 1986, Congress passed a law sponsored by Senator Barry Goldwater and Representative Bill Nichols, known as the Goldwater-Nichols Act. Among other things, it attempted to tear down the walls of rivalry that had been built up over the years among the military services that increasingly had come to hinder combat operations. Congress pointed to operations such as the ill-fated Iranian hostage rescue mission during the Carter administration, and the bombing of the Marine barracks in Beirut, Lebanon, as examples of the worst effects of interservice rivalry. Even successful campaigns such as the 1983 liberation of Grenada were seen as less than satisfying by the proponents of the measure because so many casualties might have been avoided if command arrangements had been more clear-cut.

The Goldwater-Nichols Act aimed to overcome those difficulties by legislating two fundamental measures. First, the law elevated the position of the chairman of the joint chiefs of staff and placed him in the chain of command. In the past, the chairman, while the highest ranking military officer in the U.S. armed forces, was only an advisor to the secretary of defense and the president. But he could not often express his own advice because the old laws required him to represent the views of the other service chiefs as well. This requirement resulted, more often than not, in his bringing to the nation's political leaders the least controversial positions on which he and the four service chiefs could agree. When an individual service chief did not like the direction being taken, he could obstruct progress by holding out for his own view before the chairman could take a joint position to the secretary of defense.

The other part of the wall of service separation was the control the service chiefs exerted over the forces in the field. Each component of a force in the field was tied by logistics support, personnel policies, and doctrinal practice to its service headquarters in the Pentagon rather than to the overall commander in the geographical region to which the forces were assigned. This arrangement usually resulted in theater commanders having little actual control over military operations in their theaters of operation.

The Goldwater-Nichols Act cut through the wall of service separation by elevating the position of the chairman of the joint chiefs of staff and by placing full command of all forces in the field squarely under the command of the theater commanders-in-chief. In Operations Desert Shield and Desert Storm, both General Colin L. Powell, chairman of the joint chiefs of staff, and General H. Norman Schwarzkopf, the theater commander-in-chief, exercised this new authority with tremendous effect. General Powell made the basic decisions on what the military objectives of the war were to be, the strategy to achieve them, and the forces that would be sent to the field to accomplish them. General Schwarzkopf was given wide leeway to develop the operational plan, to decide on its execution, and to resolve disagreements between air, sea, and ground components as to which would have priority at differing phases of the campaign.

BETTER IDEAS

America's superior people were empowered by better ideas. This war was not just a clash of wills, nor was it only a conflict of national interests. The Persian Gulf war brought into battle a fundamental conflict of values, strategies, and operational concepts. In the end, the allies prevailed as much because they were fighting with the right ideas as because they had great people.

This war was one of the few clear-cut ideological struggles of the post–World War II era. Saddam Hussein's idea was that if he wanted it he could take it. He was a dictator of the worst kind. Not only did he deny his people their basic rights as human beings, but he treacherously sacrificed their lives for his own selfish interests. He was willing to sacrifice hundreds of thousands of Iraqi people for his own glory. He did so not only in this fight but in his eight-year war with Iraq as well.

The allies had a clearly superior moral ground. Virtually the entire world agreed that what Saddam Hussein had done in taking Kuwait was wrong. Even those few countries that did not support the war did not deny that Saddam was wrong to take matters into his own hands by force of arms. The world recognized that his brand of aggression, like Adolf Hitler's in 1939, must be stopped or it would spread rapidly to affect the entire world. More than any other recent conflict, the Persian Gulf war was one of right versus wrong.

The second idea that prevailed was that of strategy. Saddam Hussein was pursuing a strategy of attrition, while the allies adopted a strategy of annihilation. Saddam Hussein's idea was that he did not necessarily have to win on the battlefield, he merely had to outlast the allied coalition. He was convinced that he could break up the coalition by offering separate deals to some of its less committed members. He also believed that the U.S. commitment would evaporate once casualties started to come back to the states.

He was wrong on both counts. President Bush put together an amazing international coalition in a few few months' time, and he held it together even when at times it appeared that the Soviets might break the whole thing apart with their diplomatic maneuvering. And Saddam Hussein completely missed the lesson of Vietnam. He was willing to suffer a hundred thousand casualties to inflict a few thousand on the United States in the belief that, as with Vietnam, the American people would support a war half-way until it got rough, then cut and run. This time, indeed, Americans were not going to support a president half-way through a war; they were prepared to support him all the way. The coalition set out its goals clearly at the outset of the operation and never wavered until it won.

Iraq stubbornly stuck to a losing strategy long after it became clear that it would not succeed. The amazing thing about Saddam Hussein's stubbornness is that with so many military analysts and commentators saying exactly that well before he had been cut off by the 100-hour ground campaign, he never began to pull back or even offered to do so until it was too late.

In the final analysis, the campaign was won by the side that had the better operation concept for defeating the enemy. In this case, the Iraqi concept was to hunker down and stick it out. The allies, in contrast, fought a combined campaign. There is nothing inherently wrong with an attrition strategy if the enemy can be forced to attrit itself. This attrition happened to the United States in Vietnam with disastrous results for the country. It did not happen in the Kuwait Theater of Operations because the United States had learned its operational lessons from Vietnam.

There is a debate going on in the aftermath of the war that one of the military services might have won all by itself if only it had been allowed to prosecute the war its way. Many argued that the Navy could force Iraq out of Kuwait simply by continuing the maritime embargo initiated during the late summer of 1990. Air power advocates claim that if the air campaign had been allowed to continue for just another couple of weeks, so many Iraqi tanks would have been destroyed that Saddam Hussein would have been forced out anyway. These adherents argue for a single-service approach to future wars with one arm dominating and the others playing minor roles supporting the primary air or naval force.

The fact is that no single service won this war; all of them did. None was singularly sufficient; each was absolutely necessary. It may be that naval blockades can bring a country to its knees, but in the case of the Persian Gulf war the prospects for maintaining an effective embargo around Iraq for the twelve to eighteen months that would have been necessary to do so were daunting. Even if the air campaign could have been sustained another two weeks, there is no way of knowing when an enemy will quit or how long he will stay when hunkered down. In any case, neither the politics nor the weather gave the coalition another two weeks at the end of February 1991 when the ground campaign was launched. In the end, someone had to go in on the ground and take Kuwait back; and the fight was no mere mopping up operation.

The fundamental aspect of war is that it is infinitely unpredictable. The side that best preserves its options against the unpredictable is the one that usually will prevail because war never goes completely according to plan. It was the inherent flexibility of the allied force that gave it the ability to respond to Saddam Hussein's every trick and stratagem. Indeed, most of the changes imposed on the allied plans were caused not by Iraq but by natural forces such as weather, which no one could anticipate. In the end, the ability to bring multiple arms to bear on Iraq's unitary land force meant that even if Iraq had enjoyed some measure of success early on, these forces were going to lose; the only question was when and at what cost.

SYSTEMS

The fundamental dilemma presented by the great success of Desert Storm has to do with how we deal with weapons systems for the future. The good news is that everything worked. The bad news is that we still cannot afford it all. The United States will face incredibly difficult choices in the 1990s over how to preserve the keys to this great victory even while reducing defense spending to account for the reduced threats expected to be faced for the foreseeable future. If we look at each system used in the war, there will be a desire to buy them all. If, instead, we look beyond the performance of individual weapons systems to how force packages can work together in the future, we can exploit our natural advantage in technology at an affordable cost and remain the world's only military superpower well into the next century.

We must begin by taking a new look at how we plan to deter war through strategic systems. For decades, the United States has relied on the threat of nuclear retaliation to deter adversaries from ever striking us with nuclear weapons in the first place. For a long time, we even told everyone that we reserved the right to use nuclear weapons first if our interests in Europe were threatened by massive Warsaw Pact attack. Now, those doctrines are being challenged by the irrelevance of the old Soviet threat and by the emergence of conventional warfare threats from strong Third World nations such as Iraq. We must find ways to deter future Saddam Husseins from taking other Kuwaits.

One thing the war showed us in this regard is the value of ballistic missile defenses. The Patriot was never conceived to be an anti-missile missile, but it filled that role nicely against a crude threat from Iraq's modified Scuds. Other ballistic missile threats are more sophisticated, and we will have to have systems much more capable than Patriot. They must be able to provide wide area defense and they must be rapidly deployable to any part of the world.

The war also revealed our increasing dependence on space-based systems for deterrence. The military forces received early warning of Scud launches by means of spy satellites, which detected Scud launches instantly. Launch data were relayed quickly to both the allied command in the theater and to the Israelis. This early warning made it possible to get Patriot crews ready for intercepts and to prepare populations for proper protective measures. It almost became routine after the first couple of launches.

But no one was shooting at our satellites. Those "eyes in the sky" were so valuable that had they been shut down, there would have been much more panic when the missiles struck and more resources would have been diverted to hunting down and killing those mobile Scud launchers. The military of the former Soviet Union already has a functioning anti-satellite capability, and many other countries are today developing such systems. The U.S. dependence on space-based systems is so critical that it needs to concentrate on developing counters to emerging anti-satellite systems (ASAT). There also is a need to deploy our own ASAT capabilities, and we must develop redundancy in our satellite coverage and launch capability to be prepared to fight the next war in the high ground of outer space.

In land warfare, Desert Storm demonstrated a continuing need to deploy highly lethal and agile systems capable of moving very fast across the battlefield. Given the ineffectiveness of Iraq's artillery against allied armor, it should be possible to lighten the armor protection of our heavier systems—tanks and fighting vehicles—to get even more speed and agility out of combat vehicles. The next tank must be considerably lighter, faster, and perhaps stealthier than the current M1 Abrams.

The effectiveness of the multiple launch rocket system (MLRS) should be exploited. More applications of the concept of using fewer people to deliver more firepower can be found, just as a single MLRS launcher manned by a crew of three can deliver more firepower than an entire battalion (500) of World War II artillerymen. Precision guided weapons would give MLRS the ability to hit and destroy tanks.

Ground forces in Operation Desert Storm did not have adequate surveillance and reconnaissance capabilities. No commander ever has enough information to fight his battle with complete certainty, but future wars are going to be so fast-paced that a premium will be placed on having the ability to see farther and sooner. U.S. ground forces should expand the exploitation of remotely piloted vehicles for this role and should experiment with light satellites that could be launched on short notice to provide coverage more responsive to battlefield commanders.

In the air, much can be done to exploit our technological lead over any foreseeable foe. American planes fly faster and higher, are more survivable, and can deliver more effective ordnance than any others in the world. A key to winning the air war in Desert Storm was the ability to win command of the skies so quickly. Even if the Iraqi Air Force had put up a stiff fight early on in the campaign, they would have lost, although allied aircraft losses would have been higher. We must continue to maintain our lead in the design and production of high performance aircraft.

Once air superiority is won, the effectiveness of precision bombing can have a salutary effect on the outcome of the campaign. Smart bombs killed more tanks than any other weapons. The United States leads in these technologies as well, but allied air forces possess weapons of equal effectiveness in many respects. The Iraqis also had a number of precision guided munitions they had purchased from France and the Soviet Union, so this is an area that deserves continuing efforts to maintain our lead. It will also be important to keep up with technological developments in other countries in these weapons to develop counters to their potential use against U.S. military forces.

The success of the first few days of the air campaign was, in many ways, a result of defense suppression measures taken in secret during the opening hours of the war. Active measures designed to shut down enemy air defenses included electronic warfare, Apache helicopter raids, and missile strikes. The most effective passive measure was, of course, the use of the Stealth fighter, but it is unclear how much of the success was due to the passive versus the active measures. Before we invest billions on the fielding of a new generation of Stealth fighters, we should carefully analyze the tradeoff between the two approaches. Perhaps some mix of Stealth and non-Stealth aircraft would be most appropriate for the future.

Naval combat was of course not a significant factor in the campaign of Desert Storm. But maritime supremacy was vital to the success of the effort since most allied forces deployed by sea. Carriers, submarines, and surface combatants will still be needed for the future since there are blue-water navies around the world capable of posing a significant threat to the U.S. sea lines of communication.

One glaring weakness again revealed by operations in the Persian Gulf is mine warfare at sea. The United States still does not possess adequate mine-sweeping capability even though deficiencies in this area were revealed throughout the 1980s in the very same Persian Gulf during the war between Iran and Iraq. We have been content to rely on our allies to perform needed countermine operations, and so far we have had allied support when needed. But in the future we cannot be certain that those same allies will support us against a different foe in different circumstances. The United States must develop a more robust countermine capability of its own for the 1990s.

Strategic mobility was severely stressed during Operations Desert Shield and Desert Storm. The story of the air and sea lift to deploy the force was truly remarkable. The United States is the unquestioned leader among the nations of the world in this regard. But the requirements of the future will be at least as demanding and are likely to be even more stressful. We cannot assume that our transport planes and ships will have unquestioned access to the skies and ports needed to deploy and support military forces on such a scale again. We must anticipate that there will be some interdiction of our deploying forces, and we must have sufficient back-up transport available to replace some losses.

Moreover, this war has severely stressed the existing fleet of ships and planes. We need many more fast sealift ships to get more heavy ground forces to a distant theater. Greater use can be made of maritime prepositioning ships afloat to have supplies nearby because we are not likely to enjoy an extensive support infrastructure of modern bases built into the region as we have had in Saudi Arabia. The fleet of ships bearing the bulk of the load, the slower Ready Reserve Fleet, is in need of comprehensive overhaul and must be maintained in a better state of readiness for future contingencies.

The military airlift fleet was flown to the limits of its performance capabilities during the deployment and war. Our C-141s and C-5s will need to be overhauled sooner than previously planned because so much of their design lifetime was used up in the airlift operations. A replacement aircraft is not likely to be available for some time, so we will probably have to invest in a service life extension program to essentially rebuild much of the current fleet. Finally, we must reevaluate whether we need a costly new transporter, the C-17, or if we could get more lift for the money by reopening the assembly lines for the older craft and buying newer versions of the older models.

Our ground transportation assets were inadequate to perform the task set before them. Early in the planning phase of the war, when General Schwarzkopf contemplated ordering the great deceptive shift in tank forces to the west, he quickly discovered that there were not enough heavy equipment transporter trucks in the U.S. Army to move all its tanks around. Fortunately, several smaller alliance members, including some from the Warsaw Pact, had hundreds of such trucks available since they were no longer required by their former Soviet masters in Europe. Czechoslovakia was instrumental in providing those transporters, a dependency we should not repeat in future conflicts. We ought to buy more trucks.

Special Operations forces proved their worth in the war. We may never know the complete story of how they were employed; after all, their missions are deliberately cloaked in secrecy. But apparently these commandos convinced their greatest skeptic—General Schwarzkopf—of their worth prior to the battle. They evidently were employed in a doctrinal manner, conducting strategic reconnaissance deep behind enemy lines where only human eyes and ears could do. And they conducted Direct Action missions—meaning blowing things up and killing people—where it is necessary to do so clandestinely.

The main impetus behind these successes was the maturity of the Special Operations Command (SOCOM) that was mandated by Congress in 1986. SOCOM gave such forces the bureaucratic and budgetary support they had always lacked in the past. And through their success they gained new respectability from colleagues in the conventional forces, which largely had passed them off in the past as necessary but somewhat eccentric as well.

Finally, Desert Storm demonstrated a need to continue to develop technological advances in command, control, communications, and intelligence systems. Two key capabilities available to the allies were provided by high-tech airborne radar systems. The Airborne Warning and Control System (AWACS) had the skies over the theater of operations completely wired. Anything that flew was instantaneously detected and identified by AWACS, and allied aircraft could respond much faster than the Iraqis ever knew. The equivalent for monitoring ground operations was the newly developed Joint Surveillance Target Attack System (JSTARS). This system tracked vehicles moving on the ground and was particularly effective in locating mobile Scud launchers and tank forces preparing to attack. AWACS needs updating to account for newer emerging threats, and JSTARS has proven that it should be fully developed and deployed.

More important, with all this information now available, there is a growing need for a theater-wide information network capable of distributing data in real time across the battlefield to those who need it. The current practice of having separate and unique downlink units from all these airborne and space-based sensors is already overwhelming commanders with an overabundance of ground stations. We must exploit information management technologies to reduce the numbers and varieties of such ground stations to a few common modules that can be proliferated throughout the battlefield for all users.

SUMMARY

It will not be easy to keep people, ideas, and systems in balance for the future. The threats we face are not diminishing, they are only shifting. As underlying tensions around the globe come to the surface in the absence of an overriding superpower rivalry, conflict is bound to increase. Where those conflicts threaten U.S. interests, the United States must be prepared to employ its armed forces to protect those interests.

Not every situation will be as demanding as the Persian Gulf deployment and war, but some will. It is likely that a future war will require even more of us than did this war. And surely we will not be able to assume that our next opponent will be as stupid as Saddam Hussein turned out to be. We must not become complacent about our military forces simply because of Saddam Hussein's miscalculations. We must strive to build a force that will cause future would-be Saddams to understand what can be brought to bear against them and not threaten our interests in the first place.

We won a great victory in the Persian Gulf. We preserved our interests for the foreseeable future, but in the process we unleashed new forces that will bring new pressures to bear on the region. We can have great confidence that our political leaders will work hard with others in the region to keep the peace and build a more democratic and prosperous Middle East. But we must remember that to keep the peace we must prepare for war. That old lesson is the greatest lesson of the Persian Gulf war.

PART IV

IMPLICATIONS FOR THE RESOLUTION OF CRISES IN THE POST–COLD WAR WORLD

11

Military Role in the Emerging National Security Policy

Major General Daniel W. Christman
(U.S. Army)
Lieutenant Colonel Robert D. Walz
(U.S. Army, Ret.)

The cheering for Operation Desert Storm is over. As Les Gelb said, "Don't expect any deference from Democrats on domestic issues (they'll be righter than ever for having been wrong on the Gulf), cooperation from those nations you helped save (they said thank you on Thursday), and further compliments from journalists (we're not in that business)."[1] The real test for security policy is to come. Anna Quindlen outlined this test succinctly: "Every 20 years it happens, . . . this is the peace before the storm. Now comes the testing of our mettle."[2]

To pass this test, military planners must understand what Desert Storm can tell us about strategy in the changing strategic environment. While it is too soon to identify the definitive lessons learned, some preliminary assessments are possible. Following general comments about the use of power in the "new world order," we will outline the emerging national military strategy and examine Operation Desert Storm in this light.[3]

Our thesis is simple: that the decision to use military power in the coming years will be more, not less, complex. Two reasons support this proposition. First, force reductions will leave less margin for error in the application of military power, thus deepening the interaction of political and military leaders to ensure that the political leadership understands the risks inherent in application of military power. Second, the new national military strategy requires decisions to be based on less than unambiguous warning, and it will be needed earlier to allow the use of a full range of deterrent options.[4]

THE STRATEGIC ENVIRONMENT

Before examining the uses of power in the new world order, it is appropriate to set the stage by describing the world or environment within which power is likely to be employed. At least from the perspective of the Pentagon, there appear to be seven key elements to the strategic environment:

1. We are witnessing a rapid and profound change in the former Soviet Union and in Eastern Europe that promises far-reaching effects on the entire defense establishment. The Warsaw Pact as a military alliance ceased to exist on April 1, 1991. The emergence of major new powers such as Japan, Germany, China, India, and Brazil has resulted in a multipolar rather than a bipolar environment. Some, such as Charles Krauthammer, have gone so far as to suggest that the new environment is unipolar in recognition of the unique capability of the United States to provide leadership in resolving global challenges.[5] Despite recent concerns over the Baltic states, arms control, and the direction of political and economic reform, these changes have generally had a beneficial impact on superpower relations.

2. The future direction of the military in the former Soviet Union is not as clear as previously thought. The political power and consequent size and shape of this military is in flux. Over the past several months, political events in the former Soviet Union and vacillating positions on CFE (Conventional Forces in Europe) and START (Strategic Arms Reduction Talks) have indicated the rise in influence of hard-line military leaders allied with conservative politicians.[6] The military has been used in efforts to intimidate leaders in various republics and to deal with ethnic unrest. Much of the military is also pressing to modernize its large military force. These directions could give rise to renewed emphasis on the use of the military element of power, both domestically and internationally. These trends argue for a hedge against some form of military resurgence.

3. With regional power vacuums created by diminished superpower confrontation, the possibility of continued regional instability around the globe increases. Aside from the Middle East, one must be concerned about the possibility of conflict in South Asia, continued conflict in Cambodia, ethnic and national conflicts in Eastern Europe and the Balkans, as well as conflict on the Korean peninsula. Especially worrisome is the growing proliferation of sophisticated conventional weaponry, as well as nuclear and chemical weapons. While estimates do vary, analysts assess that excluding the United States, the former Soviet Union, and Europe, 37 nations have the capability today to conduct mid-intensity conventional warfare (similar to Desert Storm, involving multiple corps on both sides); about 19 have a ballistic mis-

sile capability; approximately 20 have a chemical and/or biological capability; and 5 probably have a nuclear capability. By 2010, these numbers may increase to around 45 countries with a mid-intensity conventional capability; about 28 with ballistic missiles; approximately 32 with chemical/biological weapons; and probably 12 countries in the nuclear club.[7] The potential use of chemical and biological weapons during Desert Storm and the extraordinary precautions taken to minimize their impact were particularly good examples of this concern.

4. These trends mean that the United States must plan to counter threats across the operational continuum—from terrorism to nuclear confrontation.[8] None of the military services have the luxury of preparing for only one type of conflict. The strategic planning system that is emerging to implement the national military strategy will require military commanders to prepare flexible deterrent options to use to deter slowly rising crises. For more rapidly developing crises, the commanders must also plan large deterrent and warfighting force packages.[9] All of the military services, of necessity, must continue to complement each other as each tailors force packages to achieve the national objectives in each unique crisis.

5. The role of arms control as a component of our national security strategy has grown steadily in importance in recent years. There have been several agreements with respect to Europe. However, there seems to be the possibility for furthering stability in other regions through arms control agreements covering both conventional and non-conventional weapons. The United Nations imposition of unilateral arms control measures on Iraq in the aftermath of Operation Desert Storm could set a precedent applicable elsewhere.

6. We will also be challenged by decreasing fiscal resources as we modernize and streamline the military's organization in the years ahead. Overall, the military forces will be reduced by approximately 25 percent by 1995. For the U.S. Army, the reductions will be even greater. By 1995, the U.S. Army will reduce from a total force of 28 divisions organized into 5 corps to a force of 20 divisions including 2 "cadre divisions" organized into 4 corps. The active component forces will shrink from 18 divisions to 12, and the reserve component divisions will be reduced from 10 to 6 fully structured divisions. Two cadre divisions will also be organized and maintained at 25 to 30 percent strength.

7. The emergence of shared interests in countering Iraqi aggression has united allies and former adversaries. Syria, a former adversary, was supportive of our efforts and is considering recognition of Israel. Israel also played a constructive role by avoiding direct involvement in the conflict. The key question is whether this can be translated into

the new world order envisioned by President Bush. This quotation from the draft United Nations Resolution on the Gulf War cease-fire provides a glimpse of what the new world order may portend:

to guarantee the inviolability of the above mentioned international boundary (between Iraq and Kuwait) and to take *as appropriate all necessary measures to that end* in accordance with the Charter; . . . a plan for *immediate deployment of a United Nations Observer unit* to monitor the Khor Abdullah and a demilitarized zone.[10] (emphasis added)

The principles here embodied for the new world order are a renewed respect for international boundaries and an increased importance of the United Nations for protecting the security of nations and solving international problems. The use of the United Nations as a key component to policy is a major departure for the United States, which until recently viewed the organization as an ineffective actor on the international scene.

USES OF POWER

Much has been learned from Desert Storm. However, post-war euphoria needs to be tempered by an understanding of the uniqueness of the conflict. For example, despite the conclusions of some, Desert Storm lessons do not automatically apply to Vietnam. The Vietnamese enemy, his cause, his tactics, and the military geography all precluded the kind of campaign plan applied in Desert Storm. Other experts, including some in the U.S. Congress, maintain that the defense budget can be cut even more deeply than the secretary of defense has announced (on the order of 25 to 30 percent). The argument of these budget cutters is that if the United States could destroy the fourth largest army so easily, "what would it do against the seventh?" However, the question is not one of beating the seventh, it is deterring the first! Further, it is foolhardy to assume that because the coalition easily prevailed against Iraq, the next opponent will make the same blunders. Any future opponent will also have learned lessons from Desert Storm!

There appear to be two broad categories of lessons with relevance to future crises: those justifying the use of force and those pertaining to employment of the force. The lessons of Desert Storm, Just Cause (Panama), and El Dorado Canyon (bombing of Libya) all emphasize that combat operations should always be employed as a last resort. In the case of Libya, political and economic sanctions began as early as 1972 in an attempt to eliminate Qaddafi's support for international terrorism and subversion against moderate Arab and African governments. Military force was employed only after fourteen years of failed sanctions and the particularly heinous terrorist attack in Berlin that galvanized world opinion against state-supported terrorism. Similarly, political and economic sanctions were attempted for two years before the United States employed military force against General Noriega's Panama—again after provocations, including death and abuse of U.S. citizens. In the case of Desert Storm, the president determined that sanctions alone would not restore the legitimate government of Kuwait nor stop the destruction of that country. He employed force only after this was clear.

Popular support is another critical lesson in this category. The so-called Weinberger criteria emphasize the need for popular support before commencing a military operation.[11] This need was repeatedly underscored throughout the Gulf crisis and was perhaps best summarized by a *New York Times* writer who said, "Never go to war before insuring domestic consensus and international support."[12] Five-hundred-forty thousand Gulf veterans—soldiers, sailors, airmen, and marines—wholeheartedly concurred.

On the actual employment of force, Desert Storm demonstrated conclusively, if there was ever any doubt on this point, that the United States is not the world's policeman. Many nations are willing to work together to defend the rights of others. During the time the United States was involved in Desert Shield/Storm, there were numerous crises in which we did not take the lead: Liberia, in which we only supported the efforts of the Economic Community of West African States; Chad, where we supported the French lead; and Somalia, where Italy, Djbouti, and Saudi Arabia took the lead. The administration also discovered that supranational organizations can help in legitimizing the use of force. On this later point, however, the United States must guard against boxing itself in an implicit domestic requirement for United Nations or other nations' approval prior to taking action. There may be times when unilateral action is warranted, as in Panama.

Notwithstanding these general lessons, the bottom line for the new world order is that the republics in the former Soviet Union, despite their problems, remain a key to stability. They are no longer a "positive" military superpower in the sense that they can make happen what they desire. They are only a negative superpower to the extent they are able to thwart U.S. actions. Unlike many crises in the past, the former Soviet Union played a largely constructive role in the Gulf War, most obviously in their termination of military support to Iraq. While the Soviet Union did not provide military support to the coalition, the political support of the Kremlin for the objectives of Desert Shield was important for isolating Iraq. If the Soviet Union had continued to support Baghdad, we could have saved Saudi Arabia but liberating Kuwait would have been much more difficult. Thus, while the opportunity for convergence of interests between these new republics and Washington exists, one must be careful of the negative role they can play.

EMERGING NATIONAL MILITARY STRATEGY

Moving beyond the broad lessons of Desert Shield/Desert Storm to more specific military insights, one should turn to the evolving precepts of the national military strategy. Admiral William J. Crowe (U.S. Navy), while serving as chairman of the joint chiefs of staff, recognized that the old Cold War strategic paradigm was inflexible and outmoded. He started us down the path toward a new strategy in 1989, when our national military strategy document was updated. This process was continuing under General Colin L. Powell (U.S. Army). However, Desert Shield then hit in the midst of that transition in strategic thinking. In other words, we were designing the new strategy at the same time we were executing it.

To paraphrase Clausewitz, everything in strategy is simple; however, even the simplest of things are difficult.[13] As has been shown, the decline of the threat from the former Soviet Union, the emergence of new and changing threats to U.S. interests, and the transformation of global political and fiscal attitudes have reshaped the international security environment. In response, the military strategy to attain U.S. policy objectives, as we move beyond containment, is changing dramatically. The primary aim of the strategy—deterrence—endures. However, the concept is expanding beyond the principal threats that have shaped our strategic paradigm for the past four decades: conventional attack by the Warsaw Pact in Europe and a massive nuclear strike against the U.S. homeland. In light of these changes, strategic planning is moving toward a new regional focus. A brief examination of the concepts for use of conventional forces of our emerging national military strategy is in order before we examine their application in Desert Storm. The most significant of these concepts will be examined later in much greater detail.

Forward Presence

Longer warning time, a reduced threat in Europe, strengthened alliance partners, and declining defense budgets have changed the concept of forward defense. In the last three versions of the national military strategy, we have witnessed this former tenet move from forward defense through forward deployed forces to forward defense through forward presence to forward presence. This concept means that the demonstration of U.S. commitment will be carried out with fewer forces stationed abroad and more reliance on the forms of forward presence that are discussed in greater detail below.

Power Projection

Correspondingly, to protect U.S. global interests, we will rely on power projection of continental United States–based forces rather than the traditional rapid reinforcement of forward deployed forces. Desert Storm is an excellent example of the evolving paradigm, and it provided a unique test of our emerging regional contingency-oriented strategy—a test passed with flying colors. The major implication of this concept is the need for great flexibility in U.S. force structure and even greater reliance on demonstrating the power projection capability through military exercises such as Reforger, Bright Star, and Team Spirit.

Reconstitution

Given longer warning times for global war and significantly smaller standing forces, mobilization of established reserves is giving way to a broader concept called reconstitution. Reconstitution involves an orchestrated approach to force generation and industrial base expansion. Politically, this issue is the most difficult challenge because of the tradeoffs that must be made between research and development and production, between base closings and need for expansion capability, between foreign production and maintenance of a unilateral industrial base, and between the role of active forces and reserve component forces.

Coalition Strategy

Two issues are emerging within this traditional concept. The first is the changing strategy of NATO, for so long the dominant coalition in strategic planning. The key change to NATO strategy is that forward defense is being replaced by counterconcentration. This is one of many new themes now being addressed in a comprehensive NATO strategy review. No longer will U.S. and other allied forces be posted immediately adjacent to the border of Germany; they will be further to the rear to allow time to counterconcentrate against any would-be attacker. This theme has applicability on a global scale as well. Many high leverage, see-deep, strike-deep systems initially designed for Europe have tremendous utility for regional crises—particularly in situations in which we cannot expect to have the luxury of months of preparation time. As in Desert Storm, the destruction of enemy forces rather than the seizure or retention of terrain will be the focus.

The second issue is the nature of coalitions. Militaries are increasingly likely to be participants in ad hoc coalitions. These will be formed to meet immediate threats to a member's security and then will lapse when the threat has diminished. This approach is similar to the old balance of power system prevalent in Europe prior to the end of World War II. The critical component to any such system is a nation to play the role of the balancer, a role played by Great Britain for so long. It is obvious that in the new world order, despite the increased role of supranational organizations like the United Nations, the only nation capable of performing this function is the United States.

Arms Control

Finally, the aftermath of Desert Storm shows that arms control has applicability beyond its traditional East-West orientation. An emerging consensus appears to be forming that an arms control regime is necessary for long-term stability in the volatile Middle East. Such a regime would seek to reduce military capabilities necessary to initiate attack, enhance predictability in the size and structure of forces, reduce fear of aggressive intent, establish stable balances of forces, reduce military threats, and ensure confidence in compliance through effective verification. As Richard Burt, former chief START negotiator put it,

I believe that we will need to get on with a new agenda of arms control in the 1990s, an agenda some might call north-south arms control—that is coping with the proliferation of ballistic missiles in the Third World, of chemical weapons, of nuclear [weapons].[14]

OPERATION DESERT STORM: IMPLICATIONS FOR STRATEGY

Since traditional documents have made it very difficult to divine our military strategy, we have summarized the new national military strategy in a few words: a major shift in emphasis from reliance on forward deployed forces for forward defense against the former Soviet Union to an emphasis on projecting overwhelming force from the continental United States in response to crises that threaten U.S. interests worldwide. Strategic implications of Operation Desert Storm fall under the three key concepts that form the essence of the new strategy: forward presence, power projection, and reconstitution.

Forward Presence

Key to the U.S. role overseas in the decades ahead is forward presence. A broader concept than forward deployment, it is primarily a demonstration of U.S. political commitment. Parenthetically, this strategy represents a major change in the thinking of the armed forces, which in the past focused on forward stationing of troops in Europe and the Far East, in keeping with the dictates of our Cold War orientation and the national strategy of containment. The examples of forward presence that follow are arranged in increasing order of U.S. resource and political commitment to a region.

Military-to-Military Relations. Arguably, the most important contribution of the U.S. Central Command (the U.S. military headquarters responsible for the Southwest Asia region) in the last ten years was the patient building of relationships with the armies of the members of the coalition. There was a wealth of understanding that allowed the coalition to form, hold, and fight effectively. Equally important has been a series of exchanges the Chairman of the Joint Chiefs of Staff and chiefs of the military services have had with their counterparts all over the world, both in their countries and in the United States.[15]

Peacetime Engagement. This new term provides a useful construct for all those unglamorous day-to-day operations that help provide stability to a region.[16] Underlying this concept is the belief that building 100 kilometers of road in Honduras may be more important to the peace and stability of the region than providing a Multiple Launch Rocket System with a range of 100 kilometers. The effectiveness of security assistance programs to the Persian Gulf states and Egypt was reflected in the relative ease with which they were able to fit into the campaign plan and carry out difficult military missions in concert with U.S. forces. The military role in infrastructure building is readily apparent today in the reconstruction of Kuwait. The cleanup of the ecological damage in the Gulf under the leadership of the U.S. military and Operation Provide Comfort (Kurdish refugee relief along the Iraq-Turkey border) clearly demonstrate the role the military can play in disaster assistance and nation building or rebuilding.

Over-the-Horizon Deployments. Military power is often most effective if it is close but just over the horizon. This form of presence provides usable combat power without the adverse impact on a foreign culture that stationed forces may represent. Iraq may very well have not proceeded into Saudi Arabia due to the significant naval and air forces so quickly deployed to the Persian Gulf. On the other hand, Iraq may not have invaded Kuwait on August 2 had we not been deployed so far over the horizon. We must carefully balance the adverse impact on foreign cultures against the deterrent effect of forward deployments.

Combined Military Exercises. Bright Star conducted with Egypt, Team Spirit with Korea, and Reforger with Europe all provide many benefits both to U.S. and foreign troops. They provide U.S. soldiers acclimatization and familiarity with the military geography and armies with which they may have to work. Potential coalition partners receive training and familiarity with U.S. doctrine, equipment, and forces. The benefits for both the United States and potential coalition partners become evident and justify the small investments made when partners are required to fight together as occurred in the Persian Gulf.

Stationing. Permanent and temporary stationing is, short of combat, the ultimate demonstration of U.S. commitment and, arguably, the strongest form of forward presence. This form of presence has deterred aggression in Europe since 1945 and in Korea since 1953.

Power Projection

Power projection from the continental United States is the hallmark of the new strategy. The emphasis on power projection was a change in thinking under way months before Saddam Hussein sent his army into Kuwait on August 2, 1990. It is in this area that Desert Storm offers an especially useful case study. Desert Shield/Storm required power projection of historic proportions. Not even the early months of World War II and Korea matched the herculean efforts of the U.S. Transportation Command last fall and winter. We must have the capability to conduct another operation similar to it—in speed and size of forces—in the future. But the same conditions extant in the Persian Gulf will never be replicated. In that sense the operation is unique, and we must not fall into the trap of using Desert Storm as the model for all future contingencies.

Two facets of power projection are especially significant: the nature of coalitions and mobility. As mentioned earlier, Desert Storm highlighted the utility of coalition action and brought into sharp relief ad hoc coalition planning and execution—a much more likely occurrence in the new world order. The coalition for this operation was an unprecedented multinational force. Although frequently overlooked by pundits, over thirty-five nations provided military support (eleven nations sent ground troops into Kuwait). Several additional nations provided financial or military assistance. Even smaller, poorer nations such as Bangladesh, Morocco, Nepal, Niger, Senegal, Sierra Leone, Somalia, and Zaire sent ground forces or medical teams. East European countries such as Bulgaria, Poland, Hungary, and Czechoslovakia provided assistance. Arab nations played a major role. Together, Egypt and Syria provided around 50,000 ground forces. Saudi Arabia and other Gulf nations committed over 150,000 troops, 300 aircraft, sealift for the Egyptian and Syrian forces, as well as $36.8 billion in economic support and credit.[17]

To execute a power projection strategy, strategic mobility is vital. Over 200,000 personnel and 200,000 short tons of equipment were airlifted, a feat comparable to moving Richmond, Virginia, to the Saudi desert. More personnel and equipment were moved during the first three weeks than were moved during the first three months of the Korean conflict. During Operation Desert Shield, fast sealift ships loaded and delivered a heavy division over 8,000 nautical miles, with the first two ships arriving twenty days after the movement of the unit began. Army and Marine afloat prepositioned sustainment was delivered quickly and efficiently. Given the assets available, the sealift went exceedingly well.

However, there are challenges that must be met in the future. The ship speed and Ready Reserve Fleet (RRF) response were slower than anticipated. More than 50 percent of the RRF was not used because of obsolescence. There were significant shortfalls in capability to deliver cargo early. The Department of Defense, in response, has conducted a study, called the Mobility Requirements Study (MRS), to discover the right mix of strategic lift. Results will be provided to Congress, including how to invest $1.275 billion in fiscal year 1990 dollars that are available now; these resources must be invested quickly and wisely. While MRS will provide the details of lift requirements, Desert Shield/Storm highlighted an obvious imperative of our new strategy: additional 19–25 knot roll-on/roll-off ships and production of the new C-17 transport aircraft are absolutely essential to effective crisis execution.[18] Over and above the mobility requirements, there is also a need to improve management of our mobility programs, a task being undertaken by the Department of Defense Transportation Command.

Reconstitution

The reconstitution portion of the new strategy is designed as a hedge against an uncertain future. Current reduction plans are based on optimistic assumptions and carry substantial risk. Reconstitution and the choices that need to be made represent the greatest intellectual challenge of the new strategy.

Reconstitution means preserving the longest lead items of our security. This includes our alliance structure, forward deployments and access, and the technological and doctrinal edge that comes from vigorous innovation and development. Reconstitution involves a strategic construct labeled "graduated mobilization response," which is a long-range plan being developed for accelerating development programs, expanding and training reserve forces, and other measures necessary to keep pace with a potential threat. One of the most difficult decisions to make is whether or not to produce new systems being developed once research and development are complete. There is substantial risk associated with reconstitution because the decisions to begin the process will, of necessity, have to be based on "ambiguous indications rather than unambiguous warning."

We will continue to rely on our reserve component for combat support and combat service support, the kind of support without which Desert Storm could not have been executed. The reserves will also provide reinforcing combat forces for those scenarios in which there are longer warning times. Moreover, the nation will still require the capability to regenerate much larger forces in the event of a need to deter or fight a protracted major conflict. No one today anticipates the need to build such forces, but historical precedent and prudence indicate the need to plan for such an eventuality. Regeneration requires detailed mobilization planning, realistic call-up authority, periodic testing of the mobilization apparatus, and adequately resourced programs.

Maintenance of the current industrial base will require surge production, which is possible only if we stockpile critical components requiring long lead times. A slowly developing crisis, especially one involving a major military power such as the former Soviet Union, will require plans to expand the industrial base. Planning for production from new or alternative industrial capacity, (for example, keeping some portions of the industrial base warm and/or encouraging greater use of dual use items) is required.

CONCLUSIONS

Desert Storm forced the testing of new strategic concepts literally on the fly. The new strategy influenced the response, and in turn, the response is influencing the continued development of the new strategy. The conclusions presented here highlight how complex the use of military force in the coming decades will become.

For forty years, the paradigm governing U.S. military forces was based primarily on the fighting of a conventional land and sea battle focused on Europe against the Soviet Union. Although the doctrine produced by this paradigm was effective in Desert Storm, the need to focus beyond Europe is clear. One must mentally be prepared to live and work in the continental United States while at the same time be prepared to deploy and fight, if necessary, anywhere in the world. While all of the military services will be affected to some degree, the major impact of this sea state change will be on the ground forces. In any event, the planning necessary to implement the new strategy will be far more complex than in the past.

The military force available to the nation in the coming years will be smaller. If the nation and the services properly allocate the reduced resources available, the smaller military will permit the maintenance of ready forces able to perform as well as those in Desert Storm.

Strategic mobility has received a high priority in the draft national military strategy document and in Congress. It is absolutely essential to the success of the new strategy. Although it is relatively easy to buy more and possibly faster ships, producing the right mix of pre-positioning (both afloat and on land) and air and sea lift is not a simple task. It is difficult enough if one knows where one will fight, but it becomes monumental when the military planner cannot assume the location of the next crisis.

Political decisions made during the crisis will be studied by the United States, potential allies, and potential adversaries. While the new world order remains a vague concept, one pillar is obvious: The United States will defend treaty allies and vital interests. However, maintenance of deterrence in the future will require early political decisions, frequently based on ambiguous warning. Further, while our nation desires to act in an allied or coalition effort whenever possible, it must not preclude unilateral action. The choice of unilateral, as opposed to a coalition, response is a political one. However, the military consequences of that choice are immense. The forces built for a coalition effort are far different than ones built for a unilateral effort. The military planner must plan for both a unilateral and coalition effort, because until the actual crisis erupts, he or she cannot assume a coalition. Even more complex to the military planner is the situation faced in Desert Storm, in which one does not know if all members of the coalition will actually fight and under what conditions.

Finally, and possibly most important, the integration of the military, economic, and political instruments of power, which is necessary to the success of the military strategy, will require far greater interaction at all levels than the military officer and civilian decision maker were accustomed to previously. This complexity will require greater education and strategic vision on the part of the military officer and a keener understanding of the effect on military planning and execution of decisions made by political leadership. For all these reasons, and despite the apparent lessening of military threats, such as was presented by the former Soviet Union, planning for and actual use of military force will be far more complex in the future than in the past.

One looks with pride at Operation Desert Storm: the quality, professionalism, training, and dedication of our soldiers, sailors, airmen, and marines. But our future challenge is enormous: At the same time the defense establishment attempts to cope with the more complex new world order following Desert Storm, it is also reducing forward deployments and shaping itself for the post–Cold War world of the 1990s. According to General Gordon Sullivan, the U.S. Army's chief of staff,

That [challenge] has created some sophisticated management, organizations, and leadership problems. I think right now, the American people have a window into a very important period for the Defense Department. . . . with a smaller force the kind of quality, capability, and readiness we all displayed on Desert Storm will be even more important.[19]

How the military responds to this challenge will go a long way toward determining whether future Desert Storms will be handled as capably by our military and civilian leadership.

NOTES

1. *New York Times*, 3 March 1991, p. E-17.

2. Ibid.

3. The national military strategy is contained in the National Military Strategy Document. A description of the military element of the national security strategy, the national military strategy is a product of the Joint Strategic Planning System. It begins with reception of guidance from the president and secretary of defense and a review of the strategic environment every two years. The document is written by the joint staff after collaboration and consultation with the services and commanders of the unified and specified commands. It is then issued by the chairman of the joint chiefs of staff and approved by the president.

4. In the paradigm used during the Cold War, military actions were preplanned and based on the receipt of "unambiguous warning" of a Soviet attack. The new paradigm calls for a series of responses based on indications of an attack or onset of a crisis in an attempt to both deter an attack and posture the military effectively for combat operations should deterrence fail.

5. Charles Krauthammer, "The Unipolar Moment," *Foreign Affairs*, America and the World 1990/91, pp. 23–33.

6. Former chief of the Soviet general staff, General Moiseyev is reported to have stated that the treaty negotiated by the Ministry of Foreign Affairs has "no standing with the military."

7. Estimates prepared from various sources by the Office of the Deputy Chief of Staff for Intelligence, Department of the Army.

8. *Draft Joint Chiefs of Staff Joint Pub 3-0, Doctrine and Joint Operations* (Washington, D.C.: The Joint Chiefs of Staff, January, 1992) defines the operational continuum as consisting of three general states: peacetime, conflict,

and war. It goes on to say that there are no definite boundaries between the states and that there are several sub-states within each.

9. This new planning construct is called adaptive planning. As shown, it envisions an incremental approach in the design of force packages to allow appropriate responses to a wide range of crisis scenarios.

10. United Nations Security Council Resolution 687, April 3, 1991.

11. This was first enunciated in 1984 by Secretary of Defense Weinberger as one of six fairly limited criteria for determining recourse to the use of force. For a detailed examination of the "Weinberger Doctrine," see Alan N. Sabrosky and Robert L. Sloane, eds., *The Recourse to War: An Appraisal of the "Weinberger Doctrine,"* (Carlisle Barracks, PA: Strategic Studies Institute, U.S. Army War College, 1988).

12. R. W. Apple, *New York Times*, 3 March 1991, p. E-1.

13. The original quote is from Karl von Clausewitz, *On War*, eds. and trans. Michael Howard and Peter Paret (Princeton: Princeton University Press, 1976), 119.

14. Richard Burt, "Testimony before the Senate Foreign Relations Committee, April 17, 1991," quoted in the *Washington Post*, 19 April 1991, p. 22.

15. In fiscal year 1990 the chief of staff of the Army, for example, visited his counterparts in Guatemala (Conference of American Armies, where he met with at least a dozen of his counterparts), Egypt, Israel, Jordan, Germany, France, and Korea. Army chiefs from Korea, India, Tunisia, Bolivia, Colombia, the Netherlands, Egypt, and Peru visited the United States.

16. The term "peacetime engagement" was first used by Secretary Cheney in the Foreword to U.S. Department of Defense, *The Defense Planning Guidance, FY 1992–1997* (Washington, D.C.: Government Printing Office, 1990) to highlight the activities the armed forces must take to improve their ability to promote peace, freedom, and democracy in the Third World.

17. Paul Bedard, *Washington Times*, 27 March 1991, p. 3. Breakdown is as follows: Saudi Arabia, $16.8 billion; Kuwait, $16.0 billion; UAE, $4.0 billion.

18. Recommendation of the Joint Staff draft *Mobility Requirements Study* (Interim Response), undated, pp. 5–15.

19. General Gordon R. Sullivan (U.S. Army) speaking to the Army staff and Army secretariat at the Pentagon, Washington, D.C., March 1, 1991.

12

Use of Military Power in the Post–Cold War World: Win Big, Win Quick, and Win without Casualties

Robert F. Helms II

INTRODUCTION

The war between Iraq and the coalition of nations led by the United States is the first crisis in the post–Cold War world that has involved major nations and the use of large military forces. The war also is a watershed in that it marked a fundamental and decisive turn in the way conventional military forces will be used in the post–Cold War world. This decisive change is a reflection of the maturing of major trends that have been emerging over the past several decades.[1] This chapter uses the recent Persian Gulf crisis to examine these trends and to assess their implications for the use of military force in the post–Cold War world. The scope of this examination is limited to the use of conventional military forces as instruments of calculated aggression between modern nations. It does not include unconventional military operations such as those used in unconventional warfare, anti-terrorist, or anti-drug operations. Nor does it include internal conflicts such as civil war or fighting between factions.

The chapter first describes how the passing of the Cold War and the realization of major trends are reducing the incentives and opportunities for wars of aggression. However, it also acknowledges that the future has proven impossible to either predict or forecast accurately, and even though the probability of using war as a means for achieving aggressive aims is projected to be less, there always is the possibility that the unlikely will happen. Thus, the United States has to be prepared to use military forces to protect global interests for the foresee-

able future. As a result, the chapter also examines how these trends
are influencing the conduct of conventional wars should they occur.

ARRIVAL OF A LESS DANGEROUS WORLD

It is the hope of many that the passing of the Cold War and the
maturing of a set of major trends are intersecting to usher in a new
era, one in which there are greater levels of cooperation among nations
and military forces are used less frequently. These trends include the
rapid emergence of a truly global economy with higher levels of interdependence; the arrival of global communications; the passing of the
ideologically based competition; the coming of age for advanced conventional military weapons and supporting systems that are leveraging advanced technologies; and the rising costs of fielding and operating military forces.

Global Economy

The emergence of a global economy is influencing nations to seek
additional ways to cooperate and avoid the disruption and destruction
that is associated with war. As the world economic system continues
to mature, it can be expected to be an even more important factor that
argues against the use of military force. As described by Williamson
earlier in Chapter 1 and reinforced by Elliott during her discussion of
economic sanctions in Chapter 9, the maturing of a global economy
also provides additional ways, other than the use of military force, to
inflict pain on a belligerent nation(s) and to influence behavior. The
increasing preference of free market systems globally, to include the
former Soviet Union and throughout Eastern Europe, can be expected
to further accelerate the emergence of cooperation and attempts to
avoid military confrontations.

Global Communications

The presence of the international media was demonstrated very
clearly in its coverage of the war with Iraq. The war was visible virtually in real time in homes around the world. Consequently, the peoples of the world had access to information reported directly from the
battlefield and were not dependent on their governments for information.

The power and influence of global communications were once again
evident during the abortive August 1991 coup attempt in the former
Soviet Union. The media coverage of this event, in effect, created a

global audience that was kept abreast of rapidly changing events. In a similar manner, the peoples in the republics of the former Soviet Union, particularly in the larger cities such as Moscow, were able to keep informed and to deny those in charge of the coup the advantages of separating and isolating the population and their leaders. Unlike previous uses of the Red Army to enforce the will of the Communist Party such as the invasions of Hungary (1956) and Czechoslovakia (1968), it now is very difficult, perhaps impossible, to cut the communications links to shut out the press and keep the world from being informed of major events. Furthermore, the degree of difficulty is expected to become greater, not less, as advanced technologies continue to improve and provide for more redundancy for global communications.

Nuclear and Advanced Conventional Weapons

The dangers associated with nuclear weapons have been recognized since they were used at Nagasaki and Hiroshima in 1945. The threat of mutual destruction by nuclear weapons has been a decisive factor in defining the limits for actions that nations have been willing to undertake, particularly since the 1962 Cuban Missile Crisis. Now, however, new conventional weapons have emerged that approximate the destructiveness that was once possible only with nuclear weapons.

The 1973 Arab-Israeli war was the first demonstration of the destruction that is possible with conventional weapons using advanced technologies. While the destructiveness of conventional weapons was impressive during this war, it paled in comparison to the levels reached during the air, ground, and sea operations against Iraq. As a result, advanced conventional weapons also are becoming a major element in calculating the deterrence factor among nations and are increasing the determination of nations to avoid warfare involving modern military forces.[2]

The capabilities of these new families of conventional weapons are also rendering obsolete the need for tactical or non-strategic nuclear weapons. In the process, they are making it possible to eliminate low yield and short range nuclear weapons without losing the battlefield capabilities necessary for effective warfighting and deterrence capabilities. Indeed, the presence of these advanced conventional weapons with capabilities that approximate that of many tactical nuclear weapons increases deterrence since they can be used, as demonstrated in the war with Iraq; whereas it has been very difficult for the rational mind to imagine circumstances under which nuclear weapons would be used.

Decline of Ideological Competition

The trend away from confrontation that could lead to war also is being influenced by the decline of ideology as a basis for differences among nations. Foreign policy in the republics of the former Soviet Union is being de-ideologized and relations are being reconsidered. As the competition of communism versus democracy fades into the background, other major steps to cooperate and avoid confrontations that could lead to the use of military forces are becoming increasingly possible. The actions being taken to remove non-strategic nuclear weapons from Europe and to stand down a significant part of the strategic nuclear force in the United States and the republics of the former Soviet Union are examples of cooperative steps that are becoming possible that would have been unthinkable during the Cold War.

In a similar vein, a line of reasoning that the ways in which military force will be used have not changed in the post–Cold War world is out of step with the emerging conditions, just as Saddam Hussein was out of step when he ordered the invasion of Kuwait. Saddam Hussein was following the operational rules of the Cold War world (which no longer exists) when he directed military forces to invade Kuwait. This world, almost by definition, aligned the former Soviet Union and its allies against the United States and its allies in what has been described as a zero-sum game in virtually any crisis. Under these operational rules, it did not matter so much whether it was genuinely in the national interests of these blocs to take opposing positions; the more important issue was to oppose each other as a matter of ideological principles. The dangers of a military confrontation between these two blocs, including the possibility of a nuclear exchange, were so great that both basically were immobilized and their actions restricted to urging and providing resources to client states who became, in effect, superpower surrogates for actions in this zero-sum environment.

Under these operational rules, the Saddam Husseins of the world could inevitably count on using this situation for their own advantages. The United States, the former Soviet Union, and their allies became, in many ways, the hostages of other nations and forfeited control of their actions in situations in which the only choices were thought to be either to support their clients or suffer an ideological defeat. The possible consequences of such a defeat included the discredited concept of falling dominos, which provided much of the rationale for the U.S. involvement in Vietnam.

The passing of this zero-sum game, as the Cold War fades into the past, and the implications of the changes associated with its passing became apparent during the Persian Gulf crisis and the war with Iraq. The level of coordination and cooperation between the Soviet Union and the United States was unprecedented even though the Iraqi military was equipped, trained, and advised by the Soviet military. It must have been very painful for the Soviet military to observe the poor performance of the Iraqi military and the Soviet-provided equipment; yet they basically remained on the sidelines.

It is probable that if Iraq had invaded Kuwait in the 1960s, the 1970s, or early 1980s, the actions and reactions of the Soviet Union and the United States would have been considerably different and the probability of Saddam Hussein being successful would have greatly improved. Whether the republics of the former Soviet Union will be as cooperative or remain on the sidelines again in a similar scenario remains to be seen. However, the decline of the ideological basis for confrontations greatly increases the probability that future actions of the United States and these republics will be guided primarily by pragmatic national interests. This approach offers greater levels of confidence that the world has passed through the Cold War and has emerged in a new era.

It remains unclear how the convulsions that the republics of the former Soviet Union are undergoing will be concluded; this end state is one of the great uncertainties of the 1990s. From the perspective of the optimist, the abortive August 1991 coup attempt in the Soviet Union and the resulting flourishing of nationalism and freedom can be expected, if permitted to reach a logical conclusion, to accelerate the search for a more rational basis for national decisions. The trend also can be expected to be further reinforced as Western nations and Japan invest and become more involved in the former Soviet Union, Eastern Europe, and the People's Republic of China. At the opposite extreme, the pessimist sees opportunities for the former Soviet republics to pursue independent actions that result in conditions with the characteristics of anarchy and great instability.

The logical consequences of the trends associated with either of these views are the demise of the global power that was achieved by the former Soviet Union during the Cold War. As a result, it is probable that there will be less, not more, freedom of action among other nations for local or regional military operations. Assuming that the current movements in the direction of decentralization and free market economies continue with the attendant need for Western investments and technologies, particularly in the republics of the former Soviet Union (whatever their final end state) and Eastern Europe, it is reasonable to expect increased levels of cooperation to isolate and manage conflicts to establish vertical and horizontal controls. The realization of this scenario further reduces the incentives and opportunities for other Saddam Husseins to exploit. It also supports the positions of those who see the passing of wars between developed nations as a viable alternative for solving differences. In summary, the major trends on the Eurasian land mass and elsewhere are moving away from the use of military forces in directions of finding other alternatives for solving problems.

CONTINUING DANGERS IN AN UNCERTAIN WORLD

Of course, there is an argument that the passing of the Cold War is not necessarily leading to the emergence of a new and less threatening world. There is no assurance that the breakup of the Soviet Union will not lead to a form of anarchy among the nations that formerly comprised the USSR. The result could be wars that spill over into other areas. There also is the possibility that another event like the Iraqi invasion and occupation of Kuwait could occur. Therefore, as this argument contends, the world continues to be a dangerous place and military threats continue to exist.

However, the nature of the military threats has changed significantly in that they now exist primarily on a regional basis. This line of reasoning posits that the major threats to U.S. interests in the foreseeable future will come not from the republics of the former Soviet Union but from regional powers such as North Korea and Iraq, with the potential for threatening national interests and causing serious destabilization.

While it is possible that regional powers could have a destabilizing effect on U.S. interests, it is not at all clear that the probability of regional conflict has increased. Indeed, it seems that the chances of such conflict are becoming increasingly less with the demise of the East-West ideological competition. Most regional powers cannot afford to pay hard currency for modern military forces and have been dependent on either the United States and the former Soviet Union, or the allies of these nations, to provide military arms, equipment, and training at little or no cost. Now that the ideological incentive for providing the materials of war has decreased, these regional nations must expect to have a more difficult time in fielding modern military forces.

The argument often is made that the availability of advanced weapons is spreading as more nations such as Brazil and Israel develop the capacities for manufacturing and exporting modern arms. This argument, while correct in that more nations can produce modern weapons, fails to note that the motivation for many, if not most, of these nations to produce weapons is economic. These nations largely do not have an ideological motive for selling arms on terms that are similar to those made available by the former Soviet Union and United States during the Cold War. Additionally, not all regional powers who may want to buy advanced weapons can afford to pay market prices for arms; indeed, most cannot pay these prices. As a result, it is not at all clear that non-weapon producing nations will be able to buy and pay market prices for modern weapons in the quantities that are necessary for regional dominance. Furthermore, it is not self-evident that, even if they buy these weapons, they will be able to effectively use them.

The war with Iraq demonstrated that being able to fight and win on the modern battlefield is more than simply having the modern weapons of war available. It includes the difficult tasks of planning, coordinating, and fighting extremely complex combined arms and joint operations, which likely will include military forces of other nations. The Iraqi military was recognized as being the fourth largest military force in the world and having many top-of-the-line aircraft and tanks when the war started; yet it was totally ineffective against the military forces of the coalition.

The general conclusion is that the Iraqi military was not able to coordinate and integrate its military capabilities on the modern conventional battlefield. They simply were not prepared to use the advanced operational concepts, doctrines, and weapons found on high-tech conventional battlefields. This failure is the product of a number of factors, including the training of quality leaders and soldiers. Conversely, the coalition's military forces were able to very methodically and systematically leverage their inherent strengths of superior leadership, soldier quality, advanced technologies, secure lines of communications, and surprise against Iraqi weaknesses to achieve a quick and decisive victory. The key lesson that has implications for the future use of military force is that it is one thing to have advanced capabilities and quite another to be able to effectively use them. It is not at all clear that regional powers such as Iraq have the resources and technical skills required to field and fight military forces using high technologies effectively on future conventional battlefields.

FUTURE WARS

While the trends are moving in the directions of less conflict in the post–Cold War period, the lessons of history require continued vigilance: Rational thinking cannot be counted on to govern the actions of nations, and it would be a mistake to conclude that there will not be wars in the post–Cold War world. Furthermore, as Claude has described in Chapter 3, there is little reason to be more hopeful that a world order can be enforced by a permanent collective security agreement now than in previous years. The war with Iraq is a stark reminder that deterrence can fail, and from time to time nations may feel compelled to use military forces to defend their interests. When this situation occurs, it is quite probable that the United States, as Claude has pointed out, will continue to find itself thrust into the posture of a Great Somebody to organize and lead coordinated, selective anti-aggression actions.

The war with Iraq also introduced a set of military imperatives or standards to "win big, win quick, and win without casualties." These imperatives are the product of the unpleasant experiences of nations such as France, England, the former Soviet Union, and the United States during lengthy and indecisive uses of military forces. They also are the result of economic and political imperatives within which nations are making policy choices today and will be making them tomorrow.

Winning quick, winning big, and winning without casualties are not new standards. The Israelis have, by necessity, been following them as axioms during their periodic wars with the Arab nations. These necessities include unfavorable geographic, demographic, and economic considerations. The size of Israel does not permit trading land for time or military maneuvering. The small population of Israel relative to the more populous neighboring Arab nations dictates that Israel win its wars without large numbers of casualties. The smaller Israeli population also has meant that mobilization greatly affects the national economy when workers are required to leave their jobs and report for military service. The vulnerability of the fragile Israeli economy is a major factor in the strategic requirement for winning quick.

Deterrence of conflict is the cornerstone of Israeli strategic doctrine. A large part of deterrence is based on the perceptions of the potential aggressor. Its history of winning big during the periodic wars with its Arab neighbors increases the perceptions of Israeli invulnerability. These perceptions not only contribute to the deterrence of Arab nations but they also foster higher levels of confidence among the people of Israel and their supporters worldwide. The history of quick and decisive Israeli victories was challenged during the 1973 war. The early military successes of Egyptian armed forces and the difficulty of the Israeli military in defeating them shook the confidence of the Israeli people and their supporters. Conversely, the confidence of Arab nations was increased as a result of this war.

In many ways, the United States and the other industrialized nations find themselves in a position that is very similar to that of Israel. The unpleasant memories associated with long and indecisive wars in places like Algiers, Malaysia, and Vietnam have shaped the mind-set of the populations who were part of this history and who are determined not to repeat these experiences. The war with Iraq demonstrated the high economic costs of using modern military forces and the potential impact of modern warfare on national economies. Furthermore, neither the United States nor its allies have an industrial base that will support a long war that involves large numbers of military forces such as those that were used in either of the world wars or Korea. The spiraling costs of high-tech weapons, munitions, and supporting systems are making it very difficult to equip and maintain a ready military force that is supported by the most advanced technologies. These costs make it virtually impossible to establish and maintain large stockpiles for contingencies. These factors, in combination with an industrial base that would have difficulty making the conversion required to produce the material needed to meet military requirements and raising production levels to provide the increased demands associated with long periods of combat on modern battlefields, further argues for a quick war. If military forces are to be used, they have to be used quickly and efficiently to keep costs as low as possible. This limits the circumstances in which they can be effectively used.

Future military operations also will take place under the constant scrutiny of a skeptical audience made even more aware by global communications. The dramatic demonstration of a rapidly maturing global communications system during the Persian Gulf war is a primary factor that will make it more difficult for nations to use military force in long and indecisive wars. Indeed, it is unlikely that any nation with a free press could fight a lengthy war with the news coverage that is possible with modern communications.

War is not a predictable undertaking. Mistakes are made and lives are lost. Combat operations are filled with unpleasant sights, smells, and sounds. The normal response of military commanders for managing the press can be expected to soon create a backlash and become impossible to sustain as an increasingly adversarial relationship begins to take shape. The emergence of this situation can be expected to feed on itself and become a self-fulfilling prophecy. Critics of the war would use these mistakes to support their opposition, and in the final analysis, an anxious public would find it increasingly difficult to support the effort. There simply would be too many mistakes for the public to accept and tolerate.

Ensuring that the war effort wins quick, wins big, and wins without casualties is the safest way to avoid the dangers of lengthy and indecisive conflict. Attaining these standards denies critics the opportunities to mount an effective campaign against the war. It also provides positive reinforcements for the home front. These, in turn, feed on themselves as the public seeks "good" news and is less tolerant of "bad" news. In these circumstances, those covering the war can be expected to be more inclined to search for and report the good news, which also contributes to better relationships with the commanders and staffs fighting the war.

Winning without casualties emboldens the public and makes supporting the war effort more tolerable. The American public understands that it is not possible to fight a war without some casualties and may be expected to accept a low number of killed and injured if they consider the cause to be just. The same public cannot, however, be expected to accept large numbers of casualties, particularly if the war seems to be inconclusive or without purpose. This intolerance for large numbers of casualties extends to civilians living in the enemy's territory. It may even extend to the unnecessary killing of enemy soldiers. The need to avoid casualties to the extent possible is yet another reason to win quick.

Winning big also contributes to winning quick and winning without casualties when the opposing forces are quickly overwhelmed. This approach is the opposite of the *gradualism* that is associated with the U.S. involvement in Korea and Vietnam. The strategy of gradualism pursued during these wars sought to raise the level of effort in calculated ways to do just what was thought necessary for influencing the enemy in some desirable manner. This strategy failed badly each time and is not adaptable to the post–Cold War world. Indeed, establishing the battlefield conditions necessary for winning big, winning quick, and winning without casualties is one of the primary lessons from the war with Iraq that has major implications for the use of military forces in the post–Cold War world. However, the requirements for establishing these conditions will be taking place on a battlefield that is far different from those of the past.

Future Battlefields

The nature of the battlefield has been changed with the introduction of advanced technologies; indeed, it has been revolutionized and irrevocably transformed. These technologies are extending the battlefield in depth, width, and into the third dimension of space. Technologies are enabling soldiers to engage targets at greater ranges—firing on and killing targets beyond the range of human eyesight is more the norm on modern battlefields than the exception. Technologies are decreasing time and distance factors as automation enables data to be processed and transmitted in near real times to weapons with increased ranges and greater accuracies. Advanced technologies are turning night into day and enabling military forces to operate around the clock. The restrictions of weather are being eliminated with the applications of new technologies as well.

Advanced target detection capabilities are making it increasingly difficult to avoid detection on modern battlefields; these combine with the rapid response, improved accuracy, and greater ranges of emerging weapon systems to produce a lethality that is unprecedented in the history of warfare. Furthermore, this lethality may be expected to increase exponentially as future generations of technologies become available for use on the battlefield. U.S. tank crews who fought in the war with Iraq report firing on and killing Iraqi tanks with first round hits at great ranges, ranges so great that the Iraqis were unaware they were being fired on until other tanks around them began exploding. When the Iraqi tanks returned fire, their shells fell harmlessly well short of the U.S. positions. The Americans also tell of their surprise at the awesome firepower of the U.S. tanks as Iraqi tank turrets flew through the air like "frisbees" when hit by U.S. tanks.[3] Furthermore, this lethality is expected to increase dramatically as new target detection and data processing systems are linked to advanced weapons firing greatly improved munitions.

It is very difficult to avoid being detected and, once detected, being killed on the modern battlefield; indeed, it may be impossible. In the process, the battlefield advantages are shifting decisively from the offense to the defense in those wars in which both sides possess advanced technologies.[4] The war with Iraq very easily could lead to the wrong conclusion on this point. The United States and the other coalition military forces used an overwhelming offensive campaign to inflict a crushing and classic military defeat on the Iraqi military. On the surface, it seems reasonable to use this example as evidence that similar offenses are the key to victory. Such a conclusion would be a serious misreading of the war.

The Iraqi military had been rendered virtually ineffective by the naval blockade and air campaign when the coalition forces began the ground offensive. In the resulting situation, one force had and used advanced technologies against an opponent who was, in effect, denied any opportunities to use its advantages. Had the Iraqi military had similar technologies with the technical skills and leadership required to use them effectively, coalition forces would have had a very difficult task in conducting an offense against a prepared defense. Technologies, in effect, have become a dominant force multiplier than can be expected to be the decisive factor on future battlefields.

The ability to achieve military victory without excessive casualties to friendly and enemy forces as well as civilians is expected to be one of the criteria by which success will be measured. The criteria can also be expected to include the unnecessary destruction of industry and infrastructure. It no longer will be possible for future presidents and generals to apply maximum force to overwhelm an enemy. They also will be judged by the appropriateness of the force applied and the damage caused.

Advanced technologies will be a primary means for meeting these criteria. Technologies have the potential for enabling military forces to achieve objectives with minimum collateral damage to nonmilitary targets. For example, technologies make possible smart bombs and precision munitions that, in combination with advanced delivery systems, are capable of destroying military targets with pin-point accuracies. These capabilities, unlike the carpet bombing of earlier wars, can be used with confidence without damaging nonmilitary targets in the surrounding areas. It may also be possible for future technologies to be used in ways that now would be considered exotic. For example, it may be possible to develop systems that could shut down entire power grids, stop vehicle engines from functioning, or disrupt all communications that are transmitted over the air waves. Such technologies may make it possible to transform the use of military forces in ways that reduce the level of destruction.

As the conditions being described are realized, advanced technologies can be expected to become the dominant factor on modern conventional battlefields and the role of the soldier will continue to evolve away from physical combat toward the application of these advanced capabilities. This transformation of dominance will take place over time and proceed at a faster pace in some areas than in others; thus, it will be uneven. The logical conclusion of this process will move the soldier farther and farther away from the battle as the weapons of war become more automated and make greater uses of robotics.

Combat operations almost always will be joint; that is, they will be conducted by forces from more than one of the nation's four military services. They also will almost always involve military forces from more than one nation. As Williamson and Claude have described, it is unlikely that future military operations will be the product of truly collective security efforts. However, this conclusion does not rule out the probability of future military operations having a multinational character. Indeed, more often than not, they will involve military forces from other nations in combined operations.

The Gulf War clearly demonstrated the requirement for control of the air and the devastating results that can await the side that is at the mercy of the opposing air power. One of these lessons of the war with Iraq is the imperative of establishing and maintaining control of the air.

The battles themselves will be conducted over longer distances. They will be fast-paced, extremely violent, and the side that gains the advantage will be in a position to press it without pausing to victory. The initial battles quite likely will determine the ultimate outcome of war, and consequently it becomes an imperative to win the first battles. There will be little or no time and opportunity to recover from mistakes that, if made, could have disastrous consequences. Neither can the United States and its allies be assured of having an industrial base available that will sustain military campaigns on the scale of either of the world wars or that will outproduce the opposition. Nor will there be time to raise and prepare a force that can successfully fight and win on these battlefields; they simply are too fast-paced, complex, and deadly.

Success on these battlefields, defined in terms of winning big, winning quickly, and winning without casualties, requires extensive and thorough preparations of unit leaders and soldiers who can plan and orchestrate complex combined arms operations as part of a joint and combined military force. These battlefields do not lend themselves to military forces built around conscripts. They require well-trained professionals who have mastered the art of modern warfare. Consequently, while preparation of the battlefield has always been important, this phase of military operations becomes of paramount importance on future battlefields. The side that prepares the battlefield properly will have a great, perhaps decisive, advantage.

These preparations are wide-ranging and have to be under way well before the use of force is ever considered. They include maintaining a force that is equipped with the most advanced technologies. The force must be trained and ready to leverage the technological advantages quickly and decisively. The imperative to control horizontal and vertical escalation to win quickly and to contain the conflict requires the presence of ready forces; the nation cannot expect to have the time luxury of gearing up for a war. Its military forces must expect and be prepared to "come and fight as they are and win with what they have" in future wars. The lessons of the Gulf War challenge the strategy of mobilizing and using reserve units in complex combined arms operations. It would be immoral to place citizen-soldiers on the lethal battlefields found in modern warfare without the training that is necessary for fighting, winning, and surviving in this environment. As a result, the performance of complex military operations will increasingly become the domain of active military forces, with reserves being assigned missions that complement the skills they use every day in their civilian occupations. A rethinking of strategies for expanding the force is necessary and must be completed without undue pressures from those with political agendas.

The war with Iraq demonstrated that advanced weapons systems manned by skilled soldiers can reduce friendly casualties; in effect, technologies can be substituted for friendly lives. This lesson of the war underscores a "moral imperative" for maintaining modernized forces. It would be immoral to send U.S. soldiers, sailors, marines, and airmen into battle without every advantage that advanced technologies can provide them. Americans expect and will hold accountable those who fail to ensure that our military forces are provided the very best. For this reason alone, the nation must continue to provide the means for its military forces to maintain a critical and decisive edge in technologies.

However, it likely will not be possible for the U.S. military to maintain a critical edge without a significant change in the way that it conducts business, particularly in the way equipment is developed and bought. Higher costs and reduced budgets are converging to the extent that the military can no longer afford to be inefficient; nor does it have the resources available to maintain its own industrial base. It must now determine ways to achieve greater economies of scale by leveraging the capabilities and greater efficiencies that can be found in a close partnership with commercial industrial sectors. There are a number of obstacles such as traditions, laws, and regulations that will have to be addressed and overcome for this approach to work, but it can and must be made to work if the United States is to maintain the winning edge in advanced technologies.[5]

Technologies for advanced simulations are among the more important of these needs. The increasing costs of weapons, munitions, and the operations of military forces will require greater uses of simulators for training soldiers and leaders at all levels. Indeed, it is quite likely that simulations will become the primary means for training, with live firing and field exercises being conducted primarily to validate skills as opposed to developing them.

General Christman and Lieutenant Colonel (U.S. Army, Ret.) Walz in Chapter 11 discussed military roles in the emerging national security environment. These authors posited that, as the post–Cold War world continues to emerge, the United States expects to reduce the number of its military forces that are deployed overseas. The remaining forces will be deployed in fewer locations overseas, with more being stationed in the United States. At the same time, national interests will continue to exist around the globe and will need to be protected. There are a number of viable options that can be used in combination to reconcile the need for protecting worldwide interests with fewer forces and a reduced military presence overseas. First, the United States and its allies can be expected to continue maintaining some level of military forces deployed overseas, albeit at a level that is considerably less than during the Cold War.

Second, there is a pressing need for additional strategic air and sea lift to move military forces to locations around the world. These forces would be moved primarily from the United States but could also be moved between regions, such as the movement of U.S. forces from Europe to the Persian Gulf during the war with Iraq. If the requirements to win quickly, win big, and win without casualties are to be fulfilled, these forces must be moved rapidly and in sufficient numbers to meet and overwhelm the opponent(s) without delay. These requirements call for a mixture of advanced strategic lift that includes both air and sea capabilities. The strategic airlift will be used to quickly establish a forward presence of rapidly deployable forces in the threatened region. Strategic sealift would then be used to transport the heavy forces needed to reinforce the rapidly deployable forces and the logistics necessary to support the military operations to a successful conclusion.

Third, the military services can help their requirements for greater strategic lift by using advanced technologies to reduce the size and weight of weapons, supporting systems, and munitions without a similar decrease in capabilities. In a similar way, technologies can be used to increase the effectiveness of munitions and supporting systems. This increase in effectiveness would result in fewer munitions, weapon systems, and supporting logistics being needed to accomplish the same mission, thus reducing the tonnage and bulk that has to be transported. Automation can be used to enable fewer systems to perform the tasks once performed by many systems. Furthermore, these new systems have less weight and bulk; this also contributes to fewer strategic lift requirements.

Fourth, there likely will be attempts to continue pre-positioning critical items close to or in regions of possible use. Although this approach finds favor and is widely supported, it may prove too costly to buy equipment for pre-positioning and for the unit to have a duplicate set for training in peace time. Also, the added cost of replacing or upgrading the pre-positioned items has to be considered as new generations of technologies are developed, produced, and fielded. In summary, while limited pre-positioning may have been feasible during the Cold War, greater uses of this approach as a viable option for the post–Cold War world remain an open question that requires careful consideration before being adopted as one of the cornerstones for national military strategy.

SUMMARY

This chapter has used the Persian Gulf crisis to examine the major trends that are affecting the way nations can be expected to use military forces in the future. The scope has been restricted to the use of conventional forces and has not included unconventional military operations or internal conflict such as civil wars.

The examination of these trends leads to a conclusion, from the perspective of rational Western logic, that the utility of military force for traditional encounters such as the wars of this century is declining. The major trends that support this conclusion include the decline of ideology as a basis for competition, growing interdependence and emergence of a global economy, the destructiveness of modern weapons of war, the intrusiveness of global communications, and the world's growing public concern that unnecessary force not be used.

However, as the previous chapters have demonstrated, history teaches that rational logic does not always prevail and that nations have undertaken what would appear to be totally irrational actions. Therefore, the United States and its allies must, for the foreseeable future, continue to maintain and be prepared to use credible military forces to protect their national interests. This chapter has described how the imperatives of winning big, winning quick, and winning without casualties are changing the preparations for and the nature of warfare. These imperatives are expected to be the underlying factors on which future decisions are made for using military forces. If the Persian Gulf war teaches us that the future use of military forces is no longer business as usual, then it will have marked a watershed in the way conflicts are resolved and will be remembered as a truly historic and fundamental event that changed the course for using military forces in the post–Cold War world.

NOTES

1. See Robert F. Helms II, "An Army for Extraordinary Times" (published as "New Directions: Will the Army Jump or Be Pushed?"), *Army Magazine* 40, no. 6 (1990): 59–66, for a discussion of these trends.

2. James Blackwell, Michael J. Mazarr, and Don M. Snider, *The Gulf War: Military Lessons Learned* (Washington, DC: Center for Strategic & International Studies, July 1991), 39–43.

3. Steve Vogel, "Killer Brigade: 3d Infantry Division 'Phantoms' Hunt the Enemy," *Army Times*, 11 November 1991, pp. 10, 14–16, 22.

4. Robert F. Helms II, "Technology and Battlefields of the Future: Challenges, Opportunities, and Directions," in *U.S. Defense Policy in an Era of Constrained Resources*, eds. Robert L. Pfaltzgraff and Richard H. Schultz, Jr. (Medford, MA: Tufts University Press, 1990), 67–69.

5. Jeff Bingaman, Jacques Gansler, and Robert Kupperman, *Integrating Commercial and Military Technologies for National Strength: An Agenda for Change* (Washington, DC: Center for Strategic & International Studies, March 1991), ix.

13

Conflict in the Post–Cold War International System: Sources and Responses

Robert H. Dorff

The Iraqi invasion of Kuwait on August 2, 1990, was a sobering blow to the post–Cold War euphoria that had begun to characterize the views expressed by many analysts and practitioners of international politics. Coming hard on the heels of the collapse of the Soviet empire and the agreement on German unification, the invasion was the first concrete, major challenge to what President George Bush had been calling the "new world order." Although several analysts, including this author, had warned that a post–Cold War system might be anything but calm and predictable, it is safe to say that a majority of policymakers in the West were caught unprepared by the harsh reality of the invasion. The scramble that ensued to put together an ad hoc coalition of allies, supported by United Nations resolutions, raised numerous questions about the need for the use of force in this nascent international system of the 1990s. Moreover, the events in the Persian Gulf raised serious questions about the kinds of force that may be needed in the future.

The purpose of this chapter is to address some of those more general questions concerning the need for the use of force in the post–Cold War international system, and the types of force that may be required or expected. In the context of the theme of this book, I will attempt to ascertain whether there are lessons to be learned from the crisis in the Persian Gulf, and the coalition response to it, that may help us understand what the future uses of force may entail.

Two questions will form the core of the inquiry. First, what are the likely sources of conflict in the international system that might require some kind of application of force? Second, based on an examination of the sources of conflict, what are the types of responses that may be most likely in the changing international environment in which conflicts will arise? Our analysis should help us decide whether there are specific, or even general, lessons to be gleaned from the Gulf crisis that shed light on these two questions. Even if no generalizations are warranted, important policy implications derive from that conclusion, too.

SOURCES OF CONFLICT IN THE INTERNATIONAL SYSTEM

Before I tackle the general question of whether there are lessons to be learned from the Iraqi invasion of Kuwait and Operations Desert Shield and Desert Storm, I begin with an exploration of potential sources of conflict in the international system. I begin with the most general source, the distribution of power in the international system, and continue with some more specific possible sources. Given the extensive nature of this debate, as well as the wide-ranging disagreement entailed within it, I cannot hope to do full justice to the issues in this brief review. But by selectively examining some of the key propositions and lines of argument, I can at least lay some groundwork for approaching our more general concern with what can be learned about international conflict from the Gulf crisis.

Distribution of Power

One of the most important aspects of the debate focuses on the distribution of power in the international system as a key explanatory variable for conflict. This question is most commonly framed in terms of the polarity of the system itself, and it approaches the problem from a macro-level, systemic perspective. For decades, the debate among historians and political scientists has raged about the relative merits of a multipolar versus a bipolar distribution of power in the international system. For many years, the commonly held view was that multipolar systems, such as the classic example of nineteenth-century Europe, were inherently more stable and less prone to the use of force. Because of the fluidity of the system and the ability of various key actors to form checking and balancing coalitions within that highly flexible system, a multipolar system was likely to find an equilibrium or balance around which the extremes of conflict, especially war, could be avoided. The most commonly cited examples supporting this argument were the relatively long periods (by historical standards) of 1815–1848 and 1871–1914 in which there were no major wars among the European countries.[1]

The support for the advantages of multipolarity gained historical credence in the period from the 1950s to the 1980s as the bipolar confrontation between the United States and the Soviet Union was characterized by unusually high levels of tension, insecurity, and brinkmanship between the superpowers. To many observers, the international system was constantly poised on the very edge of major war, and lesser conflicts were typically interpreted as proxy battles between East and West that always had the possibility of escalating at virtually any moment. Given this environment of high tension and uncertainty, the conclusion seemed clear that multipolar systems were inherently more stable than the bipolar system that followed World War II.

In recent years, and well before the end of the Cold War, scholars like John Gaddis had begun to question this commonly held view.[2] One obvious reason for this questioning was the fact that by 1988 the post-war period had exceeded in length both of the earlier periods in which no major war had broken out. As Charles Kegley has described, the period from 1945 to the present constitutes the longest period of great power peace since the birth of the modern world system.[3] In a curious twist of past logic, some scholars now began to point to the bipolar system as being much more stable than a multipolar system, precisely because of the smaller number of great powers and the derivative predictability in their behavior. The East-West conflict also was viewed as placing barriers around the actions of lesser powers, in effect keeping the lid on lower level conflicts and preventing their escalation into superpower confrontation. Rather than the curse under which modern mankind was forced to live, the Cold War and its nuclear arsenals were seen as a more positive evolution toward greater international stability, predictability, and conflict avoidance.

This new direction in the long-standing emphasis on the distribution of power as an explanatory variable set the stage for what has become one of the most interesting, if not always intellectually rigorous, debates of the post–Cold War era. With the passing of the Cold War came a whole new set of discussions concerning the end of bipolarity and the reemergence of multipolarity. Some authors even spoke of unipolarity.[4] Perhaps even more interesting than the debate over the polarity itself was the debate over the implications. Some authors saw in the new multipolarity the end of international conflict and an inherently more peaceful system; still others saw quite the opposite with dire predictions of increasing conflict and a *return to the future*, meaning a return to precisely the European-based wars of the first half of this century.[5]

Although the debate about the polarity of the international system and its effects on the likelihood of conflict is an interesting and important one, there is curiously little compelling evidence that provides a meaningful basis for choosing among the competing views. As is so often the case, the answer to the question of whether bipolarity promotes or inhibits international stability rests more with the assumptions one begins with than with a clear, convincing argument. Perhaps that is one reason the debate is so interesting; there is no clear answer to who is right and who is wrong. Nonetheless, some qualified conclusions seem warranted. First, extreme pessimism and extreme optimism seem unwarranted. Although such arguments are more exciting when stated in very stark terms, the history of the debate suggests that the polarity of the system alone is not a sufficient condition for determining the likelihood of conflict. As Williamson suggests in Chapter 2 of this book, there are a number of other factors that must be considered, including the role of individuals and the effects of forces such as nationalism, technology, communication, and economics, to name a few. Pessimism or optimism about the implications of the changes cannot be clearly derived from the polarity of the system alone.

Second, the world at the present time is effectively unipolar if we are speaking of military power. The dissolution of the Soviet Union in 1991, which occurred after the conclusion of Operation Desert Storm, removed any remaining *effective* military power (the ability to employ the hardware and manpower) previously possessed by that country. This situation leaves only one military power in the world with a truly global capability, the United States. We have moved significantly away from a system in which the mere presence of two military superpowers confronting one another is in itself a potential cause of conflict. Conflict may still arise, and I will argue later that it most certainly will, but it is increasingly unlikely that it will result simply from the bipolar military confrontation between the rival superpowers.

What is it about the polarity of the international system that should concern us? Simply stated, the issue is what constitutes multipolarity. While a multipolar system in and of itself may not be less stable than a bipolar one, the real arguments for the advantages of multipolarity rest on the existence of a truly multipolar system. By this I mean that (1) power in the system is distributed in rough parity among the key international actors across most, if not all, of the relevant dimensions of power; and (2) the willingness to use that power to maintain an equilibrium is present among all of those same key actors. If the United States is the only country actually willing and able to respond to the necessity for balancing power with power, then it is highly questionable whether true multipolarity exists. Moreover, it is fundamentally more difficult for only one or even two countries to maintain effective vigilance in a system in which the potential sources of conflict have multiplied. Consequently, the end of the Cold War may not mean that multipolarity will be the problem; rather, the problem may be whether other countries are willing and able to shoulder the responsibilities of a truly multipolar system. For convenience, let us call this situation partial or immature multipolarity. The Persian Gulf crisis provides at best only modest encouragement that true multipolarity has been attained.

Partial or immature multipolarity also poses an additional potential source of conflict within the system. Among the members of the Western alliance, burden-sharing in defense is a long-standing source of friction. Over the course of the Cold War, the United States and the other members of the North Atlantic Treaty Organization frequently disagreed, and sometimes quite publicly, over the nature of the threat, the required response, and who would shoulder what share of the total defense burden. We can reasonably expect this friction to increase rather than decrease in a world in which the locus of the threats will be even more difficult to identify conclusively. While this friction may not generate conflicts over issues such as the Iraqi invasion of Kuwait, it is likely to exacerbate the problem of effective responses, both before and during future conflicts. If a concerted effort to plan and commit to multilateral responses to international crises is not forthcoming, actors who wish to disrupt the system will find the overall environment of uncertainty ripe for exploitation.

This point seems clear in the aftermath of the invasion. Although we cannot know that this situation occurred, it seems quite likely that Saddam Hussein was encouraged in his adventurous desires by the declining salience of the U.S.-Soviet confrontation. At least there was less there to discourage him than when the Cold War was still at its height. And as Gaddis reminds us, the first year of the post–Cold War era also gave us a "near-outbreak of war between India and Pakistan, an intensification of tension between Israel and its Arab neighbors, a renewed Syrian drive to impose control over Lebanon and a violent civil war in Liberia."[6] Are these events mere coincidence and unrelated to changes in the distribution of power in the international system? Possibly they are. But a more realistic answer is that they were at least encouraged by the changes that had taken place in the post–Cold War system.

While many factors played into these events, as well as the decisionmaking of Saddam Hussein, the reduction of Cold War tensions seems to have played a significant role. It is certainly worth considering whether Saddam Hussein would have made the decision to invade and been able to carry it out in the tightly bipolar military environment of the Cold War. The danger of an escalation to a full-fledged superpower confrontation may have been more than enough to spur the Soviets to intervene and counsel restraint long before an invasion became a viable option.

The shift from a bipolar Cold War system to an increasingly multipolar post–Cold War system may also have affected the events in the Persian Gulf in a somewhat more indirect fashion. Again, as Gaddis points out, the "distractions associated with the end of the Cold War in Europe during the first half of 1990 prevented both Washington and Moscow from giving the attention they should have to Persian Gulf affairs."[7] In other words, the very nature and scope of the changes taking place in the international system were enough to create an opportunity that Saddam Hussein tried to exploit. Had the Cold War still been the dominant paradigm governing the behavior of the two superpowers, it certainly seems likely that Washington and Moscow would have been paying significantly more attention to the Persian Gulf in the several months leading up to the invasion. Would this necessarily have changed events? We cannot know the answer. But we must recognize the challenge of monitoring potential crises in a system that may have many more possibilities for crises to arise now that the fear is considerably less that such conflicts will escalate into a confrontation between nations with nuclear weapons.

For all of its disadvantages, the Cold War did lend a high degree of simplicity to the overall problem of conflict management. Policymakers in the United States and the Soviet Union knew that the most significant threat to world peace and human survival lay in the nuclear arsenals controlled by them. Conflict management focused on the linkage between regional threats and the danger of their escalation into superpower confrontation. But the distractions of the end of the Cold War are symptomatic of a more general characteristic of that post–Cold War system: the uncertainty concerning the sources and nature of the threats. Even if the distribution of military power has become essentially unipolar, the possible sources of threats have multiplied significantly. Threats have not disappeared along with the Cold War; rather, they have diversified. It may be safe to say that the greatest threat, strategic nuclear war, has decreased tremendously in likelihood, but the range of other threats has expanded. Put simply, the challenges to effective conflict management have increased even as the risk of nuclear annihilation has decreased. To the extent that this results from the burgeoning multipolarity of the system, we can conclude that the multipolar post–Cold War system is a more dangerous system. The good news may be that the risk of making a mistake or miscalculation has decreased because the consequences may no longer be massive nuclear devastation. But the challenges of the new system can be met effectively only if we make the transition to a truly multipolar system. If we do not, the United States will continue to face problems of overreach, and the system will ultimately be more threatening not only to the United States but to the system itself.

Economics

Although economic issues have frequently been at the heart of conflict in the international system, recent suggestions have been made that we are entering an era in which economics will supplant geopolitics as the driving force behind the politics of confrontation. Edward Luttwak has stated this argument concisely, but other scholars have followed somewhat different and more complex lines of reasoning to arrive at similar conclusions.[8] Stephen Van Evera, for example, argues that the high-technology, "knowledge-based forms of production" in modern industrialized economies make the conquest of territory largely irrelevant.[9] Yet the decline in the utility of conquering territory to extract economic goods and resources hardly means that conflict generated by economic competition will disappear. In fact, the end of the Cold War may mean that some countries will be less inclined to show restraint in economic competition because they will no longer fear the escalation ladder leading ultimately to a nuclear war.

Nonetheless, the emergence of a global economy with its attendant economic interdependence is certainly working to enhance efforts among the industrialized countries to seek cooperative rather than conflictual solutions to problems. This situation is perhaps most evident in Europe with the accelerated movement toward economic and political union. Van Evera's arguments about the momentum toward peace fit into this general line of reasoning: War as a means of conflict resolution among modern, highly industrialized, and highly interdependent countries is simply a non-option. This line of reasoning does not mean that war can *never* occur again among these countries, but for it to occur would require some very drastic developments that most of us find difficult to imagine. It would appear, based on an assessment of current trends in the international system, that the liberal economic theorists of the post–World War II world were essentially correct in arguing that economic cooperation and integration would reduce the likelihood of war. Although the road will not be a completely smooth one, the path we are traveling does not appear to have a global war as one of the potholes. Conflict among the industrialized countries may even increase as global interdependence increases and fears of war decline, but it will most likely be conflict of a nature that does not include major war.

Yet it remains to be seen whether the arguments about the industrialized countries will hold for the less economically developed countries in the system. Desperate times lie ahead for many regions of the world, and desperate times have historically led to desperate actions and policies. The end of the Cold War may unleash some of these desperate forces, as I noted earlier. With less fear of a U.S.-Soviet military confrontation growing out of a regional conflict, regional actors may be emboldened and conflict, including the use of military force, may increase. The challenge for the industrialized countries will be to forge new instruments of conflict management out of their increased cooperation, and to apply them successfully to these potential regional hot spots.

Here, too, the events in the Persian Gulf provide some support for this concern. As Kuniholm points out in Chapter 8, economic considerations played a major role in Saddam Hussein's decision to invade Kuwait. The lure of canceling Iraq's debt to Kuwait and gaining access to its oil revenues was a significant factor in his decisionmaking—as was the end of the Cold War, which appeared to remove Soviet restraints.

The events in the Gulf also illustrate how some of the economic issues have changed very little, if at all. For example, I would argue that the very identification of the Persian Gulf as an area of strategic interest to the United States and other industrialized countries is not a reflection of a new age of economic sources of international conflict but a continued reflection of the geopolitics of the past. The oil dilemma still confronts the United States, Europe, Japan, and many countries in the Third World. What the Persian Gulf war tells us is that we will continue to pay the price, in vigilance and power projection, for our dependence on Middle Eastern oil. That will not change until and unless our patterns of oil consumption change.

More subtle kinds of economic conflict appear in the different ways in which members of the coalition reacted to the invasion and the subsequent calls for action. European dependence on oil from the region generated different interpretations of what appropriate responses to the initial invasion should be, and it played a significant role in complicating President Bush's efforts to galvanize opposition quickly and effectively. The Japanese and German response of contributing money but not military forces to the coalition operations was also a source of conflict, not only in terms of what their shares should be but also in terms of whether it was even appropriate for the United States to be playing a kind of "mercenary for hire" role in which the economic interests of those countries would be protected by U.S. armed forces. As U.S. Secretary of State Baker made apparent in his recent criticism of Japanese "checkbook diplomacy," the substitution of economic power for political and military power will not be an acceptable approach for dealing with the new multipolarity of the international system. To return to my earlier point, the major actors in the system will need to organize their respective abilities to respond to crises with the full range of power (political, military, and economic), and they must do so in a manner that reflects a true sharing of responsibility and not just an ad hoc matter of convenience or expedience.

Nationalism and Ethnicity

The crisis in the Persian Gulf also served to bring into sharper focus the tidal wave of newly resurgent forces of nationalism, religion, and ethnicity. What happened immediately prior to and during the war was only a prelude of what was to come. The brutality of Iraq's post-war response to the Kurdish uprising shows just how uncontrolled and uncontrollable these forces can be, and we have learned again that such forces were never eliminated, only suppressed, in countries like Yugoslavia. The formal dissolution of the Soviet Union has also been accompanied by the resurgence of subnationalistic and ethnic strife between and within the newly independent republics, and this resurgence has already led to an increase in acts of violence. It is in this area that I find Mearsheimer's "back to the future" logic most compelling: Not in the rekindling of continental European desires for territorial expansion, but in the forces of nationalistic, ethnic, and religious fervor among and within newly formed mini-states struggling to find viable mechanisms for governing themselves are we most likely to see hauntingly familiar themes of a past we had hoped was gone forever.

RESPONSES TO CONFLICT IN THE INTERNATIONAL SYSTEM

I come now to the question of what kinds of responses to potential and actual conflict we can expect in the post–Cold War international system. The most obvious possibility to address first is the one that received so much attention preceding the war itself and in the war's aftermath: the United Nations. Claude has already eloquently argued the case for selective anti-aggression in Chapter 3 and pointed out how this is fundamentally at odds with a system of truly collective security. There is very little that I could add to his arguments; the implication is clear that we should not expect more than is reasonable or perhaps even desirable of the United Nations and collective security generally when conflicts are likely to vary considerably in their relative importance to individual nation-states and to the international system generally.

But even in those instances in which there is substantial agreement

on the significance of the threat, the experiences of the Persian Gulf
crisis highlight the continued problem for anything even vaguely re-
sembling collective security. For the United Nations to act—politically, economically, and especially militarily (simply by condoning the
use of military force if all other options fail)—virtually requires the
presence and clear leadership of a take-charge country. In the Persian
Gulf, this country was obviously the United States. While the ways in
which the United States and the coalition forces sought the general
approval of the United Nations for pursuing sanctions as well as military options were rather novel and perhaps somewhat heartening for
proponents of collective security, the lesson to be learned is more
about the real limitations rather than the potential of that organization. To presume that the United Nations can play a leading role in
monitoring, pre-empting, and even intervening to prevent potential
crises is to put a positive spin on the story that is unwarranted by the
reality of the Persian Gulf crisis. At best, we can hope that countries
like the United States will in the future feel more of a need to defend
their definitions of a threat and the appropriate response to it in a
broader international public arena. But even this may be exaggerating
the positive, for it remains to be seen whether the largest class of
potential conflicts will fall within this same category of highly visible
and nearly unanimously perceived aggression. The less universal the
perception of the threat, the more impotent will be the role of the
United Nations, and the less likely will be the perceived need by countries like the United States to seek its seal of approval.

As we have seen in Elliott's discussion of economic sanctions in
Chapter 9, the use of economic power as a response to and deterrent
of conflict is not wholly without value. If one accepts the argument
that increasing international interdependence and the transition from
a geopolitical to a geo-economic world order will increase the value of
economic interaction for all nations in the system, one can speculate
that the use of economic sanctions will increase in importance. But as
Elliott also pointed out, economic sanctions are hard to target and
enforce, and they take a substantial amount of time to bear fruit. It
is probably safe to say that the sanctions were never given a fair
chance (in terms of time) to work. But therein lies the problem: Time
is of the essence. In the sanctions against Iraq, we saw vividly the
dilemma faced by democratic countries in such situations. Successful
action almost has to be quick and decisive or the necessary public
support will erode and eventually disappear. This situation is especially true if we assume that in most cases we will be subjected to a
barrage of stories and reports about how the sanctions are affecting
the poor, the children, the powerless . . . in other words, precisely the
innocent bystanders we want to avoid hurting any more than abso-

lutely necessary. For the democracies of the post–Cold War world, the problem is that responses requiring long-term staying power are suboptimal for achieving the objectives. The longer the conflict and the countermeasures drag on, the greater the likelihood that the popular support will begin to fade, leading to either impatience for something that works (like military action) or a lack of interest to pursue the objectives further. As the possibility of dwindling public support increases, the leaders of those countries will face pressures to move quickly to more decisive means (as President Bush did) or simply "cut bait" and let the violator off the hook.

This discussion brings us back to the question of military responses to conflict in the post–Cold War international system. Perhaps the clearest lesson we can glean from the Persian Gulf crisis is the picture it gave us of multilateral, ad hoc military responses. By this I mean multilateral military action that derives not from a collection of nations making collective decisions to join in the effort but from individual countries making their own decisions about whether to join. Just because an action involves a number of nations does not mean that it resulted from multilateral decisionmaking. In my view, the near-term outlook for truly multinational and multilateral military forces that can effectively respond to potential and real international conflicts remains poor. The more likely response will be based in the selective anti-aggression model discussed by Claude, and it will entail one or a very few countries effectively taking the lead and then persuading other important actors to join in.

There are both advantages and disadvantages to this approach. The main advantage is that it preserves a high degree of autonomy for individual countries and does not lock every country into a multilateral framework that may prove incapable of acting even when a serious threat is on the doorstep. Yet it also maintains a high degree of uncertainty as to whether any response to a crisis will be forthcoming. As I suggested earlier, it is precisely this uncertainty of a response that encouraged Saddam Hussein to reach his decision to invade Kuwait. Had he known that there would be a clear response, and especially if he had known what the United States would be able to do militarily and in forging the coalition, Saddam Hussein would almost certainly have chosen a different strategy.

What about the role of nationalism and ethnicity in generating conflict? What are the likely responses to this source of conflict? Unfortunately, I have no good answer to this. It appears that the most we can hope for in dealing with this source of conflict in the foreseeable future is to prevent any spillover to neighboring countries and within regions. It is extremely doubtful that the United States could have accomplished anything in the way of managing the intra-Iraqi and intra-regional conflicts growing out of these sources. The march to Baghdad that some people still think the United States should have undertaken in an effort to eliminate Saddam Hussein would not have solved this problem. While we may not have seen the brutal way in which Saddam Hussein turned his weapons on the Kurds, it is almost certain that the United States would have found itself in the middle of a terrible civil war. In that scenario, we would have been forced to choose between getting out and letting everything collapse, or attempting to control the outcome of the civil war through the application of military force. Let us hope that we have finally learned that such uses of military power are doomed from the start, and no country, including the United States, can resolve another country's underlying problems through outside military intervention. Removing Saddam Hussein from Iraqi politics would not have removed the underlying problems of Iraqi politics and society, nor the underlying problems of the region generally.

CONCLUSIONS

Where does this leave us in our search for some lessons in the events in the Persian Gulf from August 2, 1990, to the summer of 1991? Can we draw any truly general implications from the conflict, including its origins and the responses to it, that will help us anticipate future uses of force in the post–Cold War international system? Unfortunately, I must conclude that there is very little in the way of general lessons to be gleaned from these events. While there are some notable cautions and concerns that come into focus as a result of the war, it is perhaps most accurate to conclude that Operation Desert Shield and Operation Desert Storm were simply that: Operation Desert Shield and Operation Desert Storm.

The clearest example of the uniqueness of these events can be found in the nature of the threat and in its geographic location. It is extremely unlikely, although by no means impossible, that future conflicts will involve so stark and clear a threat as one nation invading and annexing another, as the Iraqis attempted to do with Kuwait. Even among the staunchest opponents of the United States, support in opposition to Saddam Hussein's actions was very strong. While President Bush still had to wage a long and hard battle to enlist the support of all the right players, the nature of the threat was unique in its clarity and broad impact. Radical and moderate Arabs joined together with the United States and Western allies in a coalition that can only be described as remarkable. Moreover, the fact that Iraq was a Third World country with the fourth largest standing army in the world (a "Second World" military?) made such an invasion a viable option for Saddam Hussein to consider. Most Third World countries would not be able to pose such a threat of invasion to their neighbors, let alone be able to carry it out.

The location of the threat had a twofold effect on the response. First, the fact that it was in the Persian Gulf and directly affected the oil interests of the industrialized countries meant that there was at the outset a broadly based agreement that there was a significant threat requiring some kind of response. Second, the fact that the confrontation, if it became a military one, would occur in a desert setting with contiguous high seas access meant that the capabilities of the coalition, particularly the United States, were especially well suited for a response. The rapid deployment of the U.S. 82nd Airborne Division, followed by heavy armor, large-scale ground combat troops, and the naval and marine forces made for very clear saber rattling in the early stages and an overwhelming battlefield advantage when Saddam Hussein refused to back down. Anyone who has studied the development of U.S. military strategy over the past decade will know that this situation is precisely the kind of battlefield environment for which the AirLand Battle doctrine had been devised. If U.S. policymakers had to choose a possible battlefield, they could hardly have come up with a better one. As Helms discusses in Chapter 12, virtually all of the elements of this conflict favored the nature and configuration of the U.S. military. Stand-off air and sea power could be used to prepare the battlefield for the eventual ground phase; it is small wonder that the latter seemed largely anticlimactic following the high drama and effectiveness of the former.

But what if the conflict had been threatening in a region in which strategic interests were much less clear? What if the threat had not taken the form of a direct and massive ground invasion but instead looked more like the infiltration and subversion conflicts of the Vietnam mode? And what if the conflict were taking place in a jungle or secluded mountainous terrain? A quick glance at the globe would lead us to see that the probabilities of conflict cropping up in regions very poorly suited to the kind of military power we possess is very high indeed. The likely conflicts of the future will not necessarily be perfectly suited for a U.S. military response.

On the positive side, the Persian Gulf war did demonstrate that the United States is in fact still capable of responding to serious threats around the world. As many have observed, a large part of the Vietnam legacy was dispelled with the events of 1990–1991. In addition, the events also demonstrated that it is possible to forge a viable, ad hoc multinational coalition of countries to respond to such crises. While a great part of that coalition may have been more important for its symbol than its substance, the fact remains that an important signal was sent about the possibility of effective multilateral responses to such threats. And the United States is still quite capable of pulling together a wide range of support for the pursuit of actions it deems necessary.

But is any other country or group of countries capable of performing the same role that the United States performed so successfully? Can any other international actor serve so effectively as the catalyst for action? I think it is highly doubtful that another such catalyst can be found in the world today. The changes in Eastern Europe and the Soviet Union have effectively removed the traditional counterpart to U.S. power and leadership. The United Nations remains plagued by traditional problems, as I discussed earlier. Europe is confronting serious questions of economic and political union, and it seems hardly capable of forging agreement on action among its own members let alone on a more global scale. If no other actor can perform this role, will the United States continue to do so? If it does, we are certain to see serious tensions over issues such as checkbook diplomacy and U.S. global mercenaries. A debate of this kind over the proper role of the United States in the post–Cold War international system will almost assuredly provide fertile ground for revisiting the question of U.S. isolationism. Just as Fortress America was considered as an option following World War II, it could rise again in the aftermath of the Cold War and an unwillingness of other countries to accept their full responsibilities of a more multipolar international system. The challenge to President Bush mounted by Pat Buchanan for the 1992 Republican presidential nomination is certainly a reflection of this continued isolationist sentiment among some segments of the U.S. public and opinion leaders.

Finally, it is worth returning to the issue of nationalism and ethnicity as sources of conflict in the international system. I mentioned before that such conflict is at best poorly controlled by external military means. For example, as the civil war in Yugoslavia ravaged that country and its people in 1991 there were no serious arguments put forward for a Western military intervention. Even as concern mounted over the terrible loss of human life and the fear that the conflict might spill over into other countries, the most obvious feature of the situation was the virtual impotence of other international actors (national and supranational) to do anything to halt the violence. Although the threatened use of diplomatic and economic sanctions appeared to have some positive impact on the negotiations of a peaceful settlement, it was really the dissolution of the country that halted the bloodbath. And it is not altogether certain that the violence has in fact been ended once and for all. As the world continues to shudder under the profound changes encapsulated in the phrase "end of the Cold War," the breakup of old countries into new, smaller countries, and the reemergence of long-standing but recently dormant ethnic conflict is likely to stay with us in the form of recurring cycles of violence. I see no effective means of eliminating this violence, either internally by domestic means or externally through the intervention of other countries or organizations like the European Community or the United Nations. Perhaps the post–Cold War international system will have to learn to live with this recurring conflict, in the same way that the Cold War international system learned to live with cycles of U.S.-Soviet animosity. If we cannot eliminate such conflict from the system, we must certainly strive to manage it by ensuring that no spillover effects occur and by trying to tackle the sources of conflict through economic and diplomatic means. If nothing else, the crisis in Yugoslavia does seem to suggest that the peace-keeping capabilities of the United Nations must be enhanced, and that countries like the United States should attempt to ensure that the peace-keeping role of that organization is bolstered.

The post–Cold War international system will hardly be less interesting with the disappearance of the East-West conflict. As I have tried to outline in this chapter, it will be a profoundly challenging environment for the proponents of peace and democracy. It will be a system in which the potential sources of conflict will multiply even as the risks of the ensuing conflicts diminish somewhat with the decreased likelihood of global nuclear war. For those whose role it is to monitor, anticipate, and respond to conflicts in the system, the world will be a much more difficult one to understand, analyze, and predict. Unfortunately, the range and nature of options available for responding to the expanded sources of conflict are unlikely to increase in the same way as the potential threats. The lessons of the Persian Gulf should not be drawn too conclusively about the role of the United Nations, economic sanctions, and multilateral military action in the new world order. The events in the Persian Gulf give us hope that new modes of responding to and preventing conflicts can be forged in the future, while at the same time they point up the significant challenges that lie ahead as we strive to promote and protect peaceful conflict resolution in the international system.

NOTES

1. For example, see Charles W. Kegley, Jr., ed., *The Long Postwar Peace: Contending Explanations and Projections* (New York: HarperCollins, 1991) for a discussion of these points.

2. See John L. Gaddis, "The Long Peace: Elements of Stability in the Postwar International System," *International Security* 10 (Spring 1986): 92–142.

3. Kegley, xi.

14

Conclusions and Implications

Robert F. Helms II

The chapters in this volume have described the Persian Gulf crisis from a number of perspectives and have suggested implications that will impact the search for security in the post–Cold War world. In this chapter, the major conclusions and implications for the future are summarized.

Despite the claims for the emerging of a new world order, the chapters do not offer much hope that the coalition assembled under the leadership of the United States to oppose Saddam Hussein represents a model for a permanent post–Cold War collective security arrangement. Indeed, the overall forecast is that there are more difficult times ahead for the United States and its allies in the post–Cold War world.

The lessons of history teach that despite efforts to shape international affairs according to the lessons of wars, nations have seldom been successful in controlling the events of change. Among the more notable uncontrollable consequences of wars has been the adverse impact they have had on the great powers. It is probable that an international environment is emerging in which the demise of the former Soviet Union will leave the United States as the only truly global military power. However, the situation is not all good news for the United States. There likely will be a number of lesser powers that will be seeking to gain advantages or at least to become more equal. Unlike the situation the United States experienced in 1945, there will be fewer resources available and greater constraints operating in the post–Cold War environment. Success will require a willingness to work as a member of an international team effort over a longer time period to address complex issues. Also, it likely will be necessary for the United States to be satisfied with solutions that are the result of compromises and are less than perfect.

There also will be fewer situations, if any, in which the United States will be able or willing to pursue unilateral options. Neither is the international coalition that opposed Iraq considered to be the forerunner of a permanent collective security arrangement for the post–Cold War world. Indeed, the collective effort to wage war against Iraq is considered to be an exception or aberration rather than a model of post–Cold War collective security.

There seems to be no reason to believe that nations now are more willing to assume the responsibilities and requirements for the automatic enforcement measures that would be required for collective security arrangements than they have been in the past, with few exceptions such as the North Atlantic Treaty Organization. The more promising approach will continue to be ad hoc models led by a Great Somebody to enforce selective anti-aggression such as that used in the Persian Gulf crisis. This arrangement requires that one or more nations assume the burden of being the Great Somebody that will organize and lead a multilateral effort against aggression.

There seems to be general agreement that the only nation in the foreseeable future that can fulfill the role of the Great Somebody is the United States. Consequently, for the remainder of this century and into the early decades of the next millennium, we can expect most multilateral efforts to, in effect, translate into U.S. leadership with the support and assistance that Washington can convince other nations to provide. This assumption of leadership will place the United States in the forefront of multinational efforts—which can be an uncomfortable position, as others (in both the domestic and international political environments) are prone to criticize those out in front. However, in those instances in which it is believed that critical interests are at risk, the United States can be expected to use the Persian Gulf model as a starting point for its efforts to gain international acceptance and support for selective anti-aggression actions. In the final analysis, it will be up to the Great Somebody to assume that mantle of leadership and be willing to bear the burdens that come with it; many believe that this burden will fall on the United States.

The invasion of Kuwait by Iraq was not an isolated event, and it would be a mistake to consider it to be the product of a singularly ambitious dictator. It was a product of the history of the region. The chapters in this volume have described the linkages between the history of the region and the invasion. Unfortunately, there is little optimism to be found.

The history of the Middle East is one of great power rivalry. It is a history of disappointment and turmoil in the Arab "streets" as expectations have risen and fallen with a parade of passing charismatic leaders who have promised much and delivered little. This situation is not expected to change in the foreseeable future. The problems of Islamic fundamentalism, the Palestinian issue, the questions associated with the distribution of wealth between the "have" and "have-not" nations, the continuing proliferation of arms throughout the region, the disruptive nature of terrorism emanating from the region, the quest of industrialized nations for a secure source of reasonably priced oil, and Arab suspicions of outside influences virtually assure that the Middle East and the Persian Gulf regions will remain volatile areas for the remainder of this century and well into the next millennium.

Saddam Hussein rose to power in an atmosphere of a disillusioned Arab street. He assumed a Nasser-type leadership style and appealed over the heads of political leaders to the disenchanted Arab street. Most agree that his goal was to unite the region under the leadership of Iraq. Although his quest for leadership of a unified Arab world was temporarily sidetracked during the war between Iraq and Iran, he resumed this goal after the war. The Iraqi invasion of Kuwait was an important step in his pursuit of this objective. He continued to use this style as the crisis unfolded and throughout the war. It is remarkable how well the themes played to the Arab masses. On the Arab street, there was little sympathy for Kuwait and Saddam received widespread support, particularly in Jordan and among the Palestinians.

The conditions that have supported the emergence of a series of charismatic Arab leaders continue to exist and can be expected, unless resolved, to provide the means for others to emerge in the post–Cold War world. The solutions include stable governments that support pluralism and that are more democratic, coming to grips with the Arab-Israeli problem, and more efficient ways for sharing surplus capital and increasing productivity. Until these solutions are found, the region can expect to remain clothed in turmoil and periodic outbursts of war.

Can the United States play a major role in bringing about these solutions? Certainly, past U.S. actions have not endeared the United States to the populations in the region, and there is justifiably an element of skepticism on the Arab street when it comes to the motives and fairness of Washington.

All too often, the U.S. approach has been to continue, with certain modifications, the policies of other outside powers. The inability of the United States to pursue policies that are perceived to be fair, particularly in regard to the questions of Palestinians and territory, has damaged the credibility of the United States in the Arab street. It is

very fortunate that the United States did not exceed the mandate of
the United Nations to invade and overthrow the government of Iraq
even though the opportunity clearly existed. The thinness of the coalition has been noted, and any exceeding of the limits very possibly
would have caused it to unravel.

To the credit of President Bush and the other leaders of nations
included in the coalition, they avoided this temptation and the unfavorable political fallout that would have almost certainly occurred, not
just in the Middle East and the Persian Gulf but among other nations
as well as the United Nations. If the United States is to be a Great
Somebody, it must have credibility and others must believe that it is
willing to remain within the limits that have been established by those
who are part of any multinational effort. It would be very difficult,
perhaps impossible, for the United States to once again receive a mandate from the United Nations under similar circumstances if it and
the other nations had continued on to Baghdad.

There may now be opportunities to reverse some of the adverse consequences of great power rivalry in the region and the inability of the
United States to pursue a consistent and even-handed policy over the
long term. It may be that the restraint of the United States and the
other nations of the coalition has opened other possibilities for addressing some of the difficult problems that confront the region. The
willingness of the United States to assume a position of post-war leadership in addressing the Palestinian question is but one example of
these possibilities, particularly if the process and outcomes are perceived to represent fair treatment and even-handedness. Other possibilities may include regional arms control as well as economic
cooperation and development. It is too early to forecast the ability and
willingness of the United States to take advantage of the opportunities
that it has as an honest and fair broker in the region. If the United
States is successful in pursuing such a role, the consequences can be
far reaching and can be expected to ensure a leadership role in the
region for the remainder of this century and well into the next. Conversely, failure can be expected to leave the region exposed to continued turmoil of the type that it has experienced in this century.

The jury remains out on the effectiveness of economic sanctions as
a means for resolving conflicts and behavior control among nations.
Iraq was unusually vulnerable to the economic embargo that was imposed (which was unprecedented in terms of participation and scope).
It is quite probable that it is not possible to create more favorable
conditions necessary for a successful embargo. It will never be known
if the economic embargo would have succeeded in persuading Iraq to
withdraw from Kuwait, since military means ultimately were used to
force withdrawal.

However, it is known that the economic embargo did have an impact on the combat effectiveness of Iraqi military forces. A modern military force requires a dependable logistical base and supply lines to replenish stockpiles as they are used. The embargo greatly reduced the availability of spare parts for the Iraqi military, which over time resulted in fewer operational systems. The economic embargo also had a psychological impact in that Iraqi military leaders must have understood there would be fewer, if any, replacements for those systems that were destroyed in battle or for munitions once they had been used. In effect, they were confronted with fighting, winning or losing with what they had on hand. Consequently, the available combat capabilities of the Iraqi military were becoming less with each passing day, while those of the coalition forces were increasing daily as more forces and supplies arrived in the region. This situation also increased the prospect of an Iraqi defeat on the fields of battle daily.

It is not possible to draw more than some general observations about whether economic sanctions would have been sufficient to convince Iraq to withdraw from Kuwait. However, the use of economic sanctions, in combination with military force during the crisis, does offer a model that has potential for use in other similar crises in the post–Cold War world. The lessons of the Persian Gulf war support the expectation that most attempts to oppose aggression in the post–Cold War world will consist of measures that include some form of an economic embargo in combination with military actions.

The lessons also support those who are in favor of a standing professional military force. The Iraqi invasion of Kuwait was, for the most part, unexpected. When it did occur, it contained the element of surprise. Overall, the nations of the world did not anticipate the invasion or the rapid success of Iraq in defeating Kuwait's military forces. Once the Iraqi military had defeated these military forces, the fourth largest military force in the world began consolidating its conquest and was in a position to continue the invasion into Saudi Arabia. The rapid response of the United States to first move sea, air, and light Army forces and then heavy mechanized and armor units into the region was unprecedented in history. The physical movement alone was herculean. It taxed the available strategic transportation to the limit and was a gallant effort on the part of all participants.

As professional and important to the outcome of the war as this rapid deployment of military forces was, the real outcome was determined by the professional military that had been preparing itself since the early 1970s. This military force had developed advanced operational concepts and doctrines that enabled it to fight as a joint force and with other nations to leverage its inherent advantages against the enduring weaknesses of its opponents. These inherent advantages include developing and using advanced technologies. It had developed and fielded the weapons and supporting systems that are needed for these advanced battlefield doctrines. These were on hand and readily available. There was no waiting for the industrial base to transform itself and begin production of the requirements for war. It also had recruited and manned its formations and staffs with individuals who had mastered the use of advanced systems and operational concepts. Finally, the professional military had trained itself to achieve a peace-time readiness that is unprecedented in the history of the United States.

It is difficult to imagine another set of circumstances in which a peacetime military force would be better prepared than U.S. forces were at the beginning of the crisis. Furthermore, the military commanders were able to use the interlude between their arrival in the region and the outbreak of war for training and further fine-tuning their battle skills, operational concepts, and campaign plans. At the same time, the combat capabilities of the Iraqi military were becoming less as a result of the economic embargo. The military situation enabled coalition military forces to systematically and very methodically first neutralize and then strip away any of the advantages that the Iraqi military forces might have had at the outset of the crisis. When this process was completed, coalition military forces had established the conditions for achieving a new set of imperatives for using military force in the post–Cold War world: "winning big, winning quick, and winning without casualties."

The lessons of the Persian Gulf war have far-reaching implications for the future use of military force. The ability of the United States to respond quickly and effectively with military forces would not have been possible without the presence of existing and ready military forces. Since this military force existed, the political leaders could exercise the option of a credible military response to deter further Iraqi aggression first and then to defeat it quickly without significant friendly casualties. As a result, the potential for the conflict to spread to other countries was kept lower. The political and diplomatic costs of the war were also reduced as other nations were emboldened to support the war effort or at least not to oppose it. Even the economic costs of the war were kept lower by the quick and decisive military victory. If the military force deployed into the region had been ill prepared in terms of equipment or training, all of these costs could have been expected to be considerably higher and the war outcome, to include the consequences, less certain.

The war also demonstrated the dominant role of technologies on the modern battlefield. However, there is a need for exercising caution lest the wrong conclusions be drawn about the ability of military forces to overwhelm opposing forces with the application of advanced technologies. The Iraqi military force was advertised to be the fourth largest in the world and to possess some of the most modern tanks and aircraft. This force was so decisively overwhelmed and defeated that there may be a temptation to conclude that advanced technologies can be used to achieve similar results elsewhere. These results may be possible, but the war with Iraq is not a good case study for drawing such conclusions.

The Iraqi Air Force fled the war in the early stages and, in doing so, left the ground elements to the mercy of coalition air power. In the open terrains of the Middle East, the side that controls the air historically has dictated terms for the land war. The Iraqi military, while large and possessing some of the more modern weapon systems, was immobilized. It generally was inept in advanced operational concepts, using technologies on a modern, integrated battlefield, and it had no air cover. This force basically dug itself in and attempted to outlast coalition forces by letting them punch themselves out. It is one thing to have a large military force with advanced systems and quite another to use it effectively against a skilled opponent.

The implication for other nations that it is very difficult, if not impossible, to fight a modern military force with the capabilities that were fielded by the coalition is obvious. It no longer is possible to trade off modernization with the massing of large military forces armed with outdated weapons. This implication of the war's outcome should cause other would-be aggressors to pause and consider the possible consequences before undertaking hostile actions. There is no reason for optimism that the results will be any more successful than those of Saddam Hussein. Unfortunately, it almost certainly will lead some nations to seek opportunities to buy weapons systems with the latest technologies, even though there is no assurance that they can field a military force with the ability to effectively use these technologies. Fortunately, it may cause more rational leaders to pause and better understand the futility of military aggression in a high-tech environment, and to seek other alternatives for resolving disputes.

One important issue that needs to be addressed involves the question of what would have been the outcome if Iraqi military forces had capabilities and abilities that were similar to those of the coalition. The outcome surely would have been more difficult to achieve and more costly in terms of lives, time, and economic factors. It probably would not have been possible to achieve the imperatives of winning big, winning quick, and winning without casualties. It is quite likely that the outcome would have been a high-tech standoff as neither side was able to mount and sustain effective offensive operations to a successful conclusion. This situation is not unlike the conditions dictated by the machine gun on the battlefields of World War I in which neither side was able to conduct a decisive offensive campaign; such may be the conditions on future battlefields when both sides are armed with and know how to use advanced technologies. The emergence of these conditions, in combination with other factors such as increasing interdependence, should cause nations to seek other means for resolving differences in the post–Cold War world.

Finally, the war with Iraq is seen as providing justification for maintaining modern military forces. Indeed, the war has provided a moral rationale for the resources necessary for maintaining modern military forces. The war clearly demonstrated that technologies can be used to save lives, and this lesson must not be lost on the American public as the memories of the war fade into the background. Although the maintaining of modern military forces is costly, it can be expected to be more costly not to pay the price.

The chapters presented in this volume have outlined a series of challenges that confront the United States and its allies as they move out of the Cold War and toward a new world order. They also have described a number of opportunities that can and should be built on in the quest for a stable national security in the post–Cold War world. The challenge confronting these nations is to find ways to identify and exploit the opportunities while preventing the obstacles from blocking progress. The chapters included in this volume are intended as a contribution to meeting these challenges.

References

Anthony, John Duke. 1975. *Arab States of the Lower Gulf: People, Politics, Petroleum.* Washington, DC: The Middle East Institute.

Art, Robert. 1991. "A Defensible Defense: America's Grand Strategy after the Cold War." *International Security* 15: 5–53.

Bill, James, and Carl Leider. 1984. *Politics in the Middle East.* 2d ed. Boston: Little, Brown.

Bingaman, Jeff; Jacques Gansler; and Robert Kupperman. 1991. *Integrating Commercial and Military Technologies for National Strength: An Agenda for Change.* Washington, DC: Center for Strategic & International Studies.

Blackwell, James. 1991. *Thunder in the Desert: The Strategy and Tactics of the Persian Gulf War.* New York: Bantam Books.

Blackwell, James, and Barry M. Blechman, eds. 1990. *Making Defense Reform Work.* Washington, DC: Brassey's (U.S.).

Blackwell, James; Michael J. Mazarr; and Don M. Snider. 1991. *The Gulf War: Military Lessons Learned.* Washington, DC: Center for Strategic & International Studies.

Bradsher, Henry. 1983. *Afghanistan and the Soviet Union.* Durham, NC: Duke University Press.

Broder, David S. 1991. "With Cheney in Charge." *Washington Post*, February 27.

Brzezinski, Zbigniew. 1983. *Power and Principle: Memoirs of the National Security Adviser, 1977–1981.* New York: Farrar, Straus, Giroux.

Busch, Briton Cooper. 1967. *Britain and the Persian Gulf, 1894–1914.* Berkeley: University of California Press.

Bush, George. 1990. "The UN: World Parliament of Peace." Address to UN General Assembly, New York, October 1. U.S. Department of State, Current Policy No. 1303.

Carter, Jimmy. 1982. *Keeping Faith: Memoirs of a President.* New York: Bantam.

Carver, Jeremy P. 1991. "The Gulf Crisis: Does Article 41 Have a Future?" Remarks to the International Law Association, British Branch, January 16. Unpublished.

———. Remarks on "The Gulf War: The Law of International Sanctions," Proceeding of the 85th Annual Meeting of The American Society of International Law, Washington, DC, April 18, 1991.

Center for Strategic and International Studies. February 1969. *The Gulf: Implications of British Withdrawal.* Special Report Series No. 8. Washington, DC: Georgetown University Press.

Claude, Inis L., Jr. 1962. *Power and International Relations.* New York: Random House.

———. 1986. *American Approaches to World Affairs.* Lanham, MD: University Press of America.

Daily Progress. 1991. Charlottesville, VA, January 19.

Darby, Phillip. 1973. *British Defense Policy East of Suez, 1947–1968.* London: Oxford University Press.

Donovan, Robert. 1982. *Tumultuous Years: The Presidency of Harry S. Truman, 1949–1953.* New York: Norton.

Eilts, Hermann. 1980. "Security Considerations in the Persian Gulf." *International Security* 5(2): 79.

Fromkin, David. 1980. "The Great Game in Asia." *Foreign Affairs* 58(4): 936–951.

Gaddis, John Lewis. 1986. "The Long Peace: Elements of Stability in the Postwar International System." *International Security* 10(Spring): 92–142.

Gavin, R. J. 1975. *Aden under British Rule, 1839–1967.* London: Hurst.

Genco, Stephen J. 1974. "The Eisenhower Doctrine: Deterrence in the Middle East, 1957–1958." In *Deterrence in American Foreign Policy: Theory and Practice,* eds. Alexander George and Richard Smoke. New York: Columbia University Press.

Graham, Robert. 1979. *Iran: The Illusion of Power.* New York: St. Martin's Press.

Harrison, Selig. 1981. *In Afghanistan's Shadow: Baluch Nationalism and Soviet Temptations.* Washington, DC: Carnegie Endowment for International Peace.

Hawley, Donald. 1970. *The Trucial States.* London: Allen & Unwin.

Helms, Christine. 1981. *The Cohesion of Saudi Arabia: Evolution of Political Identity.* Baltimore: Johns Hopkins University Press.

Helms, Robert F., II. 1990. "An Army for Extraordinary Times" (published as "New Directions: Will the Army Jump or Be Pushed?"). *Army Magazine* 40(6): 59–66.

———. 1990. "Technology and Battlefields of the Future: Challenges, Opportunities, and Directions." In *U.S. Defense Policy in an Era of Constrained Resources,* eds. Robert L. Pfaltzgraff and Richard H. Schultz, Jr. Medford, MA: Tufts University Press.

Holden, David. 1966. *Farewell to Arabia.* London: Faber & Faber.

———. 1971. "The Persian Gulf: After the British Raj." *Foreign Affairs* 49(4): 721–735.

Hoopes, Townsend. 1973. *The Devil and John Foster Dulles*. Boston: Little, Brown.

Hourani, George. 1951. *Arab Seafaring in the Indian Ocean in Ancient and Medieval Times*. Princeton: Princeton University Press.

Hufbauer, Gary Clyde; Jeffrey J. Schott; and Kimberly Ann Elliott. 1991. *Economic Sanctions Reconsidered*. 2d ed., 2 vols. Washington, DC: Institute for International Economics.

Huntington, Samuel P. 1991. "America's Changing Strategic Interests." *Survival* 33: 3–17.

Ingram, Edward. 1979. *The Beginning of the Great Game in Asia, 1828–1834*. Oxford: Clarendon Press.

Jervis, Robert. 1976. *Perception and Misperception in International Politics*. Princeton: Princeton University Press.

———. 1991. "The Future of World Politics: Will It Resemble the Past?" Unpublished manuscript.

Johnson, Maxwell. 1983. *The Military as an Instrument of U.S. Policy in Southwest Asia: The Rapid Deployment Joint Task Force, 1979–1982*. Boulder, CO: Westview.

Kaiser, David. 1990. *Politics and War: European Conflict from Philip II to Hitler*. Cambridge, MA: Harvard University Press.

Keddie, Nikki. 1983. "The Iranian Revolution in Comparative Perspective." *American Historical Review* 88(3): 579–598.

Kegley, Charles W., Jr., ed. 1991. *The Long Postwar Peace: Contending Explanations and Projections*. New York: HarperCollins.

Kelly, J. B. 1968. *Britain and the Persian Gulf, 1795–1880*. Oxford: Clarendon Press.

———. 1980. *Arabia, the Gulf and the West: A Critical View of the Arabs and Their Oil Policy*. New York: Basic Books.

Kennedy, Paul. 1987. *The Rise and Fall of the Great Powers: Economic Change and Military Conflict from 1500 to 2000*. New York: Alfred A. Knopf.

Kissinger, Henry A. 1957. *A World Restored: Metternich, Castlereagh, and the Problems of Peace, 1812–1822*. Boston: Houghton Mifflin.

———. 1979. *White House Years*. Boston: Little, Brown.

———. 1982. *Years of Upheaval*. Boston: Little, Brown.

Kraehe, Enno. 1983. *The Congress of Vienna, 1814–1815*. Vol. 2 of *Metternich's German Policy*. Princeton: Princeton University Press.

Krauthammer, Charles. 1991. "The Unipolar Moment." *Foreign Affairs* 70(1): 23–33.

Kuniholm, Bruce. 1984. *The Near East Connection: Greece and Turkey in the Reconstruction and Security of Europe, 1946–1952*. Brookline, MA: Hellenic Press.

Landen, Robert G. 1967. *Oman since 1967: Disruptive Modernization in a Traditional Arab Society*. Princeton: Princeton University Press.

Lauterpacht, E.; C. J. Greenwood; Marc Weller; and Daniel Bethlehem, eds. 1991. *The Kuwait Crisis*, vol. 1: *Basic Documents*, and vol. 2: *Sanctions and Their Economic Consequences*. Cambridge: Grotius Publications.

Legvold, Robert. 1991. "The Gulf Crisis and the Future of Gorbachev's Foreign Policy Revolution." *The Harriman Institute Forum*, October.

Lewis, Bernard, ed. 1976. *Islam and the Arab World: Faith, People, Culture.* New York: Alfred A. Knopf.

Long, David. 1978. *The Persian Gulf: An Introduction to Its Peoples, Politics, and Economics*, rev. ed. Boulder, CO: Westview Press.

Love, Kennett. 1969. *Suez: The Twice Fought War.* New York: McGraw-Hill.

Luttwak, Edward N. 1990. "From Geopolitics to Geo-Economics: Logic of Conflict, Grammar of Commerce." *The National Interest* 20(Summer): 17–23.

McLachlan, Keith. 1980. "Oil in the Persian Gulf." In *The Persian Gulf States: A General Survey*, eds. Alvin Cottrell et al. Baltimore: Johns Hopkins University Press.

Malloy, Michael P. 1990. *Economic Sanctions and U.S. Trade.* Boston: Little, Brown.

Mearsheimer, John J. 1990. "Back to the Future: Instability in Europe after the Cold War." *International Security* 15(Summer): 5–56.

Miklos, Jack. 1983. *The Iranian Revolution and Modernization: Way Stations to Anarchy.* Washington, DC: National Defense University Press.

Mitchell, George J. 1991. "The Other Business of the Nation Won't Wait." *Washington Post*, January 30.

Mortimer, Edward. 1982. *Faith and Power: The Politics of Islam.* New York: Vintage.

Mueller, John. 1989. *Retreat from Doomsday: The Obsolescence of Major War.* New York: Basic Books.

Newell, Nancy, and Richard Newell. 1981. *The Struggle for Afghanistan.* Ithaca, NY: Cornell University Press.

Newsom, David. 1981. "America Engulfed." *Foreign Policy* 43(Summer): 17–32.

Nimetz, Matthew. Under Secretary of State for Security, Science, and Technology. U.S. Department of State. 1980. *U.S. Security Framework.* Current Policy no. 221. Washington, DC: Bureau of Public Affairs, September 16.

Nye, Joseph. 1990. *Bound to Lead: The Changing Nature of American Power.* New York: Basic Books.

Porter, Michael. 1990. *The Competitive Advantage of Nations.* New York: Free Press.

Ramazani, Rouhollah. 1975. *Iran's Foreign Policy, 1941–1973: A Study of Foreign Policy in Modernizing Nations.* Charlottesville: University Press of Virginia.

———. 1979. *The Persian Gulf and the Strait of Hormuz.* Alphenaan den Rijn, The Netherlands: Sijthoff & Noordhoff.

———. 1982. *The United States and Iran: The Patterns of Influence.* New York: Praeger.

Reich, Robert. 1991. *The Work of Nations: Preparing Ourselves for 21st Century Capitalism.* New York: Alfred A. Knopf.

Rubin, Barry. 1980. *Paved with Good Intentions: The American Experience and Iran.* New York: Oxford.

Rubinstein, Alvin. 1982. *Soviet Policy toward Turkey, Iran, and Afghanistan: The Dynamics of Influence.* New York: Praeger.

Sabrosky, Alan N., and Robert L. Sloane, eds. 1988. *The Recourse to War: An Appraisal of the "Weinberger Doctrine."* Carlisle Barracks, PA: Strategic Studies Institute, U.S. Army War College.

Saikal, Amin. 1980. *The Rise and Fall of the Shah.* Princeton: Princeton University Press.

Saunders, Harold. 1981. *The Middle East Problem in the 1980s.* Washington, D.C.: American Enterprise Institute for Public Policy Research.

Savory, Roger. 1980a. "The History of the Persian Gulf: A.D. 600–1800." In *The Persian Gulf States: A General Survey,* eds. Alvin Cottrell et al. Baltimore: Johns Hopkins University Press.

———. 1980b. "The History of the Persian Gulf: The Ancient Period." In *The Persian Gulf States: A General Survey,* eds. Alvin Cottrell et al. Baltimore: Johns Hopkins University Press.

Sick, Gary. n.d. "The Evolution of U.S. Strategy toward the Indian Ocean and Persian Gulf Regions." Unpublished manuscript.

Sisco, Joseph. 1980. Comments before Hearings before the Committee on Foreign Relations. *U.S. Security Interests and Policies in Southwest Asia,* pp. 42–50. Washington, DC: Government Printing Office.

Taylor, Alan R. 1991. *The Superpowers and the Middle East.* Syracuse, NY: Syracuse University Press.

Thomas, Raju. 1981. "The Afghanistan Crisis and South Asian Security." *Journal of Strategic Studies* 4(4): 415–434.

United Nations. 1991. *United Nations Security Council Resolutions Relating to the Crisis in the Gulf.* UN Department of Public Information, DPC/1104, November; Add. 1, December.

United Nations Security Council Resolution 687, April 3, 1991.

U.S. Congress. Senate. Committee on Foreign Relations. *U.S. Military Sales to Iran.* Staff Report to the Subcommittee on Foreign Assistance. Washington, DC: Government Printing Office, 1976.

U.S. Department of Defense. 1992. *Joint Chiefs of Staff Publication 3.0: Doctrine for Unified and Joint Operations.* Washington, DC: Government Printing Office.

———. 1991. *The Defense Planning Guidance, FY 1992–1997.* Washington, DC: Government Printing Office.

Van Evera, Stephen. 1990. "Primed for Peace: Europe after the Cold War." *International Security* 15(Winter): 7–57.

Vance, Cyrus. 1983. *Hard Choices: Critical Years in America's Foreign Policy.* New York: Simon & Schuster.

Vogel, Steve. 1991. "Killer Brigade: 3d Infantry Division 'Phantoms' Hunt the Enemy." *Army Times,* November 11, pp. 10, 14–16, 22.

von Clausewitz, Karl. 1976. *On War.* Eds. and trans. Michael Howard and Peter Paret. Princeton: Princeton University Press.

Watson, Bruce. 1982. *Red Navy at Sea: Soviet Naval Operations on the High Seas, 1956–1980.* Boulder, CO: Westview.

Williams, Juan. 1991. "Race and War in the Persian Gulf." *Washington Post,* January 20.

Yapp, Malcolm. 1980a. "The History of the Persian Gulf: British Policy in the Persian Gulf." In *The Persian Gulf States: A General Survey*, eds. Alvin Cottrell et al. Baltimore: Johns Hopkins University Press.

———. 1980b. "The History of the Persian Gulf: The Nineteenth and Twentieth Centuries." In *The Persian Gulf States: A General Survey*, eds. Alvin Cottrell et al. Baltimore: Johns Hopkins University Press.

———. 1980c. *Strategies of British India: Britain, Iran and Afghanistan, 1798–1850*. Oxford: Clarendon Press.

Zahlan, Rosemarie Said. 1978. *The Origins of the United Arab Emirates: A Political and Social History of the Trucial States*. New York: St. Martin's Press.

Index

About the Editors and Contributors

JAMES BLACKWELL is a Senior Fellow at the Center for Strategic and International Studies where he is the Director for Political-Military Studies. He is the author of *Thunder in the Desert: The Strategy and Tactics of the Persian Gulf War*, and is co-editor, with Barry Blechman, of *Making Defense Reform Work*. He has also published numerous articles in professional journals, among them *Parameters*, *Military Technology*, *NATO's 16 Nations*, and *National Defense*. Dr. Blackwell has appeared on network television and radio worldwide, and served as CNN's military analyst during the Persian Gulf crisis.

MAJOR GENERAL DANIEL W. CHRISTMAN is currently the Commanding General of the U.S. Army Engineer Center and Fort Leonard Wood, and Commandant, U.S. Army Engineer Center, Fort Leonard Wood, Missouri. He was formerly the Director of Strategy, Plans, and Policy in the Department of the Army Headquarters. He has previously served in important national security positions such as Staff Assistant for Strategic Arms Limitation Talks with the National Security Council; Army advisor to the Chairman of the Joint Chiefs of Staff, Admiral William J. Crowe; and Assistant to the Attorney General of the United States for National Security Affairs.

INIS L. CLAUDE, JR. is Professor of Government and Foreign Affairs, Emeritus, at the University of Virginia. He is the author of many books and monographs in the field of international relations, and among his most recent are *American Approaches to World Affairs*

(1986), *The Record of International Organizations in the Twentieth Century* (1986), and *States and the Global System* (1988).

ROBERT H. DORFF is Associate Professor in the Department of Political Science and Public Administration at North Carolina State University. He is coauthor of *A Theory of Political Decision Modes* (1980), and his published research has appeared in such journals as the *American Political Science Review*, the *British Journal of Political Science*, the *Journal of Politics*, and the *Journal of Theoretical Politics*.

KIMBERLY ANN ELLIOTT is a Research Associate at the Institute for International Economics in Washington, D.C. She has written and co-authored several articles and books on economic sanctions and American trade policy, including *Economic Sanctions Reconsidered* (1990), *Trade Protection in the United States* (1986), *Auction Quotas in United States Trade Policy* (1987), and *Reciprocity and Retaliation: Do "Tough" Trade Policies Work?* (forthcoming).

CHRISTINE M. HELMS is an independent consultant and freelance writer who has travelled extensively in the Middle East and interviewed many of the region's leaders. Dr. Helms previously worked at the Brookings Institution and the Smithsonian Institution. During the recent Gulf crisis she testified before Congress on the impact of sanctions against Iraq and also met with President Bush. Author of numerous articles regarding Middle Eastern matters, her publications include *The Cohesion of Saudi Arabia* (1981), *Iraq: Eastern Flank of the Arabic World* (1984), and *Arabism & Islam: Stateless Nations & Nationless States* (1990).

ROBERT F. HELMS II is Program Director, Military Issues and Studies, Center for Social Research and Policy Analysis, at the Research Triangle Institute at Research Triangle Park, North Carolina.

BRUCE R. KUNIHOLM is Director of the Institute of Policy Sciences and Public Affairs at Duke University, and Professor of Public Policy Studies and History. Among his publications are *The Origins of the Cold War in the Near East: Great Power Conflict and Diplomacy in Iran, Turkey, and Greece*; *The Persian Gulf and United States Policy*; and *The Palestinian Problem and U.S. Public Policy*.

ALAN R. TAYLOR is a Professor of Middle East studies at The American University's School of International Service in Washington, D.C. He is author of *The Superpowers and the Middle East, The Arab Bal-*

ance of Power, *The Islamic Question in Middle East Politics*, *The Zionist Mind*, and *Prelude to Israel*.

LIEUTENANT COLONEL ROBERT D. WALZ retired from the U.S. Army on April 1, 1992 and has accepted a position as Instructor of National Security Affairs at the U.S. Army Command and General Staff College. He was formerly a strategy and policy analyst with the Strategy, Plans, and Policy Directorate in the Department of the Army Headquarters.

SAMUEL R. WILLIAMSON, JR. is the Vice-Chancellor and President of The University of the South in Sewanee, Tennessee. He has published widely in the field of international history and strategic politics. He is the author of *The Politics of Grand Strategy: Britain and France Prepare for War, 1904–1914* (1990) and *Austria-Hungary and the Origins of the First World War* (1991); editor of *The Origins of a Tragedy: July 1914* (1979); and co-editor, with Peter Pastor, of *Essays on World War I: Origins and Prisoners of War* (1983).